# A HANDBOOK OF ESSENTIAL LAW

## FOR THE IRISH HOTEL AND CATERING INDUSTRY

Third Edition

# A HANDBOOK OF ESSENTIAL LAW

## FOR THE IRISH HOTEL AND CATERING INDUSTRY

Third Edition

*FRANCIS J. DEMPSEY*

PUBLICATIONS

© CERT Ltd 1998

Published by CERT, CERT House, Amiens Street,
Dublin 1, Ireland.
Telephone: (01) 855 6555. Fax: (01) 855 6821.

Design and typesetting by DK&A Design, Dublin.

ISBN 1-870387-63-5

(ISBN 1-870387-38-4: Second Edition)

(ISBN 1-870387-08-2: First Edition)

This book has been prepared as a guide only (and not as a
definitive text) to very complex legal issues affecting hotel
and catering law. The author and CERT do not accept
responsibility for any errors or omissions. In cases of
individual concern, you are advised to consult an
appropriate legal practitioner.

# CONTENTS

TABLE OF STATUTES     xi

PREFACE TO THE THIRD EDITION     xiii

PREFACE TO THE FIRST EDITION     xiv

ACKNOWLEDGEMENTS     xvi

1: INTRODUCTION TO IRISH LAW     1-15
    Classification of Law     1
    Sources of Law     2
    The Courts of Law     8
    Personnel of the Law     14

2: FORMING THE BUSINESS     17-30
    Sole Trader     17
    General Partnership     19
    Limited Partnership     22
    The Company     23
    Private Limited Companies     24

3: FURTHER FORMALITIES     31-51
    Registering a Business Name     31
    Passing Off     34
    Registration of Premises under Tourist Traffic Acts, 1939-95     35
    Registration of Food Premises     45
    Insurance for Business     49

4: THE LAW OF CONTRACT     53-72
    The Concept of a Contract     53
    Contract Form     54
      Essential Elements of a Contract     54
      Capacity to Contract     61
      Invalid Contracts     63
      The Termination or Discharge of a Contract     64
      Remedies for Breach of Contract     66

Statute of Limitations, 1957 and Contracts 67
Unfair Terms in Consumer Contracts 67

5: THE LAW OF TORTS 73-93
Specific Torts 73
Negligence 74
Occupier's Liability 76
Employer's Liability 81
Defamation 88
Nuisance 89
Trespass 90
Intention in Tort 91
Defences in Tort 92
Remedies in Tort 92
Tort Distinguished from Breach of Contract 93
Tort Distinguished from Crime 93

6: LAW FOR THE IRISH HOTEL AND CATERING INDUSTRY 95-147
The Hotel Proprietors Act, 1963 95
Keeping a Register of Hotel Guests 102
The Retail Prices (Food in Catering Establishments)
    Display Order, 1984 103
The Retail Prices (Beverages in Licensed Premises)
    Display Order, 1976 105
Consumer Information and Protection 107
Consumer Information Act, 1978 107
Sale of Goods and Supply of Services Act, 1980 110
Package Holidays and Travel Trade Act, 1995 110
Fire Safety Legislation 119
Fire Safety in Places of Assembly (Ease of Escape)
    Regulations, 1985 125
Department of the Environment Codes of Practice 126
The Fire Services Act, 1981 and Licensing under Other Statutes 126
Food Hygiene Regulations, 1950–89 127
Prohibition and Restriction on Smoking in Public Areas
    and Facilities 144

7: Intoxicating Liquor Licensing – Part I     149-164
    Introduction and General Provisions    149
    Categories of Licence    149
    Tax Clearance Certificates    150
    Prohibition on the Sale of Intoxicating Liquor to Persons
        Under 18 Years    152
    Children on Licensed Premises    152
    Employment of Persons Under the Age of 18 Years
        on Licensed Premises    154
    Obtaining a Declaration Relating to Proposed Licensed
        Premises    154
    Procedure for Obtaining a Declaration    155
    Objections to the Granting of a Declaration    155
    Procedure for the Renewal of Intoxicating Liquor Licences    155
    Objections to the Renewal of a Licence    156
    Procedure for Making an Objection to the Renewal of
        Licences    157
    Hours of Trading in Licensed Premises    158
    General Licensing Considerations and Offences    160

8: Intoxicating Liquor Licensing – Part II    165-189
    Specified Purpose Licences, Certificates and Orders    165
    Spirits Retailer's On-Licence    165
    Hotel Licences    169
    Special Restaurant Licence    171
    Wine Retailer's On-Licence    175
    Restaurant Certificate    178
    Limited Restaurant Certificate    180
    General Exemption Order    181
    Special Exemption Order    182
    Exemption for Special Events    185
    Occasional Licence    186
    Festival Clubs    188
    Night Clubs    188

9: Entertainment Licences    191-198
    Public Dancing Licences    191

Temporary Dance Licence                                191
Annual Dance Licence                                   192
Public Music and Singing Licence                       194
Temporary Public Music and Singing Licence             195
Performing Rights                                      196

10: EMPLOYMENT LAW – PART I                         199–203
    The Contract of Employment                         199

11: EMPLOYMENT LAW – PART II                        205–280
    Employment Legislation                             205
    Minimum Notice and Terms of Employment             205
    Working Time, Rest and Holidays                    212
    Unfair Dismissal                                   223
    Employment of Children and Young Persons           231
    Maternity Protection                               236
    Adoptive Leave                                     246
    Redundancy                                         249
    Collective Redundancies                            251
    Payment of Wages                                   254
    Equal Pay                                          259
    Employment Equality                                262
    Sexual Harassment                                  265
    Safety, Health and Welfare at Work                 268
    Part-Time Workers                                  270
    Joint Labour Committees                            272
    Labour Relations Commission                        274
    The Labour Court                                   276
    Rights Commissioners                               278
    Employment Appeals Tribunal                        280

SELECT BIBLIOGRAPHY                                     281

INDEX                                                  283

# TABLE OF STATUTES, STATUTORY
# INSTRUMENTS AND ORDERS

Accidental Fires Act, 1943, .......... 101
Adoption Act, 1991 .......... 247
Adoptive Leave Act, 1995 .......... 214, 246–9
Aliens Order, 1946 .......... 102
Anti-Discrimination (Pay) Act, 1974 .......... 259–62, 264–5, 276
Civil Liability Act, 1961 .......... 75
Companies Acts, 1963-90 .......... 23, 24, 25, 26, 29, 85
Companies (Amendment) Act, 1983 .......... 24
Companies (Amendment) Act, 1990 .......... 26
Consumer Information Act, 1978 .......... 107–10
Copyright Act, 1963 .......... 196–8
Courts Act, 1996 .......... 11
Courts and Court Officers Act, 1995 .......... 12–13, 14
Courts (No. 2) Act, 1986 .......... 155, 156
Employment Equality Act, 1977 .......... 262–5, 276
European Communities (Hygiene of Foodstuffs) Regulations, 1998 ..... 135, 140–4
European Communities (Official Control of Foodstuffs) Regulations, 1998 .. 135–9
European Communities (Single-Member PLCs) Regulations, 1994 .......... 29–30
European Communities (Unfair Terms in Consumer Contracts) Regulations, 1995
.......... 67–72
Finance Act, 1992 .......... 150
Fire Authorities (Emergency Operations) Regulations), 1987 .......... 119
Fire Safety in Places of Assembly (Ease of Escape) Regulations, 1985 .... 119, 125–6
Fire Services Act, 1981 .......... 119, 126–7, 172, 191
Fire Services Act, 1981 (Prescribed Premises) Regulations, 1987 .......... 119
Food Hygiene (Amendment) Regulations, 1989 .......... 130
Food Hygiene Regulations, 1950-89 .......... 18, 45, 48, 127–35, 172
Gaming and Lotteries Acts, 1956-79 .......... 127
Holidays (Employees) Act, 1973 .......... 212
Hotel Proprietors Act, 1963 .......... 95–102, 111
Industrial Relations Act, 1946 .......... 276
Industrial Relations Act, 1969 .......... 276
Industrial Relations Act, 1976 .......... 276
Industrial Relations Act, 1990 .......... 272–4, 277–8
Intoxicating Liquor Act, 1927 .......... 179
Intoxicating Liquor Act, 1960 .......... 170
Intoxicating Liquor Act, 1988 .......... 36, 37, 152–3
Intoxicating Liquor Acts, 1833-1988 .......... 149
Licensing Acts, 1833-1995 .......... 127

Licensing (Ireland) Act, 1902 .................................................................. 149, 170
Limited Partnership Act, 1907 ......................................................................... 22
Local Government (Planning and Development) Acts, 1963-93 ....................... 172
Maternity Protection Act, 1994 ........................... 214, 224, 225, 236–46, 271, 280
Maternity Protection of Employees Acts, 1981-91 ......................................... 236
Minimum Notice and Terms of Employment Acts, 1973-91
    .............. 200, 203, 205–12, 224, 226, 251, 271, 280
Occupier's Liability Act, 1995 ...................................................................... 76–81
Organisation of Working Time Act, 1997 .................................................. 212–23
Package Holidays and Travel Trade Act, 1995 ........................................... 110–19
Partnership Act, 1890                                                                          19-22
Payment of Wages Act, 1991 ................................................................ 254–9, 279
Petty Sessions (Ireland) Act, 1851 .....................................................139, 223, 235
Protection of Employees (Employers' Insolvency) Acts, 1981-91 ...... 249, 272, 280
Protection of Employment Act, 1977 ............................................................. 251
Protection of Young Persons (Employment) Act, 1996 ............................... 231–6
Public Dance Halls Act, 1935 ................................................ 127, 183, 189, 191–4
Public Health Acts Amendment Act, 1890 ............................................. 127, 194
Redundancy Payments Acts, 1967-91 ......................................... 200, 249–54, 280
Registration of Business Names Act, 1963 ...................................18, 19, 27, 31–4
Registration of Clubs Acts, 1904-86 ............................................................. 127
Retail Prices (Beverages in Licensed Premises) Display Order, 1976 ............. 105–7
Retail Prices (Food in Catering Establishments) Display Order, 1984 ........... 103–5
Safety, Health and Welfare at Work Act, 1989 ............................ 83–8, 243, 268–9
Safety, Health and Welfare at Work (General Applications) Regulations, 1993
    ................. 268–9
Sale of Goods Act, 1893 ............................................................................... 101
Sale of Goods and Supply of Services Act, 1980 ...................................... 110, 111
Single European Act, 1986 ................................................................................ 6
Special Restaurant Licence (Standards) Regulations, 1988 ............................ 172
Standard Time Act, 1968 ............................................................................. 158
Statute of Limitations, 1957 ................................................................. 67, 92, 208
Terms of Employment (Information) Act, 1994 .................. 205, 208–12, 271, 280
Tobacco (Health Promotion and Protection) Act, 1988 ................................. 144
Tobacco (Health Promotion and Protection) Regulations, 1995 ................... 144–7
Tourist Traffic Acts ................................................................ 18, 35–45, 95–6
Unfair Dismissals Acts, 1977-94 ........................... 200, 203, 223–31, 246, 279, 280
Worker Participation (State Enterprises) Acts, 1977 ........................................ 272
Worker Protection (Regular Part-Time Employees) Act, 1991 ............. 212, 270–2

# PREFACE TO THE THIRD EDITION

New developments in the law continue apace. The introduction of new statutory provisions, the updating and reform of existing legislation, and other changes in the law, make this edition not just timely, but necessary.

It has never been more important for those employed in or otherwise connected with the hotel and catering industry in Ireland to have knowledge of the law governing this industry.

There is a growing awareness by the general public of their legal rights and while this is as it should be, a more litigious public makes it all the more important for those engaged in business to recognise easily and readily the serious and costly consequences of legal liability. This, the third edition, remains faithful to and builds upon the aims of its predecessors and continues to endeavour to make the relevant law accessible to its readership.

Francis J. Dempsey
LL.B., M.I.Mgt., M.H.C.I.M.A., P.G.C.E.

1 May 1998

# PREFACE TO THE FIRST EDITION

No legal text, however good its pedigree, is an adequate substitute for professional legal advice tailored to the needs of a specific case. That said, it is hoped that this handbook, the first of its kind on the subject in the Republic of Ireland, will be a useful source of reference for students of hotel and catering studies and for those engaged in the hotel and catering industry, whether at management, supervisory or operative level. It is hoped, too, that it will find its way into the hands of the general reader.

The inevitable consequence of writing a book to accommodate the legal requirements of any specialist business is the creation of an expectation that every possible legal aspect of that business will be included. Such an expectation is unrealistic. Where one has to exercise personal choice in the matter of including or excluding material, there is, naturally, concern that that which is eventually selected for inclusion should survive critical scrutiny. It is hoped that one's individual interests have coincided, at least in the majority of instances, with what is broadly required.

This handbook avoids the strict format of a conventional legal text, with the intention of making the material more readily accessible to its intended readership.

The aims of this handbook are:

1. To make available a variety of legal information not easily accessible until now in any single source.
2. To facilitate the recognition of the legal implications of situations that may arise in the day-to-day conduct of business in the hotel and catering industry in the Republic of Ireland.
3. To provide the knowledge to foresee, and thereby avoid by appropriate remedial action, the unwanted consequences of situations with a legal dimension.
4. Where litigation is inevitable, to enable those involved to instruct a solicitor with greater accuracy and thoroughness.

Every effort has been made to achieve these aims in a manner that combines the necessary accuracy with the desirable accessibility and brevity.

Before acting on information contained in this handbook, readers should seek professional legal advice.

Francis J. Dempsey
LL.B., M.I.Mgt., M.H.C.I.M.A., P.G.C.E.

1 August 1990

# ACKNOWLEDGEMENTS

I should like to acknowledge and record my indebtedness and gratitude to the many individuals who were so generous with their time, expertise and patience during the preparation of this work. While I hope this acknowledgement will be accepted by everyone concerned, the extent of my indebtedness to some warrants particular mention and thanks:

- Dennis Driscoll, Senior Lecturer in Law and former Dean of the Faculty of Law, National University of Ireland, Galway, of whose erudition, advice and friendship I have been the beneficiary for many years.
- Bernard O'Hara, Head of the School of Business Studies and Humanities, Galway-Mayo Institute of Technology.
- Jonathan Williams, Literary Agent, Dublin.
- James Woods, District Court Clerk, Limerick.
- Bryan McMahon, Professor of Law, University College, Galway.
- Michael Houlihan, Solicitor, Messrs. I.M. Houlihan and Sons, Ennis, Co. Clare.
- Eamon Shackleton, Director of Operations, Irish Music Rights Organisation, Dublin.
- Andrew Halloran, Supervising Environmental Health Officer, Community Care, Galway.
- John O'Shaughnessy, Chief Fire Officer, Galway.
- Thomas O'Donoghue, Solicitor, Galway County Council.
- James McGuigan, Bord Fáilte Éireann, Dublin.
- John Ronayne, Senior Appeals and Monitoring Officer, Bord Fáilte Éireann, Dublin.
- Jerome Ford, Higher Executive Officer, Department of Enterprise, Trade and Employment.
- Ray Ellard, Chief Environmental Health Officer, Food Unit, Department of Health and Children.

This publication could not have been completed without the cooperation and support of CERT, Bord Fáilte Éireann, Irish Hotels' Federation, Patrick F. O'Reilly & Co., Solicitors, colleagues at the

Galway-Mayo Institute of Technology, and CERT staff and personnel in the Irish hotel and catering industry.

It is wholly appropriate and a positive delight to express my profound gratitude to my family for their support, encouragement and affection. Individually and collectively, nuclear and extended, they are my inspiration and my motivation — God bless them.

# Chapter 1

# INTRODUCTION TO IRISH LAW

There are many ways in which the word 'law' may be defined for different purposes and in different contexts. The present context, however, suggests that law may be defined 'as a collection of rules and principles for the regulation of human behaviour in society and which Irish courts will strive to enforce'.

## CLASSIFICATION OF LAW

It is possible to identify an extensive range of legal topics, each with its own set of rules: criminal law, evidence, tort, contract, family law, constitutional law, company law, labour law, and so on.

Law is often classified as being either substantive or adjectival. Both these terms need clarification. Adjectival law deals with the procedures that have to be taken in a legal action. Since it involves the rules of law governing evidence and court practice and procedure, it could be referred to as procedural law. Substantive law, on the other hand, can be subdivided into public law and private law. Public law governs the relationship between an individual and the state, and covers, for example, criminal law, tax law, constitutional law and social welfare law. Private law concerns relationships amongst individuals; for example, contracts, trusts, torts, succession and family law.

Law can also be divided into criminal law and civil law. Criminal law is the mechanism by which society punishes the wrong-doer and protects the innocent. It is administered through the offices of the Garda Síochána and the Director of Public Prosecutions. A person prosecuted in a criminal action is subject to the rules of criminal law and may be found guilty or not guilty. The usual consequence of a guilty verdict is a fine or imprisonment, or perhaps both. In determining the defendant's guilt or innocence, the state must prove that the person is guilty beyond all reasonable doubt — a much higher standard of proof than that required in a civil case.

In contrast to criminal law, the object of which is to punish, the purpose of civil law is to provide for the resolution of disputes and the compensation of the wronged individual. The terms used to describe the parties in the civil action are 'plaintiff' or 'complainant' for the person bringing the action, and 'defendant' for the person against whom the action is taken. The state does not play any part in bringing a civil action to court, and an aggrieved party who does not institute proceedings on his or her own behalf will receive no redress. Where the plaintiff is successful, the usual remedy is the award of financial compensation. Alternatively, what might be sought by the plaintiff is an injunction requiring the defendant to do something he/she is not doing and should be doing, or prohibiting him/her from doing something he/she is doing and should not be doing. A civil action is often referred to as civil suit, and the defendant to such an action is said to have been sued by the aggrieved party or plaintiff.

## SOURCES OF LAW

There are a number of important sources of law in Ireland:

- the Constitution
- legislation, sometimes called statute law
- common law, sometimes called case law, or judicial precedent or judge-made law
- law of the European Union.

### The Constitution

The Irish Constitution, Bunreacht na hÉireann, was adopted on 29 December 1937 and replaced the Constitution of the Irish Free State 1922. The Constitution is the fundamental law of the state and all legislation enacted by the Oireachtas which is in conflict with it is deemed to be invalid.

As well as providing the framework within which the state must operate, the Constitution provides for the fundamental rights of each citizen. Where an individual believes that his or her constitutional rights have been infringed, he or she may initiate a constitutional action in the High Court to have such rights recognised. Before signing a bill that has completed its passage through the Houses of the Oireachtas, the President, after consultation with the Council of State (an advisory body), may refer the bill or parts of it to the Supreme Court to test its constitutionality.

The Constitution deals with such matters as the nation and the national territory; the office and function of the President; the nature, power and functions of the Oireachtas; government and the courts; and with property, personal rights, the family, education and religion.

The Constitution can be changed only by a referendum put to the people.

## Legislation

Statutes are acts of the Oireachtas and are an important source of law. By virtue of the Constitution, the primary law-making body in the state is the Oireachtas. This is a three-tier entity consisting of the President, Dáil Éireann and Seanad Éireann. Statute law is required to be consistent with the Constitution; if it is not, such law is invalid. Statutes are subject to the interpretation of the courts, and these interpretations themselves become the source of legal principles and rules.

A distinction is made between primary legislation enacted by the Oireachtas and subordinate or delegated legislation. Delegated legislation is where laws are laid down by a body or person to whom the superior legislature, the Oireachtas, has handed down authority to make such laws. This type of legislation can be categorised as follows:

1. **Executive subordinate legislation.** This permits the executive government to activate parts of legislation by order.
2. **Statutory instruments.** A minister is empowered to make statutory instruments relating to his or her department.
3. **Municipal subordinate legislation.** Local authorities are empowered by virtue of various statutes to make local bylaws.
4. **Autonomous subordinate legislation.** Limited powers are conferred on

private individuals by legislation (such as the Companies Acts, 1963-90) to enable them to exercise control over their own affairs.

Before a statute becomes law, it is known as a bill and must success-fully pass through five stages in the Houses of the Oireachtas, be agreed to by the Dáil and Seanad and be signed by the President. It is then promulgated by the President, who publishes a notice in *Iris Oifigiúil* stating that the bill has become law.

## Common Law

The English common law system was introduced into Ireland towards the end of the twelfth century. Ireland, therefore, belongs to the com-mon law family that has strongly influenced the legal systems in many parts of the world, including the United States of America, Canada, Australia, New Zealand, India and many African states.

A feature of the common law is its adherence to the doctrine of precedent. In essence, this is where the lower courts in the legal sys-tem must follow the decisions of the higher courts on questions of law.

The status of a decision laid down by a court depends greatly on the status of that court. Therefore, a decision arrived at by the Supreme Court will bind all the courts below it. Decisions by the Court of Criminal Appeal will bind the Central Criminal Court, the Special Criminal Court, the Circuit Court and the District Court. The Supreme Court is not bound by its own previous decisions, although it will not depart from them without good reason.

English decisions arrived at before 1922 are part of Irish law to the extent that they have not been overruled, are not contrary to subse-quent legislation nor unconstitutional. English decisions since 1922 are regarded as persuasive but not binding.

The purpose of the rule of precedent is to ensure continuity and certainty in the law and also to ensure that judges are consistent in reaching decisions on similar facts. To be a binding precedent, a case must have been decided by an earlier court on identical or sufficiently similar facts. This raises the question of whether the facts of one case are sufficiently similar to another to allow the precedent to apply.

## Law of the European Union

Ireland became a member of the European Community on 1 January 1973. In order to do so, it was necessary to amend the Constitution to permit the laws of the Community to be part of Irish law. The effect of this is that the law of the Community takes precedence over Irish law. If there is a conflict between Irish law and Community law, the latter prevails.

Since Ireland joined the Community, legislation from Brussels has had a significant impact on the Irish legal system. Quite apart from the foundation treaties of the Community, there has been a constant flow of regulations, directives and decisions, thereby ensuring an ever-increasing importance for European Community law as a source of law.

The Treaty of European Union (TEU), often referred to as the Maastricht Treaty, came into operation on 1 November 1993. At this point it became legally correct to refer to the European Community (EC), rather than the former description, European Economic Community (EEC). The word 'economic' was removed to reflect a change of emphasis towards non-economic provisions. It also became common to refer to the European Union instead of the European Community, although there are, in fact, three communities, the European Coal and Steel Community (ECSC), Euratom and the EC, still in existence. However, the European Community is still the most important pillar of the European Union, and the EC Treaty, as amended by the Treaty of European Union, still dominates.

The primary sources of European Union law are the treaties. These are:

The European Coal and Steel Community Treaty, 1951

The European Economic Treaty, 1957 (Treaty of Rome)

Euratom Treaty, 1957 (Atomic Energy)

Convention on Certain Institutions Common to the European Communities, 1957

Merger Treaty, 1965

Acts of Accession of 1972 (UK, Ireland, Denmark), of 1979 (Greece), of 1985 (Spain, Portugal), of 1994 (Austria, Finland, Sweden).

Budgetary Treaties of 1970 and 1975

The Treaty Amending the Treaties Establishing the Community with respect to Greenland, 1985

The Single European Act, 1986

The Treaty of European Union, 1992 (Maastricht Treaty)

These treaties are often described as the constitution of the European Union, and any legislation passed by the institutions of the Union must not contradict the provisions of the treaties.

The Council of Ministers and the Commission are empowered to make the laws necessary to achieve the objectives of the treaties. These secondary sources of law are described as follows:

- **A regulation.** This is binding in its entirety and directly applicable in all member states. It takes effect in each member state without any further action required of the member state. A regulation must be published in the official journal of the European Union and comes into force on a specific date.
- **A directive.** This is binding as to the result to be achieved, but it is left to each member state to decide the form and method of its implementation. In Ireland some legislative act is required to implement a directive, e.g. an Act of the Oireachtas or a statutory instrument.
- **A decision.** This is binding in its entirety on those to whom it is directed. A decision may be directed to apply to a particular person, a corporate body or, indeed, a member state.

It should be noted that recommendations and opinions have no binding force.

The institutions of the European Union are the Commission, the Council of Ministers, the European Parliament and the Court of Justice.

- **The Commission.** This consists of twenty members (two each from France, Germany, Italy, Spain and the United Kingdom and one from each of the other member states, Belgium, Denmark, Greece, Ireland, Luxembourg, Netherlands, Portugal, Austria, Finland and Sweden) appointed by the agreement of the governments of the member states. The Commission has the responsibility to ensure that the Treaty of Rome is observed. The commissioners serve for a five-year term, which is renewable. The Commission has a president and five vice-presidents, whose terms of office are two years, also renewable.

- **The Council.** Each member state is represented on the Council of Ministers, which is not a fixed body but consists of ministers/representatives of the governments of each member state, with membership being dictated by the issues under discussion, e.g. agriculture, finance, employment. The Council is presided over by the president. This position rotates in alphabetical order around the member states every six months. Only one voting delegate per member state is allowed. Meetings are held in private unless the Council unanimously decides otherwise.

- **The Parliament.** The parliament is directly elected by the people of the member states. This assembly is a deliberating rather than a decision-making body and its powers are regarded as advisory and supervisory. Ireland elects fifteen members from four constituencies: Munster (4), Dublin (4), Leinster (4) and Connaught/Ulster (3).

  In all, there are 626 Members of the European Parliament (MEPs) made up as follows: Germany (99), France, Italy and the United Kingdom (87 each), Spain (64), Netherlands (31), Belgium, Greece and Portugal (25 each), Sweden (22), Austria (21), Denmark and Finland (16 each), Ireland (15), Luxembourg (6). The Parliament is based in Strasbourg, with some sessions held in Luxembourg, and most committee meetings are held in Brussels. Members are elected for a five-year term.

- **The Court of Justice.** This consists of fifteen judges, with one judge from each member state. Appointed for a term of six years, the judges elect their own President of the Court, who serves in that position for three years. However, it is possible for the period in office to be renewed. To be considered for appointment, persons 'should be independent and qualified for the highest judicial office within their own respective countries'. However, it is important to note that, whereas Irish judges are selected from barristers and, to a lesser extent solicitors, judges of this court are chosen from a much wider field, including academic lawyers. Judges must not be influenced by their national origins, but must strive for a community approach in reaching a decision. The Court is not bound by the rules of precedent, as Irish courts are. The Court of Justice has the task of ensuring that the Treaty of Rome is observed in its interpretation and implementation.

## THE COURTS OF LAW

The constitution provides for the establishment of a Supreme Court and a High Court. These are known as superior courts. The lower courts are known as inferior courts. The courts system is hierarchical. At the top is the Supreme Court, followed by the Court of Criminal Appeal; next is the High Court, then the Circuit Court and at the bottom the District Court.

### District Court

This is the lowest court in the land. The State is currently divided into 24 District Court districts, comprising the Dublin Metropolitan District and 23 other districts. These 23 districts are further divided into over 200 District Court areas. This Court has a President who is, *ex officio,* a Judge of the Circuit Court. Since the enactment of the Courts and Court Officers Act, 1995, the District Court can have up to 50 judges. In addition, however, where a judge is absent from duty for any reason, the government is empowered to appoint persons to act as temporary District Court Judges. Barristers and solicitors of ten years experience can be appointed to this court. Although District Court Judges normally retire at 65 years, their tenure may be extended to age 70. Furthermore, under the 1995 Act, Section 47 (3) provides that: 'The age of retirement shall be 72 years for a person who holds office on or before the coming into operation of this Section as a Judge of the High Court, the Circuit Court, the District Court, the Court of Justice, the Court of First Instance attached thereto or an Advocate-General of the Court of Justice and who is subsequently appointed to be a Judge of the Supreme Court or High Court.'

In civil cases, the court's jurisdiction is limited in relation to the nature and amount of the claim. In most cases, such as contract and tort, it has jurisdiction if the claim does not exceed £5,000. In criminal cases, it has jurisdiction in two types of cases. First, for minor offences triable in a summary manner, the penalty varies according to the gravity with which the legislature viewed the offence when drawing up the particular statute. In summary cases, according to the offence, fines may vary up to a maximum of £1,500 and/or twelve months' imprisonment. Secondly, for indictable offences that are dealt with summarily and that carry a maximum fine of £1,500 and/or twelve months' imprisonment in all cases. The District Court can impose consecutive sentences not exceeding two years.

The District Court also has a function in relation to serious offences when it conducts a preliminary hearing to ascertain if the prosecution has sufficient evidence to warrant returning the accused for trial to a higher court. A jury trial in a civil or criminal matter is not available in the District Court.

## Small Claims Procedure

The small claims procedure is a recently introduced mechanism for handling small claims within the District Court structure. The procedure was introduced on 16 December 1991 on a pilot scheme basis in the Dublin Metropolitan district, the District Court area of Cork city and the District Court area of Sligo and, following the success of the scheme, was extended countrywide on 8 December 1993. It is designed to handle consumer claims speedily, cheaply, with minimal formality and without the need for a solicitor.

The procedure is administered by the Small Claims Registrar (the District Court Clerk), whose function is to process small claims and, if possible, reach a satisfactory settlement without recourse to a court hearing. The Registrar will handle small claims in which the amount of the claim does not exceed £600. A small claim under this procedure is one that relates to:

(a) **a consumer contract** — between a consumer and a vendor in respect of any goods or services purchased (but excluding a claim arising from an agreement under the Hire Purchase Acts, 1946 and 1960 or from an alleged breach of a leasing agreement)

(b) **a tort** — in respect of minor damage caused to property (but excluding personal injuries)

(c) **a tenancy** — in respect of the non-return of any sum paid by the tenant to the landlord as rent deposit or any sum of money known as 'key money'.

To be eligible to use the small claims procedure, a consumer must have bought the goods or services (which are the subject of the dispute) for private use from someone selling/providing them in the course of a business. It is important to stress that the procedure is confined to disputes between consumers and persons/companies in business and cannot be used by one business person against another.

The consumer making a claim is referred to as the 'applicant' and the person/company against whom/which the claim is made is called the 'respondent'.

The claim is made on a special application form (SC1) which is available from the Small Claims Registrar at the local District Court office. When completed, the form must be lodged with the Registrar, together with the £6 fee. The Registrar then sends a copy of the application to the respondent (retaining the original), together with a notice of claim against the respondent (form SC2), notice of acceptance of liability (form SC3) and notice of dispute (form SC4).

If the respondent admits the claim against her/him and

(a) agrees to pay the amount claimed, or
(b) consents to judgment being given against her/him, or
(c) wishes to pay the amount claimed by instalments

she/he must complete and return the notice of acceptance of liability (form SC3) to the Registrar within fifteen days of the service of the notice of claim and copy claim upon her/him.

Where the respondent disputes the claim or wishes to make a counterclaim, she/he must complete and return the notice of dispute (form SC4) to the Registrar, again within fifteen days of the service of the notice of claim. Where a counterclaim is made, it must be accompanied by a fee of £6. Upon receipt of the notice of dispute, the Registrar will furnish the claimant with a copy.

If the respondent fails to return either the notice of acceptance of liability or the notice of dispute to the Registrar within fifteen days of the service of the notice of claim and fails to contact the Registrar within that period, she/he is held to have admitted the claim. The claimant may then apply for judgment by swearing an affidavit of debt and lodging this with the Registrar, together with a request for judgment and a small claims decree. When a decree is issued, the Registrar will notify the respondent accordingly.

In cases where the claim is disputed, the Registrar will attempt to negotiate a settlement between the parties. Where an attempt at settlement fails, the case will be referred to the District Court for a hearing. The Registrar is empowered at any time on his own initiative and, if requested by either party, to refer to the District Court for hearing any application under the small claims procedure.

At the hearing, the Registrar will outline to the court the alleged facts. The applicant and the respondent may be called in turn to give their versions of the facts in dispute and may be questioned by the judge. The judge will then decide the claim.

Where the applicant's claim is successful, the respondent normally will be allowed four weeks in which to pay the amount of the award (unless an arrangement to pay by instalments is agreed). If the respondent does not pay up, the applicant can apply to the Registrar to have the order of the court executed by the sheriff. An appeal by either party of a decision of the District Court may be made to the Circuit Court. The full rules relating to the small claims procedure are contained in the District Court (Small Claims Procedure) Rules, 1993 (S.1. No. 356 of 1993).

## Circuit Court

The Circuit Court consists of a President who is, *ex officio,* a Judge of the High Court and not more than 27 ordinary judges. This figure reflects an increase in the number of Judges as provided for under the Courts Act, 1996. Here again, where a Judge is absent from duty for any reason, the government is empowered to appoint a temporary Judge.

The Circuit Court is organised on a regional basis, with the State currently divided into eight circuits: the Cork, Dublin, Eastern, Midland, Northern, South-East, South-West and Western Circuits. At least ten Judges, including the President of the Circuit Court, are permanently assigned by the government to the Dublin Circuit and at least three to Cork. The Judge assigned to each circuit travels to different towns within that circuit a number of times each year. Barristers and solicitors of ten years' experience can be appointed a

Circuit Court Judge. Circuit Court Judges retire at the age of seventy years. (Note that the eligibility of solicitors for appointment as Circuit Court Judges is authorised by provisions contained in the Courts and Court Officers Act, 1995 — see also under High Court).

In contract and tort cases, the Circuit Court has jurisdiction where the claim does not exceed £30,000, or it has unlimited jurisdiction by consent of the parties. In criminal matters, the Circuit Court can hear all indictable offences except murder and treason. In criminal cases, the judge sits with a jury of twelve persons, but juries have been abolished in civil cases in the Circuit Court since 1971. The court can hear both civil and criminal appeals from the District Court. Such appeals are a full rehearing of the case and the parties are entitled to call fresh evidence.

## High Court

This court consists of a president and up to twenty-four judges. By virtue of their offices, the President of the Circuit Court and the Chief Justice are also members of the High Court.

In the event of the illness of a High Court Judge or where, for any other reason, a sufficient number of High Court Judges is not available to carry on the work of the Court, the Chief Justice, at the request of the President of the High Court, may request a Supreme Court Judge to sit as an additional judge of the High Court. Furthermore, where a Judge of the High Court is appointed President of the Law Reform Commission, the maximum number of ordinary judges of the High Court will be increased to twenty-five.

Barristers of twelve years' experience are eligible for appointment as a High Court Judge. Since the enactment of the Courts and Court Officers Act, 1995, solicitors became eligible for the first time for appointment as Circuit Court Judges. Section 28 of this Act provides that a judge with four years' service in the Circuit Court shall be eligible for appointment as a Judge of the High Court or Supreme Court. This provision, therefore, will qualify a solicitor who has been appointed a Circuit Court Judge for appointment to the High Court and Supreme Court after four years' service as a Judge of the

Circuit Court.

High Court Judges retire at the age of seventy. However, where a Judge of the High Court held office at the time of the enactment of the Courts and Court Officers Act, 1995, the retirement age of such judge will be seventy-two years.

Normally the High Court sits with a single judge presiding, but occasionally it may sit with three judges. The High Court has unlimited jurisdiction and can award unlimited damages. When it is hearing a criminal case, it is known as the Central Criminal Court. The Central Criminal Court hears the most serious cases, such as murder (although serious cases with a terrorist element are dealt with in the Special Criminal Court).

The High Court has the power to use a jury in cases of defamation, false imprisonment or intentional trespass to the person (assault), but must use a jury in criminal cases where the accused person pleads 'not guilty'. Until 1988, a plaintiff in a civil action for personal injuries was entitled to a jury, but this right has been abolished.

In the limited number of cases in which a jury is used in civil actions, a verdict will be upheld where there is a majority of nine out of twelve. A majority of ten out of twelve is required in criminal cases.

The High Court may be required by a District Court justice to give its opinion on a point of law.

## Court of Criminal Appeal

This court hears appeals from conviction upon indictment from the Central Criminal Court, the Circuit Court and the Special Criminal Court. The judges, one of whom is the Chief Justice or another Supreme Court judge, and two High Court judges sit together in this court.

The Courts and Court Officers Act, 1995 provides for the abolition of the Court of Criminal Appeal and the transfer of its jurisdiction to the Supreme Court. At the time of publication, this was yet to be effected.

## Supreme Court

This is the final court of appeal in Ireland in criminal, civil and constitutional cases. The court consists of the Chief Justice and seven Supreme Court judges. The President of the High Court, by virtue of his office, is also a member. The court will sit with three judges or, in important cases, with five judges. It cannot sit with an even number of judges.

By invitation, Judges of the High Court sit in the Supreme Court. Barristers of twelve years' experience, Judges of the High Court, and Circuit Court Judges of four years' experience may be appointed to the Supreme Court. Supreme Court Judges retire at the age of seventy, except those who were already in office at the time of the enactment of the Courts and Court Officers Act, 1995, when retirement for such judges is seventy-two years.

### PERSONNEL OF THE LAW

The Irish Constitution provides for the appointment of an Attorney General whose function is to act as legal adviser to the government. Although not a member of the government, the Attorney General is nevertheless required to resign from office when there is a change of government. The appointment is made by the President, on the nomination of the Taoiseach.

The Director of Public Prosecutions, whose office was established by statute in 1974, is responsible for the prosecution of serious crimes.

The practising legal profession in Ireland is divided into two branches — solicitors and barristers. The training and qualification of solicitors is the responsibility of the Incorporated Law Society of Ireland, while that of barristers is the responsibility of the Honourable Society of King's Inns. A solicitor prepares a case for trial and deals directly with his or her client. He/she has a right of audience in all the courts, but usually instructs a barrister to represent his/her client in the higher courts. A barrister is normally engaged in the presentation of cases in court and is often a specialist in a particular facet of law.

There are two types of practising barrister — the senior and junior counsel — and this division of the profession indicates expertise and seniority. The work of the barrister takes two forms: the most important aspect is as an advocate on behalf of his or her client in open court; secondly, the barrister may be engaged in drafting pleadings and giving legal opinions. A barrister is not permitted to work directly for the client, but is engaged by the solicitor.

A solicitor may be engaged in a considerable amount of non-contentious office work, such as handling the sale and purchase of houses and land, drawing up wills and forming companies and partnerships. Barristers do not have a monopoly on handling cases in court, and therefore solicitors, too, do a certain amount of this type of work.

Judges are appointed by the President, on the advice of the government. They can be removed from office by the President 'for stated misbehaviour or incapacity' only on a resolution of both Houses of the Oireachtas.

# Chapter 2

# FORMING THE BUSINESS

Some people argue that the most important decision to be made by the prospective business person is the one to go into business in the first place. However, once this decision has been taken, an important question will immediately arise: what legal form should the enterprise take? There are a number of options, some of them suitable only for specialised purposes, but the choice for the hotelier or caterer will normally be made from the following: (a) sole trader, (b) partnership, or (c) company (including the single-member private limited company).

## SOLE TRADER

A sole trader is a person who sets up in business on his own account and is the proprietor. He can, of course, employ as many people as he wishes, but the essential feature is that he alone is responsible for the running of the business and has no association with others in that regard.

In general, the sole trader is not burdened by a vast array of legal red tape, although it must be said that the extent to which he is free of legal restrictions relates very closely to the type of business he wishes to operate. Many businesses require those engaged in them to hold particular qualifications or to obtain special licences. For those engaged in the hotel and catering industry, there are likely to be more legal formalities to comply with than for those trading as grocers, newsagents, clothing retailers and the like. Such legal formalities particular to various aspects of the hotel and catering industry could include, for example, applications for licenses to sell intoxicating liquor and to hold public dances and discos, and the registration of premises under the Food Hygiene Regulations and the Tourist Traffic Acts.

One legal formality that may be complied with concerns the name by which the business is to trade and be known. If a sole trader intends to conduct business under his own name, e.g. Brian O'Connor, then he may go ahead and do so. But, if he wants to trade under an invented name, such as The Tasty Tuckbox Restaurant, he must register it under requirements laid down in the Registration of Business Names Act, 1963 (see page 31).

Those who are contemplating setting up in business as a sole trader should give some thought to the relative merits and limitations of such an enterprise.

## Factors in Favour of Sole Tradership

- Apart from the considerations already mentioned, there are no formalities.
- Profits after tax accrue entirely to the sole trader.
- The proprietor's business affairs are as confidential as he or she wishes them to be.
- He or she does not have to consult or agree with others in making decisions.
- The sole trader can easily transfer or sell the business.
- The sole trader has complete managerial control.

## Factors Against Sole Tradership

- There is unlimited liability for all the debts and obligations of the business, even to the extent of forfeiting personal property (this constitutes, by far, the greatest disadvantage). But see single-member private limited companies (page 29).
- The business has no separate legal identity distinct from the owner.
- The sole trader must have, or be able to raise, the capital necessary to finance the business.
- All business losses must be borne by the sole trader.

## GENERAL PARTNERSHIP

The Partnership Act, 1890 defines a partnership as 'the relation which subsists between persons carrying on a business in common with a view of profit'. This definition identifies the need for three essential ingredients to be present before a partnership can exist. There must, of course, be a business, and this is a term that embraces professions, trades and occupations; at least two people must be involved; and the object of the enterprise must be to make a profit.

### Forming a Partnership

No particular form of agreement is required. Although usually it is constituted by contract expressed as a deed, a partnership can be set up by a verbal contract or even can be inferred from facts and circumstances. The existence of a partnership is therefore a question of fact and does not in every case require the expressed intention of the participating parties. Clearly, a verbal contract covering a matter of such potential importance as a partnership agreement creates scope for difficulties. The main disadvantage is the problem of proving its provisions in the event of a dispute; in the absence of corroboration, one partner's word is as good as another's.

With the exception of partnerships of solicitors and accountants, the maximum number of partners permitted is limited to twenty and the business thus formed is more correctly referred to as a firm. If the partners do not trade under their own names, they will be required to register under the Registration of Business Names Act, 1963 (see page 31).

### Liability of Partners

The liability of partners for the debts and obligations of the firm is a joint matter. This does not affect the extent of an individual partner's liability since each partner is individually and severally liable for all the debts of the firm. The meaning of the term 'joint', in this context, is that a plaintiff can bring only one action against the members of the firm.

## Authority of Partners

The authority of a partner may be of two kinds:

(a) **Actual or express authority,** which derives from the authority given to a partner by the terms contained in the partnership agreement, and

(b) **Ostensible or apparent authority,** which is the authority with which a partner is vested by virtue of his or her status as a partner.

The type of authority exercised, whether actual or ostensible, can therefore be seen to have implications for the firm.

If a partner acts on behalf of the firm within the scope of his express authority, there is little difficulty in seeing that his actions will bind the partnership. If he acts beyond the scope of his actual authority but within the scope of his ostensible authority, he will also bind the firm, unless the party with whom he has contracted had notice of the partner's actual authority.

The distinction between actual and ostensible authority is best illustrated by an example:

> Tom, Dick and Harriet are partners in a firm of builders' providers. Their partnership agreement has a clause which states that 'No partner without the express agreement of all partners is permitted to advance credit in excess of £500 in value to any customer of the firm'.
>
> Dermot, a local hotelier and a personal friend of Dick, is in the process of refurbishing a section of his hotel. He approaches Dick for the supply, on credit, of building materials worth £2,000, to be paid for within three months.

In this example, if Dick refuses to supply the goods to Dermot, he will be following the requirements of the partnership agreement. If, however, he supplies the materials, he will nevertheless bind his firm by his actions, because, as far as Dermot is concerned, Dick, being a partner, appears to have authority to advance the requested credit. Therefore, Dermot could ignore any request by the partnership to pay up before the agreed time.

## Power of Partners

Usually a partner can:

- Purchase goods for the firm
- Sell the goods of the firm
- Receive payment of debts and give receipts

- Engage employees for the firm
- Draw, accept and endorse bills and cheques
- If the partnership is a trading firm, borrows money on the firm's credit, or pledges goods belonging to the firm.

It should be noted that the partnership agreement may curtail or extend the powers identified here.

## Dissolution of a Partnership

A partnership may be brought to an end in several ways:

- At the will of a partner, where no fixed term has been agreed upon; if the partnership is constituted by a deed, the partner must give notice in writing.
- On the expiry of the time agreed upon as the term or, if for a single undertaking, on the completion of the undertaking.
- By the death or bankruptcy of a partner, unless the agreement provides otherwise.
- At the option of the other partners, if one partner has suffered his or her share of the partnership property to be judicially charged for his or her separate debt.
- By the occurrence of an event that makes the partnership illegal.
- By the permanent insanity of a partner.
- By the permanent incapacity of a partner to perform his or her part of the partnership contract.
- When business can be carried on only at a loss.
- When the court thinks it just and equitable to decree a dissolution.

## Procedure on the Dissolution of a Partnership

When the partnership is dissolved, the firm's assets are liquidated and used:

- to pay creditors
- to repay any loans from partners
- to repay the capital to partners.

If there is any profit on the realisation of the assets, it is divided among the partners in the same ratio as they share profits.

## Advantages of a Partnership

- If the business gets into financial difficulty, no single partner has to bear the total loss if the others have sufficient means to honour their share.

- There is no requirement to publish accounts.

- The more partners, the more capital is available to the business, and the greater the potential for a more varied business expertise.

## Disadvantages of a Partnership

- Unlimited liability (but see, generally, Limited Partnership below).

- A partnership is not a separate legal entity (see Private Limited Companies, page 24).

- Profits must be shared among all the partners in accordance with the partnership agreement or, in the absence of an agreement, equally.

- The continuity of the partnership may be affected by the occurrence of certain events (see Dissolution of a Partnership, page 21).

## LIMITED PARTNERSHIP

The Limited Partnership Act, 1907 provides a mechanism whereby a partner may limit his or her liability for the debts and obligations of the firm. The expression 'limited partnership' is somewhat misleading since it gives the impression that the entity has limited liability. This is not the case. The limitation on liability is afforded to certain persons, who by their actions comply with the Act to acquire limited liability.

## Limited Partner Defined

A limited partner is one who contributes to the partnership, when he or she joins it, a stated amount of capital in cash or property valued at a stated amount and whose liability for the debts and obligations of the firm is limited to the amount contributed.

## Rules Relating to Limited Partnership

In general, the same law is applicable to limited partnerships as to general partnerships, but certain provisions of the Limited Partnership Act, 1907 contain express modifications to partnership law. These modifications are as follows:

- One or more of the partners must be general partners who are liable for all the firm's debts and obligations.

- One or more of the partners must be limited partners, who, on entering the partnership, contribute capital beyond which they are not liable to contribute for the firm's debts.

- A limited partner must not take part in the management of the partnership business, and if he does, he will become liable for all the debts and obligations of the firm incurred during that time.

- A limited partner may assign his or her share of the partnership with the consent of the general partners.

- Neither the death, the bankruptcy nor the insanity of a limited partner will dissolve the firm.

## Requirement of Registration

Every limited partnership must be registered with the Registrar of Companies. Such registration requires that the Registrar be provided with the following information, signed by all the partners:

- The name of the business

- The nature of the business

- The principal place of the business

- The name of each partner

- The duration of the partnership

- The date of commencement

- A statement that the partnership is limited

- A description of each limited partner

- The amount contributed by each partner and the method of payment.

## THE COMPANY

The law relating to companies incorporated in Ireland is governed by the Companies Act, 1963, which was amended by a series of other Acts in 1977, 1982, 1983, 1986 and by two very important Acts in 1990. These are collectively referred to as The Companies Acts, 1963-90.

The administration of the provisions of these Acts is the responsibility of the Minister for Enterprise, Trade and Employment, who appoints a Registrar of Companies to run the Companies Registration Office in Dublin Castle.

## Possible Options

A company may be unlimited, or limited by shares, or limited by guarantees. It may be public or private. A private company is defined in the Companies Act, 1963 as a company that has a share capital and that by its articles of association

- limits the number of its members to 50 (but not including employees and past employees whose membership commenced while they were employed by the company)
- prohibits itself from making any invitation to the public to subscribe for its shares or debentures
- restricts the right to transfer its shares.

Any other company is deemed to be a public company. However, the Companies (Amendment) Act, 1983 provided the first statutory definition of a public company as being 'a company which is not a Private Company'. This Act differentiates between a 'public limited company' and all other companies. The principal characteristics of the public limited company are that:

- it indicates its status by the use of the words Public limited company (or uses the abbreviation plc)
- it is limited by shares
- it has an allotted share capital of a nominal amount of not less than £30,000 (or such greater amount as may be specified from time to time by the Minister for Enterprise, Trade and Employment).

### PRIVATE LIMITED COMPANIES

These are by far the most popular means of operating a company in Ireland today and outnumber public companies by a ratio that is close to two hundred to one. The emphasis here, therefore, will be confined mainly to dealing with the formation of a private company, the liability of whose members is limited by shares.

When a company is limited by shares, the liability of its members is limited to the amount that they have agreed to pay for their shares. If they have paid for their shares in full, they will have no further liability to the company. Any amount unpaid must be paid up, even if the company gets into financial difficulty and looks like being liquidated or is in fact liquidated. The word 'limited', therefore, in this context means that liability to repay the business's debts is limited to the amount remaining unpaid on shares. If the business goes bankrupt, the personal possessions of the members cannot be seized to pay the company's debts, unless of course there was fraud involved. Limited liability may also be lost where the membership of a private company falls below two (or below seven in a public company) and where such company carries on business for more than six months after that occurrence. (But see special provisions relating to single-member private limited companies, at the end of this chapter.) Every member who is aware that the company is operating in such circumstances becomes liable for all debts incurred during that time. Furthermore, a limited company has a legal existence that is separate from its members. Like an individual, the company can enter into a contract with other organisations and individuals, can sue and be sued and prosecuted, without involving its members in the proceedings.

In return for an investment in the company, a member is usually entitled to the following rights:

- to receive a share in the company's profits (called a dividend)
- to attend meetings of the company
- to vote at company meetings
- to receive company reports and accounts.

## Restriction on Directors

Under the provisions of the Companies Act, 1990, there is a restriction on the directors of insolvent companies becoming directors of other companies for a period of five years. However, the High Court has the power to set aside this restriction if it is established that a director has acted honestly and responsibly in the conduct of the affairs of the insolvent company. Furthermore, the restriction will not apply in a case where the other company has an allotted share capital of £20,000 (and is a private company) or £100,000 (and is a public company) and in both cases the allotted share capital is fully paid up.

## Appointment of Company Examiner

Under the Companies (Amendment) Act, 1990, the High Court has the power to appoint an examiner to a company where it appears that such company is unable to pay its debts, and no notice of a resolution for its winding-up has been given more than seven days before the application and no order has been made for its winding-up.

The petition for the appointment of an examiner may be made by the company, the directors, a creditor, or members holding not less than one-tenth of such of the paid-up capital as carries the right to voting at general meetings. The court may grant the petition if it considers that this would be likely to contribute to the company's survival. From the date of presentation of the petition to the expiry of the ensuing three months (or the withdrawal or refusal of the petition), the company is under the protection of the court, which has the following effects:

- No proceedings for its winding-up may be commenced or resolution for winding-up passed (any resolution so passed will have no effect).

- No receiver may be appointed.

- No legal process can be put into force against the company's property without the examiner's consent.

- No action may be taken to realise any security which is charged on its property without the examiner's consent.

- Where any person other than the company is liable to pay all or any part of the company's debts, no legal process can be put in force against such person's property and no legal proceedings of any kind may be commenced against such person in respect of such debts.

- Repossession of goods in the company's possession under a hire-purchase agreement cannot be effected without the examiner's consent.

## Forming a Private Limited Company

A private company must have at least two members and not more than fifty (subject to the exception relating to employees referred to above) and must be registered in compliance with the requirements for registration laid down in the Companies Acts, 1963-90. (But see special provisions relating to single-member private limited companies, at the end of this chapter.)

Before a company can be registered, the following documents must be delivered to the Registrar of Companies:

1. **THE MEMORANDUM OF ASSOCIATION.** The memorandum must be signed by at least two persons and must contain five clauses:

- *The Name Clause.* This sets out the name of the company and ends with the word 'limited', or in Irish 'Teoranta'. The company may carry on its business under a name other than its registered corporate name, but it is then subject to the requirement of the Registration of Business Names Act, 1963 (see page 31).

- *The Objects Clause.* This must state the objects for which the company was formed. Provided it is lawful, there is complete freedom as to what the objects clause may contain. However, once the objects clause is stipulated in the Memorandum of Association, the company is strictly confined by the clause.

- *The Limited Liability Clause.* This is a statement to the effect that the liability of members is limited.

- *The Capital Clause.* This must state the amount of the nominal capital, the number of shares into which it is divided, and the amount of each share.

- *Association Clause.* Here the subscribers make a declaration that they wish to be formed into a company and agree to take shares in that company

2. **THE ARTICLES OF ASSOCIATION.** These, too, must be signed by at least two persons. A standard form of Articles is provided in the schedule to the Companies Act, 1963, known as Table A, and this will apply to a company limited by shares, except to the extent that it is specifically excluded or modified by the Articles adopted by the company. It should be noted that adopting Table A verbatim is not necessary. The possibilities of an individual construction of Table A are open to the founder of a company. The Articles set out the rules for the management of the company's affairs and include such matters as the appointment, powers, duties, and removal of directors, the holding of and conduct at company meetings; and the acquisition, transfer and forfeiture of shares. For example, the Articles might be drafted so as to give security of tenure to directors or to a particular director, or a right to appoint or remove one or more directors. The Articles of Association of a private limited company must also include the provisions referred to above (namely, those defining the private company, limiting the number of members to fifty, restricting the transfer of shares, and prohibiting any invitation to the public to subscribe for shares). The Articles are subservient to the Memorandum, and if there is any inconsistency between the two documents, the Memorandum of Association will prevail.

**Note: The Memorandum of Association and the Articles of Association together are regarded as the company's constitution.**

3. **THE STATUTORY DECLARATION.** This is a statement, made on oath to the effect that all the requirements of the Companies Acts relating to registration have been fully complied with. It may be made by the solicitor acting in the formation of the company, or by a person named in the Articles as a director or secretary of the company.

4. A statement in a prescribed form containing particulars of the persons who are to be the first directors, including their names, addresses, nationalities and occupations, and the names and addresses of the secretary or joint secretaries. This statement must be signed by or on behalf of the subscribers to the memorandum and it must be accompanied by a consent signed by each of the persons named as a director, secretary or joint secretary to act in that capacity.

5. Details of the company's registered office.

6. The prescribed fee for registration and stamp duties.

If these documents are in order, the Registrar will proceed to register the company and will issue, in due course, the 'Certificate of Incorporation'. This document could be described as the company's 'birth certificate' and is conclusive evidence that the requirements for registration under the Companies Acts have been met in full. The private limited company then can commence business.

## Advantages of a Private Limited Company

1. Perhaps the single most outstanding advantage is the concept of limited liability (but note — page 25 — how this may be lost).
2. The ability, through the act of incorporation, to keep the company's affairs separate from those of the shareholders.
3. The business is not affected by the death of anyone connected with it.
4. The acquisition or disposal of shares can be arranged easily.
5. The business, as distinct from the legal, advantages include: a higher level of status or image attached to a company; the management structure is more clearly defined; and capital investment may be acquired more easily.

## Disadvantages of a Private Limited Company

1. Limited liability status can be diluted by the increasingly common practice of

lending institutions requiring personal guarantees from directors and major shareholders.

2. The company is required to file annual returns and submit audited accounts to the Companies Registration Office, thereby necessitating the continuing services of an accountant.

3. Once incorporated, the company will probably need continuing professional advice to meet its legal obligations.

## Single-Member Private Limited Company

The European Communities (Single-Member Private Limited Companies) Regulations, 1994 became law on 1 October 1994 and gave effect to Council Directive No. 89/667/EEC. These regulations introduce the facility, which is also widely available throughout the European Union, whereby a sole person, whether natural or legal, will now be able to form or become a single-member private limited liability company. The regulations are to be construed as one with the Companies Acts, 1963-1990.

## Forming a Single-Member Company

Notwithstanding the provisions of the Companies Act, 1963, one person may, for any lawful purpose, by subscribing his or her name to a Memorandum of Association and complying with the requirements of the Companies Acts and these regulations, form a private limited liability company.

An already existing private limited liability company with two or more subscribers can become a single-member company when the number of its members is reduced to one and all the shares in the company are registered in the name of a sole person. When a company becomes a single-member company in this manner, it is required to give notice of this fact to the Registrar of Companies within 28 days after the date on which the number of members is reduced to one, giving the name of the sole member and the date on which it became a single-member company. Notification must be in writing and in a form prescribed in the regulations. Failure to comply with these requirements will render the company and every officer of the company who is in default guilty of an offence.

Similarly, a single-member company shall cease to be a single-member company on such date as the number of members increases to more than one, but will continue to be a private limited liability company while the number of members does not exceed fifty. The same notification requirements to the Registrar of Companies, as described above, apply also in these circumstances.

## Further Provisions

The regulations provide that, subject to certain modifications, all the provisions of the Companies Acts which apply to private companies limited by shares or by guarantee will apply to single-member companies. For example, the sole member, if he or she so decides, can dispense with the holding of general meetings, including annual general meetings. However, certain notifications will have to be made. The detailed regulations pertaining to general meetings (including annual general meetings) are contained in the European Communities (Single-Member Private Limited Companies) Regulations, 1994 (S.I.No.275 of 1994).

Single-member companies will, for the time being, continue to require two directors. At the time these regulations were introduced, the then Minister for Enterprise and Employment gave an undertaking to request the Company Law Review Group, in a future phase of its work, to examine the feasibility of reducing the minimum number of directors in these types of companies to one.

## Penalties

A person guilty of an offence under any provision of these regulations shall be liable, on summary conviction, to a fine not exceeding £1,000.

# Chapter 3

# FURTHER FORMALITIES

## REGISTERING A BUSINESS NAME

The need to protect the public (and creditors) from the excesses of a dishonest or unscrupulous trader, who might seek to conceal his true identity by trading under a fictitious name, is recognised in the Registration of Business Names Act, 1963. This statute lays down the requirements and procedure to be followed when registering the name of a business.

## Is Registration Always Necessary?

Not every business name is required to be registered. If a business is being run under

(a) the true surname of a sole trader, or

(b) the true surnames of all the persons in a partnership, or

(c) the corporate names of all partners that are corporations, or

(d) the corporate name of a body corporate,

registration under the Act is not required.

In the case of (a) and (b), the addition of the true Christian name(s), forename(s) or initials of these is permitted. Any other addition to the name(s) necessitates registration, as does the use of an invented name, such as 'The Hideaway Hotel'. In the case of (c), involving a partnership consisting of bodies corporate (e.g. companies), any addition to the corporate name necessitates registration. With regard to (d), so long as the corporate body (e.g. company) trades under its corporate (company) name, without any addition, it too will be exempt from the requirement of registration.

## Registration Particulars Required by Registrar

Where the registration of a business name is required, the following particulars must be furnished in writing and delivered by hand or by post to the Registrar of Companies, Dublin Castle:

- The business name.
- The general nature of the business.
- The principal place of the business.
- The date of the adoption of the business name.
- Where the registration is by a firm, the present Christian name (or forename) and surname, any former names, nationality (if not Irish), usual residence, other business occupation(s) (if any) of each of the individuals who are partners, and the corporate name and registered office of every corporate body that is a partner.
- Where registration is by a sole trader, the present Christian name (or forename) and surname, any former name, nationality (if not Irish), usual residence, other business occupation(s) (if any) of such an individual.
- Where registration is by a body corporate, the corporate name and the registered or principal office in the state.

The foregoing particulars must be signed as follows:

(a) In the case of a sole trader — by that individual.

(b) In the case of a body corporate — by a director or secretary.

(c) In the case of a firm (partnership), either

    (i) by all the individuals who are partners, and by a director or secretary of all bodies corporate that are partners, or

    (ii) by an individual who is a partner, or a director or secretary of some body corporate which is a partner (this latter must be verified by a statutory declaration).

The application must be accompanied by the appropriate registration fee — currently £15.

## Registration Certificate

When a business name has been registered, the Registrar will issue a certificate of registration. This certificate must be displayed in a prominent manner in the principal place of business and in every branch office or location where the business is normally carried on.

## Index of Business Names

The Registrar is required under the Act to keep an index of all business names. Any person may inspect the documents kept by the Registrar, on payment of the fee prescribed from time to time and, on the same terms, may obtain a certificate of registration of any business or require a copy of, or extract from, any document.

## Further Provisions of the Act

- Registration must be made within one month of the adoption of the business name.

- Any changes in the particulars registered must be notified in writing and must be delivered by hand or by post to the Registrar within one month of the change.

- All documents used by a business registered under this Act, such as business letters, circulars and catalogues on which the business name appears, must set out the true name(s) and nationality (if not Irish) of the person(s) trading under the business name.

- The Minister for Enterprise, Trade and Employment may refuse to permit the registration of any name which, in his or her opinion, is an undesirable business name, but such refusal may be appealed to the High Court.

## Offences and Penalties

- For making a false statement in the provision of particulars for registration, a period of imprisonment not exceeding six months may be imposed in substitution of or in addition to a fine of £100.

- For failing to publish in business letters, circulars and catalogues the true name(s) and nationality (if not Irish) of person(s) trading under a business name, there is a fine not exceeding £25.

Upon conviction for the following offences, a maximum fine of up to £100 may be imposed:

- for failing to furnish particulars
- for failing to notify changes in registered information
- for failing to display a certificate of registration in a prominent place
- for failing to notify the Registrar that a business has ceased trading under a

registered business name

- for continuing to use a business name after the name has been refused registration.

## Who may be Held Liable?

Every individual, in the case of a sole trader, and every partner may be held liable under this Act and, where a body corporate is guilty of any offence, every director, secretary or officer who is knowingly a party to the default will be similarly liable.

## Authority to Use a Registered Business Name

The Registration of Business Names Act, 1963 makes it clear that the registration of a business name confers no absolute authority to use that name. Registration of the business name is merely that, and such registration cannot be advanced by anyone as proof of their entitlement to use it.

The Registrar makes no comparison with the trademarks index or the company index. Therefore, the acceptance by him, for registration, of a particular business name should not be taken to mean that no rights already exist in the name. In view of this, anyone considering registering a business name should investigate the possibility of others having established rights to the proposed name, before incurring any expenses in connection with the business.

## PASSING OFF

Although, strictly speaking, a matter for discussion under the Law of Torts (see generally Chapter 5), the foregoing mention of the Registration of Business Names Act makes it appropriate to deal here with the tort of 'passing off'.

Any person who takes advantage of the good reputation of an already established business by adopting the same or similar business name, logo, packaging, trademark or other representational materials may be liable in tort for 'passing off'.

It is not necessary for the plaintiff to prove that he or she suffered loss, or that anyone was actually deceived, or that there was fraud on the part of the defendant. The plaintiff must prove, however, that the presentation of the goods or services is such as to be calculated to mislead the public into believing that such goods or services are the products of the long-established business.

The usual remedy sought by a plaintiff is an injunction to prevent the continuation of the passing off.

## REGISTRATION OF PREMISES UNDER TOURIST TRAFFIC ACTS, 1939-95

### Background and Role of Bord Fáilte Éireann

The Irish Tourist Board, as it was then called, was established by the Tourist Traffic Act, 1939 and subsequently was renamed Bord Fáilte under the Tourist Traffic Act, 1952. It was not until the enactment of the Tourist Traffic Act, 1955 that it acquired the name by which it is now known — Bord Fáilte Éireann.

Bord Fáilte Éireann is a body corporate and consists of not more than nine members. Each member is appointed by the Minister responsible (at present the Minister for Tourism, Sport and Recreation) and holds office for a period not exceeding five years. On the expiration of his or her term of office, a member is eligible for reappointment.

Bord Fáilte Éireann is required to furnish the Minister with such information in relation to its operation as he or she may from time to time require and, in addition, must provide the Minister with an annual report, which has to be laid before each House of the Oireachtas.

Under the Tourist Traffic Acts, Bord Fáilte Éireann is charged with a general duty 'to encourage and promote the development of tourist traffic in and to the state'. Although the activities identified here are not intended to be exhaustive, they give some idea of the wide-ranging functions of Bord Fáilte Éireann, whose brief extends to include the following:

- To inspect, register and grade all types of tourist accommodation.
- To assist in the provision and improvement of holiday accommodation and tourist facilities and amenities.
- To provide and assist schemes for the training of tourism personnel.
- To protect and maintain places of historic, scenic and scientific interest and to facilitate visitors by the provision of signs and means of access.
- To advertise the advantages and amenities of holiday resorts in Ireland.
- To prepare and publish guidebooks and other information for tourists.
- To establish, equip and operate tourist information bureaux both inside and outside Ireland.
- To cooperate with other bodies in connection with tourist publicity.
- To provide consultancy and advisory services to tourism.

It should be noted that, subject to compliance with procedures laid down in the Tourist Traffic Acts, Bord Fáilte Éireann has power compulsorily to acquire land for the purpose of exercising any of its duties and functions.

Since the enactment of the Tourist Traffic Act, 1995, the way in which Bord Fáilte Eireann discharges its functions has, in a number of matters, altered. Specifically, the 1995 Act enables Bord Fáilte Éireann to exercise its powers and perform any of its functions under the Tourist Traffic Acts, 1939-87 regarding the registration and grading of accommodation and under the Intoxicating Liquor Act, 1988 in relation to Special Restaurant Licences, by or through contractors.

In its implementation of the provisions of the Tourist Traffic Act, 1995, Bord Fáilte Éireann has subcontracted its accommodation assessment and classification functions to a contractor, but has retained an overall monitoring role. In a separate arrangement, a number of accommodation associations have been recognised by Bord Fáilte Eireann as self-regulating bodies for the purpose of approving the various types of bed and breakfast accommodation. However, Bord Fáilte Éireann will continue to be responsible for ensuring that standards meet the needs of visitors and tour operators.

Tourism Quality Services (Ireland) Ltd, 25 Herbert Place, Dublin 2 (Tel. 01-6625784) is the contractor retained by Bord Fáilte Éireann to carry out the assessment, registration and classification of hotels, guesthouses, caravan and camping parks, holiday cottages and holiday apartments; and the registration of holiday hostels, youth hostels and holiday camps. In addition, the company will award certificates to restaurants applying for a liquor licence under the Intoxicating Liquor Act, 1988 (Special Restaurant Licence — see page 171).

While Tourism Quality Services (Ireland) Ltd. will process and register applications in all the above accommodation categories, as well as administering registration renewals, Bord Fáilte Éireann continues to retain important functions. Where an application for registration is rejected, any subsequent appeal against this decision is made to an officer of Bord Fáilte Éireann. Similarly, where there is an appeal against the cancellation of a Bord Fáilte Éireann certificate, an officer of Bord Fáilte Éireann will also carry out this appeal.

The other accommodation associations recognised by Bord Fáilte Éireann are:

- Farm and Country Standards Ltd (Irish Farm Holidays Association), 2 Michael Street, Limerick. (Tel. 061-400700). Awarded the contract for approving/listing all existing farmhouses and the inspection of new farmhouses.

- Quality Approved Bed and Breakfast Ltd, Bachelor's Walk, Ballyshannon, Co. Donegal. (Tel. 072-52760). Awarded the contract for approving/listing all existing town homes and country homes and the inspection of new town and country homes.

- Specialist Accommodation Approvals, P.O. 5451, Dublin 3 (Tel. 01-8338227). Awarded the contract for approving specialist accommodation, i.e. houses of architectural/historical character, specialist activity and pubs with accommodation and the inspection of any new premises wishing to enter these categories.

All these agencies operate under licence from Bord Fáilte Éireann, but Bord Fáilte Éireann owns the requirements for each category of accommodation.

## Range of Registers

Tourism Quality Services (Ireland) Ltd. maintains a separate register for each of the following types of accommodation: hotels; guesthouses; holiday hostels; youth hostels; holiday camps; caravan and camping parks; holiday cottages; and holiday apartments. In order to be eligible for registration under a particular category, there are specific and detailed regulations with which the premises seeking registration must be able to comply. These regulations prescribe the general character of the premises, the type of accommodation and services and the other qualifications required. The regulations for each type of accommodation are readily available, for a nominal charge, from Tourism Quality Services (Ireland) Ltd.

## Application Procedure for Registration

The proprietor of any premises may apply to Tourism Quality Services (Ireland) Ltd. for registration, nominating the particular register that is appropriate to the type of premises. Every application must:

- be made in writing and in the form prescribed
- include the full name, address and description of the proprietor; the name of the premises and its address or situation; and such other particulars as may be required
- be accompanied by the prescribed application fee
- be accompanied by a statement of the charges that the applicant proposes to make for rooms, meals, services (as applicable) provided in the premises during the period between registration (if granted) and the following December.

When an application for registration is received, the premises are inspected by a representative of Tourism Quality Services (Ireland) Ltd. If, following the inspection, the premises are deemed eligible for registration, the applicant is so informed and, in order to effect registration, is required to pay the prescribed registration fee. Failure to pay the registration fee within three months of being served with notice that the premises are eligible for registration will render the application void.

Where an application for registration is rejected, the applicant must be served with notice of this decision and has fourteen days in which to make written representations with a view to showing that his or her premises are eligible for registration. If the applicant exercises this right of appeal, a second inspection of the premises will be carried out by an officer of Bord Fáilte Éireann. If the applicant does not appeal within the prescribed fourteen days, or appeals and once again is unsuccessful, Bord Fáilte Éireann will refuse to register the premises. Where the appeal is successful, the premises will be registered on payment of the registration fee. The registration process cannot be completed until the fee is paid. Irrespective of the date on which the premises are first registered, the renewal of registration falls due on the following 31 December.

## Procedure for the Renewal of Registration

The registered proprietor of premises may apply to Tourism Quality Services (Ireland) Ltd., on or before 15 October (or, with the consent of Tourism Quality Services (Ireland) Ltd., on or before 15 November) in any year, for the renewal of the registration of the premises as from 31 December.

An application for renewal must:

- be made in writing and in the form prescribed
- contain the prescribed particulars
- be accompanied by the required fee
- be accompanied by a statement (referred to as a scale of charges) of the charges that the applicant proposes to make for rooms, meals and services (as applicable) provided on the premises during the period of registration.

If Tourism Quality Services (Ireland) Ltd. is satisfied that the premises have not ceased to be eligible, then it will renew the registration. In cases where Tourism Quality Services (Ireland) Ltd. considers that the premises have ceased to be eligible, an inspection will be carried out. Following this inspection, the premises are either deemed eligible for registration or rejected yet again. If the latter is the case, Tourism Quality Services (Ireland) Ltd. is required to state the grounds upon which the premises are considered ineligible. An appeals procedure may be followed, similar to that which applies to an original application (i.e. directly to Bord Fáilte Éireann) and allowing for a second inspection.

The renewal of registration may also be refused where the applicant has (without the consent of Tourism Quality Services (Ireland) Ltd.), in the trading period prior to renewal, 'wilfully failed to adhere to charges not exceeding those specified in the scale of charges furnished by him or her' with his or her previous registration.

## Rules relating to Registration Certificates

Whenever Tourism Quality Services (Ireland) Ltd. registers any premises under its authority, it will issue, free of charge, a certificate of registration to the registered proprietor. The following provisions apply to the registration certificate:

(a) The certificate must be in the prescribed form and must contain a statement of the premises to which it relates, the name of the registered proprietor, and such other information as may be required.

(b) The certificate must be signed by an authorised representative of Tourism Quality Services (Ireland) Ltd.

(c) The certificate must (unless it is returned to Tourism Quality Services (Ireland) Ltd. for any purpose) be displayed in a prominent place at or near the main entrance to the premises to which it relates, during the period of registration certified by it.

(d) The certificate must be returned to Tourism Quality Services (Ireland) Ltd. immediately after the registration expires or when requested by Tourism Quality Services (Ireland) Ltd.

Failure to display the certificate in accordance with (c) above is an offence and, on summary conviction, carries a fine not exceeding £200, with a further fine of £10 for every day during which the offence continues (but not exceeding £200). Failure to return the certificate immediately upon its expiry or when requested by Tourism Quality Services (Ireland) Ltd. is also an offence. The penalty here on summary conviction is a fine not exceeding £50, with an additional fine of £5 for every day during which the offence continues (but not exceeding £200).

## Cancellation of Registration

Tourism Quality Services (Ireland) Ltd. is at liberty to carry out an inspection of premises at any time. If, following such inspection, Tourism Quality Services (Ireland) Ltd. is of the opinion that the premises have ceased to be eligible for registration, a second inspection will be carried out. Following the second inspection, and where the company's opinion is unchanged, the proprietor will be notified of the decision and has thirty days to make written representation to maintain registration. If the proprietor does not avail of this appeal mechanism, his or her registration is cancelled. Where the propietor responds within the thirty-day period by making a written representation contending the decision about the continuing eligibility of his or her premises, a third inspection will be carried out, this time by an officer of Bord Fáilte Éireann. If Bord Fáilte Éireann, as a result of the third inspection and the representation made to it, is of the opinion that the premises have not ceased to be eligible for registration, the proprietor must be informed accordingly. However, failure to satisfy the Bord following the third inspection will result in cancellation of the registration. Where cancellation occurs, it will have effect from a date determined by the Bord, but not earlier than fourteen days after the decision to cancel is made. Furthermore, Bord Fáilte Éireann must serve a notice of cancellation on the proprietor not later than seven days before the date decided.

The Bord may at any time cancel the registration of premises if it is of the view that the proprietor has (without consent) wilfully failed to adhere to charges not exceeding those specified by him/her.

## Restriction on the Description of Premises

It is an offence for the proprietor or occupier of any premises to describe or hold out or permit any person to describe or hold out such premises as:

(a) Hotel

(b) Guesthouse

(c) Holiday hostel or holiday home

(d) Youth hostel

(e) Motor hotel; motel; coach hotel; motor inn; motor court; tourist court

(f) Caravan site; caravan park; caravan camp; caravan centre; caravan estate; caravan court; caravantel; camping site; camping park; camping centre; camping estate; camping court; autocamp

(g) Approved holiday cottage; approved holiday house; approved holiday home;

approved holiday villa

(h) Holiday apartment; tourist apartment; apartotel; holiday flat

unless the premises are registered in the appropriate register for the particular accommodation and the proprietor or occupier is registered as the proprietor. The penalty on summary conviction is a fine not exceeding £500 and, in the case of a continuing offence, a further fine not exceeding £20 for every day during which the offence continues (but not exceeding £300).

Where a person is acting in contravention of the matters outlined above, the Circuit Court, on the application of Bord Fáilte Éireann, may prohibit the continuance of the contravention.

## Grading

From time to time Tourism Quality Services (Ireland) Ltd. may grade the premises registered in any of its registers and, similarly, may withdraw a grade or allot a different grade, as it considers appropriate.

It is an offence for the proprietor of premises to describe or hold out his or her premises as being of a grade other than that allotted to the premises. Such an offence carries a penalty on summary conviction of a fine not exceeding £500.

On 1 January 1994, a new star system of grading for hotels and guesthouses was introduced. Hotels are now graded from five stars at the top down to one star, while guesthouses are graded from four stars down to one star. Under this star system, a hotel or guesthouse cannot be demoted to a lower grade. If a hotel or guesthouse does not maintain the physical and operational standards set down for its particular grade, its grade will be taken away. This is to protect the integrity of each particular grade within the star system.

## Inspection of Premises

A registration representative is entitled at all reasonable times (subject to the production by him or her, if so required, of his or her appointment in writing as a registration officer) to enter and inspect any registered premises, or premises in respect of which an application for registration has been made. He or she may require the registered proprietor (or applicant for registration, as the case may be) or any person employed on the premises to furnish such information as may be reasonably necessary for the purpose of the Tourist Traffic Acts.

Every person

- who obstructs or impedes a registration representative in the exercise of his or her duty, or
- who fails or refuses to give a registration representative on demand any information that he or she is entitled to demand, or
- who wilfully gives false or misleading information in a material particular to a registration officer

will be guilty of an offence and will be liable, on summary conviction, to a fine not exceeding £50.

## Inspection of Register

Any person may inspect any register, or obtain a certified copy of any entry in a register, or obtain a certificate that any particular premises are not registered in a specified register, on payment of such fee as may be prescribed from time to time by Tourism Quality Services (Ireland) Ltd.

## Display of Charges

Tourism Quality Services (Ireland) Ltd. may require the proprietor of registered premises to display in such places as it thinks proper, lists of current charges for rooms, meals or other services. Failure to comply with this requirement is an offence carrying a fine not exceeding £100, together with a further fine not exceeding £10 per day (to a maximum of £100) for every day during which the offence is continued.

## Display of Certain Information

A registered proprietor must display in the interior of the premises such information as Tourism Quality Services (Ireland) Ltd. may require in writing from time to time. Such display must be made in the manner and in such places as the Bord may require. A proprietor who does not comply with this requirement is guilty of an offence and is liable, on summary conviction, to a fine not exceeding £100.

## External Signs

Tourism Quality Services (Ireland) Ltd. may supply the proprietor of registered premises with a sign suitable for display outside the premises. Such a sign must be displayed in a prominent position at or near the main entrance to the premises. Failure to display the sign as required is an offence, for which the penalty is a fine not exceeding £100. Unless Tourism Quality Services (Ireland) Ltd. gives its consent, no other sign denoting the standard of the premises may be displayed. Contravention of this requirement also carries a fine not exceeding £100.

## Publication of the List of Registered Premises

A list showing all the registered premises in each of the different categories of accommodation is published by Tourism Quality Services (Ireland) Ltd. at least once every year. However, where the registered proprietor requests Tourism Quality Services (Ireland) Ltd. to omit his or her premises from the list in respect of any year, Tourism Quality Services (Ireland) Ltd., having regard to all the circumstances, may accede to this request. The list may include information relating to the standard of the premises, the charges made and any other information of interest to tourists.

## Publication of the List of Unregistered Premises

Tourism Quality Services (Ireland) Ltd. may publish a list of premises that provide accommodation for tourists but which are not registered by it. The company may include in the list information relating to the accommodation available, the charges made and any other information of interest to tourists. No premises will be included in the list except at the request or with the consent of the proprietor.

## Service of Notice

Where a notice is required to be served on any applicant for renewal of registration, the notice must be served in one of the following ways:

(a) by delivering the notice to the applicant

(b) by delivering the notice to any person, not less than sixteen years of age, who is in the employment of the applicant, or

(c) by sending the notice by post in a prepaid letter addressed, in the case of an applicant for registration, to the place where he or she carries on business or at his/her last known place of abode or, in the case of an applicant for renewal of registration, at the premises in respect of which the application has been made.


## REGISTRATION OF FOOD PREMISES

The Food Hygiene Regulations, 1950-89 require every health board in the country to keep a register of food premises (form F.H.B.) containing such information as may be required from time to time by the Minister for Health and Children or by the health boards.

A person who proposes to set up any registrable food business in a premises must apply for registration of the premises (on form F.H.C.) to the local health board at least one month before the commencement of the business. In respect of each application, the applicant must pay the board a fee as follows:

(a) where the food premises is a restaurant, take-away food premises, fishmongers, poulterers, butchers, pork butchers or wholesalers — £100, and

(b) in all other cases — £200.


### Procedure for the Registration of Food Premises

When an application for registration is made, the health board must adopt one of the following procedures within one month:

(a) Where all the appropriate provisions of the regulations have been complied with, the health board will register the premises and shall notify the applicant.

(b) Where one or more of the appropriate provisions has not been complied with, but the health board considers it expedient to permit the food business to be carried on, subject to arrangements being made to comply fully with the regulations, the board shall

- register the premises provisionally for a period not exceeding six months
- notify the applicant that the premises have been provisionally registered
- inform the applicant of the measures to be taken to comply fully with the regulations.

(c) Where one or more of the appropriate provisions have not been complied with, or the health board considers it inappropriate to allow the business to be carried on in the premises because of the degree of risk to public health, it shall refuse to register the premises and shall issue a notice to the applicant informing him or her of the refusal and the grounds for it.

## Procedure Subsequent to Provisional Registration

Where a health board has permitted a provisional registration of food premises, it shall adopt one of the following procedures before the expiry of the period of provisional registration:

(a) If all the provisions of the regulations are complied with, the health board shall register the premises unprovisionally and shall inform the applicant of such.

(b) If one or more of the appropriate provisions has still not been complied with, but the health board considers it expedient to continue to permit the food business to be carried on, it shall register the premises provisionally for a second and final period not exceeding six months and shall inform the proprietor of such continuance.

(c) If one or more of the appropriate provisions are still not complied with and the health board considers it inappropriate to permit the food business to be carried on in the premises, it shall refuse to register the premises for any further period and shall issue the applicant with a notice of refusal and the grounds for it.

Where provisional registration is continued for a specified period as provided for at (b) above, the health board, before the expiration of that period, shall

(i) if all the appropriate provisions are complied with, register the premise unprovisionally and shall inform the applicant that the premises has been so registered.

(ii) if one or more of the appropriate provisions is still not complied with, refuse to register the premises for any further period and shall issue the applicant with a notice of refusal and the grounds for it.

In determining whether the appropriate provisions are complied with in respect of the food business being carried on, regard shall be had to the nature and extent of such food business.

## Alteration and Cancellation of Entries in the Register

Where a food business in a registered food premises is transferred from the registered proprietor to another person, the latter must notify the health board in writing of the transfer within one month. The health board must then alter the register of food premises to take account of the transfer.

On the application in writing of the registered proprietor, or of his/her personal representative or, in the case of a body corporate, of the liquidator, the health board may at any time alter or cancel any entry in the register of food premises.

The chief executive officer of a health board, without application from the registered proprietor, may cancel the registration of a food premises at any time if he or she is satisfied:

(a) that the registered proprietor, if an individual, has died or, if a body corporate, has been dissolved and no person has within three months after such death or dissolution notified the health board that the food business has been transferred to him or her;

(b) that a food business is no longer being carried on in the premises;

(c) that a food business of the same nature and extent as was proposed when the premises was registered, is no longer being carried on;

(d) that there has been a transfer of the food business in the food premises from the registered proprietor to another person and the latter has failed to notify the health board of the transfer, as required;

(e) that there are no longer suitable facilities for compliance with the appropriate provisions in respect of the food business being carried on.

In the case of (b), (c), (d) and (e) above, the chief executive officer of the health board must notify the registered proprietor in writing of his or her intention to cancel registration at least fourteen days before doing so. Where an entry in the register of food premises is altered or cancelled, the chief executive officer must also notify the registered proprietor in writing.

## Cancellation and Suspension of Registration by Minister

Where the registered proprietor of a food premises has been convicted of offences in contravention of the regulations, the health board shall, within one year of the conviction, make such investigations as it thinks fit to determine if any of the regulations are not being complied with. If, following investigation, the health board is not satisfied that the regulations are being fully complied with, it will notify the registered proprietor of its intention to apply to the

Minister for Health and Children (but not sooner than one month after the notification) for an order cancelling the registration of the premises. The notification (which is sent on form F.H.D.) identifies the regulations that are not being complied with.

If, after the expiration of one month from serving the notice, the health board is of the opinion that any of the regulations are still not being complied with, it may apply to the Minister for Health and Children for an order cancelling registration of the premises.

Where such an application is made to the Minister, he or she may:

- by order, cancel the registration of the food premises from a specified date and have copies of the order sent to the health board and to the registered proprietor of the food premises, or

- by order, suspend the registration of the food premises from a specified day for a specified period and have copies of the order sent to the health board and to the registered proprietor, or

- inform the health board and the registered proprietor that he or she does not propose to make an order cancelling or suspending the registration of the food premises.

There is also provision in the Food Hygiene Regulations for the Minister to initiate the procedure outlined above for the cancellation or suspension of the registration of food premises (form F.H.E.). If the Minister is not satisfied that the regulations are being complied with, he or she may, at the expiration of the period of suspension ordered, extend the suspension further or, indeed, cancel the registration.

Any person aggrieved by an order of the Minister may, not later than fourteen days after the making of the order, apply for an annulment of the order to the judge of the District Court in the court area where the premises are situated. The District judge may either annul or confirm the order as he or she thinks fit.

Any person who is aggrieved by a decision of a health board in relation to the refusal of the board to register a food premises or to make provisional registration of a food premises unprovisional, or in relation to the cancellation of the registration of a food premises, may appeal in writing to the Minister against such decision within one month (or such longer period as the Minister may, in any particular case, allow) from the date on which notice of the decision is issued. The appeal must be sent by post and must be addressed to the Minister for Health and Children, Department of Health and Children, Hawkins House, Dublin 2. The person making the appeal must furnish immediately on request to the Minister any information he or she may require to enable him or her to decide the appeal. If the request for information is not responded to and complied with, the Minister may deem the appeal to be withdrawn. In dealing with the appeal, the Minister may:

(a) confirm the decision of the health board, or
(b) direct the health board to take such action as he or she thinks fit in relation to the registration of the food premises.

A health board must immediately inform the aggrieved person of, and comply with, any decision of the Minister for Health and Children.

## Regulations Governing Occasional Food Premises

A food business shall not be carried on in an occasional food premises more often than one day in any period of three months, except under and in accordance with a permit of the local health board.

The permit issued by the board will be on form F.H.A. and may contain conditions, including those limiting the nature of the food business that may be carried on.

Where the health board issues a permit relating to an occasional food premises, the food business must not be carried on for more than two months at any time and for not more than four months in any calendar year.

A person applying to a health board for a permit to carry on a food business in an occasional food premises must pay a fee of £50 to the board in respect of each application.

### INSURANCE FOR BUSINESS

It is perhaps true to say that it is possible to insure almost anything against any eventuality — at a price! The prudent hotelier, restaurateur, publican or general business person should ensure adequate insurance cover for their particular needs. Professional advice is necessary and its requirement cannot be overemphasised. Insurance is a major business expense. There is a competitive insurance market and brokers should be actively encouraged at each annual renewal to seek the lowest available price quotation appropriate to the risk to be covered. It is noteworthy that the higher the premium payable, the greater the commission received by the broker. Among the many risks to be covered by the business person, the following should be considered:

1. **Public Liability.** This is to cover liability for death, injury or illness to a member of the public caused by defects in the business premises, products, services or because of the negligence of the proprietor or his/her employees. The smallest business should have cover of at least one million pounds.

2. **Employer's Liability.** This is similar to public liability and covers claims by employees against their employers.

3. **Personal Accident Insurance.** This can be taken out by almost anyone, but is of particular use to business proprietors to cover future financial security in the event of a disabling illness or accident.

4. **Fire, flood, storm, water damage, consequential loss of profits, and the commercial use of motor vehicles.**

5. **Fidelity Insurance.** To cover a proprietor in the event of embezzlement or fraud by staff.

6. **Money.** This is to cover loss of cash from the premises and in transit to and from banks and other financial institutions.

7. **Travel.** Where a proprietor or employees have to travel on business or promotional trips, this type of insurance gives cover for death, illness or loss of luggage.

8. **Permanent Health Insurance.**

9. **Voluntary Health Insurance.**

10. **Pension-type Insurances.**

Extreme care should be exercised in arranging any type of insurance cover. It is important to ensure that property and loss of profits are insured for amounts that are adequate to cover their value. Otherwise, in the event of a claim, the insurance company may use the average rule and reduce the amount it will pay. An average clause in a contract of insurance means there is an apportionment of the loss between the insurer and the insured, having regard to the extent to which the risk has been under-insured. For example, in property insurance where the property is of greater value than the sum for which it is insured, the policy-holder is, in effect, his or her own insurer of the difference and must bear a rateable share of any loss.

Conditions attached to policies should be studied carefully, and the proprietor or manager of the business should make sure that they are observed.

# Chapter 4

## THE LAW OF CONTRACT

The frequency with which people enter into contracts in their daily lives is generally not appreciated and the many transactions of which contracts are the basis are largely taken for granted. Ordering a meal in a restaurant, buying a pint of beer in a pub and purchasing a loaf of bread in a supermarket are all everyday occurrences conducted without thought of any contractual implications. For the person in business — whether hotelier, restaurateur, caterer or publican — the impact of contract law is inescapable. Contracts are entered into for the supply of foodstuffs, drink and equipment, for services such as laundry, maintenance and cleaning, for the professional advice of solicitors, accountants and consultants, and, of course, for the employment of staff. Each of these contracts confers rights and imposes obligations on the parties involved.

Countless contracts are negotiated, completed, and honoured daily. Some others are made and broken, but only those pursued through the courts are ever heard of. In some cases, the amount in dispute would not make a claim worthwhile; in others, the individual may feel intimidated by the prospect of going to court; where a business is involved, concern about adverse public relations might be a deterrent. There is a body of legal principles to govern those contracts that are in dispute and that reach the courts.

### THE CONCEPT OF A CONTRACT

A contract is an agreement that legally binds the parties who have entered into it. The theory is that the agreement is the outcome of consenting minds, each party to the contract being free to accept or reject the terms offered by the other. However, the notion of consenting minds is misleading because the parties will be judged by what they have said, written or done and not by what is in their minds. Furthermore, the freedom of the parties to contract as they please must be tempered by limitations imposed by the common law and legislation.

## CONTRACT FORM

The majority of contracts are known as simple contracts and require no special formality. They may be (a) oral, (b) in writing, (c) partly oral and partly in writing, or (d) inferred from conduct.

It is often thought that an oral contract is worthless and has no legal standing. This is not correct. Obviously, an oral contract may be difficult to prove, but this difficulty does not make it illegal or invalid. On the other hand, it should not be thought that because a contract is in writing, it is incapable of giving rise to problems. In cases where the contract is partly oral and partly in writing, the difficulties of both species may affect the contract. Furthermore, the conduct of an individual may impose a legally binding obligation, as, for example, when she or he helps herself or himself to petrol at a self-service filling station.

However, the law will not recognise some contracts unless they are

(a) **in writing:** examples of these are hire purchase and credit sales agreements.

(b) **evidenced in writing:** examples of these are contracts for the sale of land or of an interest in land. The contract in its entirety does not have to be in written form, but there must be written evidence of the essential parts of it. These types of contract are outside the scope of this book.

## Essential Elements of a Contract

For a contract to be valid and binding on the parties, it must contain three vital elements:

1. Agreement.
2. An intention to be legally bound.
3. Consideration.

If even one of these elements is missing, no contract exists. Each element requires elaboration.

## 1. Agreement

In order that a contract may exist, the parties must reach a definite agreement. In a dispute, the courts will analyse the negotiations, correspondence and statements made between the parties to ascertain whether one party has made an offer that is unconditionally and unambiguously accepted by the other. It is sometimes very difficult to identify the twin elements of offer and acceptance so essential to the contract and to identify which of the parties has made an offer. A useful test to adopt is to pose the question 'Which party first puts his/her proposition in such a form that the other party by a mere assent can cause a contract to emerge?' It is essential for the courts to determine whether the negotiations between the parties ever amounted to agreement and therein lies the importance of offer and acceptance.

### (a) OFFER

An offer is a definite and unambiguous statement of the terms on which the person making the offer (the offeror) is prepared to be bound. The offer must be communicated to the other party (the offeree) and may take any form — oral, writing, or inferred from conduct. It may be directed to an individual, or to a group of individuals, or to the world at large.

An offer must be distinguished from (i) an invitation to treat, (ii) a request for information, and (iii) a statement of intention.

(i) **AN INVITATION TO TREAT**. This is a preliminary stage in negotiation and does not constitute an offer. For example, in a restaurant where service is provided by waiting staff, the display of the menu amounts only to an invitation to treat and is not an offer. If the menu were regarded as an offer, anyone ordering from it would constitute an acceptance that, in turn, would create a binding contract, and the restaurant would be legally bound to supply the item ordered. It is very often the case that high customer demand for a particular dish will result in the unavailability of it for other customers, and problems of seasonality or a breakdown in supply could also create gaps in the menu. Such events would place an undue burden on proprietors if the law were to regard the menu as an offer.

The display of prepacked foods in a self-service restaurant is an invitation to treat and here again it is the customer who makes the offer to purchase by taking the food to the cashier. The contract is not completed until the cashier accepts the payment, and the customer therefore may reject the food and return it to the display cabinet without incurring any contractual obligation. The outcome is likely to be different, however, if the customer requests a portion to be cut from a larger dish or requests an item to order. This may be regarded as an offer to purchase the item and the provision of it by the service assistant may be considered an acceptance of the offer.

The price list displayed at a fast food outlet is yet another example of a mere invitation to treat which does not amount to an offer. The customer's selection of a menu item is an offer to purchase and the cooking and serving of it obliges the customer to pay.

Goods displayed in a shop window amount to an invitation to the public to buy them. The offer is made by the customer, and the shopkeeper has no contractual obligation until he or she accepts the offer.

An advertisement in a newspaper or magazine is also an invitation to treat. The rationale for this is understandable in the light of the previous examples. If the advertisement were regarded as an offer, the advertiser would have a contractual obligation to every person who responded to the advertisement with an order for the goods, irrespective of his or her ability to supply a sufficient quantity of them.

An offer to invite tenders is also an invitation to treat. In any advertisement inviting tenders, it should be made clear that the costs of preparing such tenders will not be allowed.

**(ii) A REQUEST FOR INFORMATION.** A request for information does not constitute an offer and cannot be regarded as such. An inquiry about prices, or product availability, or a request for a brochure will not incur a contractual obligation. A prospective hotel guest who inquires about room rates and vacancies is merely requesting information. The hotelier's response may be a specific reply to the inquiry and, here again, no obligation is created. However, the hotelier's reply may include a definite offer of accommodation, whereupon acceptance by the prospective guest will create a contract.

**(iii) A STATEMENT OF INTENTION.** A declaration by a person that he or she intends to do something is not regarded as an offer.

## TERMINATION OF AN OFFER

An offer may be terminated in the following ways:

- *Rejection.* An offer is terminated when the person to whom it is offered refuses to accept it.

- **Lapse of time.** Failure to accept an offer within a stipulated period will terminate the offer. In the absence of a stipulated period, an offer may lapse because of a person's failure to accept the offer within a reasonable time. What is reasonable will depend on the subject-matter of the contract. In a contract for the sale of perishable goods, fresh salmon for example, two or three days would probably be reasonable, whereas an offer for the sale of shares could lapse in a matter of minutes or hours.

- **By death.** The death of a prospective hotel guest will terminate the offer, but if the hotel is owned by a company, the death of the person running it will not normally affect the offer.

- **Revocation.** An offer may be revoked at any time by the offeror before it is accepted by the person to whom it is offered. Communication of the revocation must reach the 'offeree' before he/she has accepted the offer. Such communication may be made directly by the offeror to the offeree or to the offeree by some third party. The revocation of an offer by post is effective only when the letter has been delivered. A promise to keep an offer open for a fixed period does not prevent its revocation within that period. However, a person may buy a promise to keep an offer open for a fixed period and such an offer cannot then be revoked without breach of this so-called 'option contract'.

- **Counter offer.** This occurs where the offeree changes the terms of the offer; for example, agrees to pay £50 for the use of a double bedroom when the original offer was a single room for £50. This amounts to a counter offer and has the effect of destroying the original offer and creating a new offer.

### (b) ACCEPTANCE

An offer is contractually binding when it is accepted by the offeree and the acceptance is communicated to the offeror. There are, therefore, two basic requirements of a valid acceptance: (i) there must be acceptance in fact; (ii) the acceptance must be communicated to the offeror.

**(i) ACCEPTANCE IN FACT.** The acceptance may be in writing, oral, or inferred from conduct. It must also be unqualified and correspond exactly to the terms of the offer. If the original terms are varied, then this is regarded as a counter offer and the person making the counter offer is putting forward a new offer.

**(ii) COMMUNICATION OF ACCEPTANCE.** The general rule here is that acceptance is not effective until it is communicated to and received by the offeror. The acceptance may be communicated by the offeree or by someone with authority. The offeror may indicate the method to be used to communicate the acceptance; for example, 'please reply by telephone on or before 12 December'.

However, if the offeree adopts an equally efficient method, this will be sufficient unless the offeror insists on a particular method of reply. Clearly if the offeree adopts a method of acceptance in contravention of the conditions of the offer, there is no valid acceptance. A condition that silence will be taken as constituting acceptance cannot be imposed by the offeror without the offeree's consent. An acceptance is not effective if it is communicated in ignorance of the offer. This rule prevents an individual from accepting an offer of which he or she is unaware. For example, if lost property is returned to its owner without knowledge that the owner has offered a reward, there is no legal entitlement to claim the reward. There are two exceptions to the rule that acceptance must be communicated. Firstly, in cases where the offer consists of a promise to pay money in return for the performance of a particular act or undertaking, the performance of the act is deemed to be a sufficient acceptance. Secondly, where the parties contemplate acceptance by post, the acceptance is deemed to be effective where and when the letter is posted. If the letter is lost in the post, the validity of the contract is not affected, provided it is clear from the circumstances of the case that the postal service is to be used and the loss or delay is not the offeree's fault by, for example, incorrectly addressing the communication. This is often referred to as the 'postal rule'. It is worth noting that 'posting' in this context means 'to put into the control of the post office in the usual manner of posting' and not merely handing the letter to a postman.

## 2. Intention to be Legally Bound

This is the second element that must be present for a contract to be legally binding. If there is no intention to create legal relations, there can be no binding contract. However, the courts do not seek to determine whether the parties intended in their minds to be legally bound by what they agreed to, for this would be an impossible task. Instead, the test employed is to determine whether, from their words, conduct and the surrounding circumstances of the negotiations, a reasonable person would come to the conclusion that the parties intended to be legally bound. The courts, in examining this intention, make a distinction between agreements occurring in a social or domestic setting and those occurring in a commercial or business setting.

### (a) SOCIAL OR DOMESTIC AGREEMENTS

Where an agreement is of a social or domestic nature, such as those arising amongst family members, there is a presumption by the courts that the parties do not intend to be legally bound. This presumption can be rebutted by bringing forward evidence that demonstrates that the parties did intend to be bound by their agreement. The existence of an enforceable contract depends, therefore, on what inference can reasonably be made from the circumstances of the agreement. Generally, domestic agreements made between a husband and wife living together are presumed not to be enforceable, but financial agreements between separated spouses are usually binding.

### (b) COMMERCIAL OR BUSINESS AGREEMENTS

It is unnecessary in commercial or business agreements for the parties to state to each other that they intend to be legally bound. In such agreements, the courts take a contrary view to that adopted in relation to social or domestic agreements and they presume that the parties do intend to be legally bound. However, here too such a presumption can be rebutted by evidence that demonstrates that the parties do not intend to be legally bound. An example of this in business is the so-called Gentleman's Agreement, where the parties make it clear that they intend no legally binding undertaking between them. An agreement followed by the words 'but don't hold me to it' would have a similar effect.

## 3. Consideration

Every contract (oral or written) that is not in the form of a deed under seal must be supported by consideration. This means that, in an action in contract, the plaintiff must be able to show that he or she gave or promised to give some advantage to the defendant in return for the defendant's promise. The advantage moving from one party to the other party is known as 'consideration'. When trying to ascertain if consideration is present in any particular situation in a dispute, it is useful to look for the promises made by the parties. An illustration may be helpful at this point.

The Silver Sandcastle Hotel agrees to provide overnight accommodation to Henry for £50. It is clear that each party to the agreement has made a promise to the other. The hotel has promised to supply Henry with accommodation. Henry has promised to pay £50. Therefore, each party is at the same time

(i)   A promisor (the giver of a promise) and

(ii)  A promisee (the recipient of a promise)

- The hotel is the promisor of accommodation; Henry is the promisee for the accommodation.

- Henry is the promisor of £50; the hotel is the promisee for the £50.

In return for the hotel's promise to provide accommodation, Henry is to give £50. This is the consideration for Henry's promise.

Similarly, in return for Henry's promise of £50, the hotel is to provide accommodation. This is the consideration for Henry's promise.

As a general rule, a person cannot sue on a contract unless he can show that he gave consideration. There is, however, an exception to this rule where the contract is in the form of a deed. A deed does not require consideration and will be binding if it complies with the requirement of a valid deed. It must be

- in writing
- signed
- with a seal affixed
- delivered.

A number of rules governing consideration have been developed from decisions reached by the courts.

(a) *The consideration must be real or sufficient.* The court will not investigate the adequacy of the exchange that took place between the parties, but only that some value, however small, was given. For example, if a hotelier chooses to provide the presidential suite of his hotel at the rate of £1 per day, the courts will not intervene unless there has been fraud, duress, misrepresentation or some other matter which vitiates the contract.

(b) *Consideration must have been provided by the plaintiff.* An individual may sue on the contract only if he or she has provided consideration. He or she cannot sue if the consideration was provided by someone else.

(c) *Consideration must not be past.* An individual is not entitled to sue on the basis of consideration given before the agreement was made. For example, Seán mows the lawn at Mary's guesthouse when Mary is in hospital. When she gets home, Mary promises Seán £50 for his work but she never pays. Seán cannot sue because the consideration he provided, i.e. mowing the lawn, was provided before Mary's undertaking of payment, and is therefore past consideration.

(d) *Consideration must not be vague, illegal or impossible to perform.*

(e) *Consideration must be given to enforce the waiving of a contractual obligation.* When an individual to a contract waives a right that he has under the contract, he is perfectly entitled to reinstate that right later, unless the other party to the contract has provided some consideration.

## Capacity to Contract

In general, all persons have full power to enter into any contract they wish. However, different rules apply to the following categories:

1. Infants
2. Married women
3. Mentally ill and intoxicated persons
4. Companies.

### *1. Infants*

An infant in Irish law is a person who has not yet reached his/her eighteenth birthday. The contracts of infants usually may be examined under three headings: (a) those that are void, (b) those that are binding, and (c) those that are voidable (note that a voidable contract remains valid unless and until the option of avoiding it has been exercised by the person so entitled).

### (a) **The void contracts of infants are:**

   (i)    any contract that could not fail to operate to the infant's disadvantage

   (ii)   any contract for goods supplied or to be supplied other than necessaries (see page 62)

   (iii)  any contract for the repayment of money loaned or to be loaned, and promises to pay interest, commission, or other payments in respect of such loans.

### (b) **The binding contracts of infants are:**

   (i)    any contract to pay for necessaries supplied

   (ii)   certain contracts that are for the infant's benefit; for example, contracts of employment or apprenticeship or for education.

But if the terms of these contracts are oppressive, they will not be binding.

## (c) **The voidable contracts of infants**

These are contracts which are binding on the parties (including the infant) unless or until the infant avoids them either during infancy or within a reasonable time after reaching the age of eighteen. Such contracts are those of continuing liability such as:

- partnerships
- holding shares in a company
- leases.

A repudiation of such a contract can be made only after the infant reaches the age of eighteen. If the repudiation is made during infancy, it remains suspensive and may be recalled when the person reaches eighteen.

### NECESSARIES

The necessaries of an infant are such things as are reasonably essential in view of the infant's station in life and that are actually required by him/her when the contract is made. The burden is on the supplier to prove that the infant (a) needs the goods and (b) that they are suitable to his/her way of life.

Where it has been established that an infant has been supplied with necessaries, thereby making the contract binding on him/her, his/her obligation is to pay a reasonable price. This is not necessarily the full contract price and, in fact, may be significantly lower than the contract price. It should be appreciated that what constitutes necessaries for one minor may not be considered necessaries for another.

## 2. *Married women*

Married women are under no contractual impediment and may freely enter contracts in their own right and be bound by the terms of their agreements.

However, it is often the case that a married woman may be acting as an agent for her husband. For example, she may book a hotel room on her husband's behalf and at his request. In this case, the husband is responsible for the payment of the bill.

A husband may also be liable to pay the hotel expenses incurred by his wife, even if he is not with her on the occasion. This will arise if the wife has previously stayed at the hotel and the husband has always paid her account. In law this is known as an agency by estoppel and the husband will continue to incur liability to pay until he expressly notifies the hotel that he will no longer be liable.

### 3. Mentally ill and intoxicated persons

If a person is so mentally ill at the time the contract is made as not to be able to understand the nature of the contract, or is in such a state of intoxication as not to know what he or she is doing, the contract is voidable, provided it can be shown that the other party is aware of his/her condition at the time the contract is made. However, such persons must pay a reasonable price if they are supplied with necessaries.

### 4. Companies

Companies can make only those contracts that are authorised by their constitutions, i.e. the Memorandum and Articles of Association. A contract made by a company without authority is said to be *ultra vires* (beyond the legal power of the company).

A company, being an artificial legal person, needs to operate and function through its directors and employees. By acting through such persons, a company may enter into and be bound in contract. It is important, therefore, when dealing with a company, to be sure that the person who appears to be acting on behalf of the company has the authority to do so.

## Invalid Contracts

Even in circumstances where the three essential elements are present, a contract may be ineffective because it contains a component that renders it invalid. For example, the contract may be void because of mistake, or it may be voidable if it was induced by duress, undue influence or misrepresentation. On the other hand, a contract may be unenforceable because an essential formality was not adhered to. Moreover, the subject-matter of the contract may make it illegal. Each of these concepts is governed by its own set of legal rules.

Occasionally a contract of employment may contain a clause that attempts to restrain an employee on the termination of his employment from working for a rival employer or from opening his own business in competition with his former employer. This type of clause is termed a 'restraint of trade'. The courts will not always uphold these clauses. However, they may be valid if the restraint is regarded as reasonably necessary to protect the interests of the person seeking to enforce it and if it is not injurious to the public or unreasonable with regard to the person restrained. An employer is entitled to protect his trade secrets and trade connections and to prevent his customers from being spirited away by a former employee who could use his knowledge, e.g. of customer lists, to attract business to his enterprise and away from his former employer.

## The Termination or Discharge of a Contract

Where the obligations of one party to the contract are fully performed, the rights of the other party are extinguished. When all the rights and obligations have been extinguished, the contract is regarded as having been discharged.

There are a number of ways in which a contract may be discharged:

- Performance
- Agreement
- Frustration
- Breach.

## 1. Performance

When the parties to a contract have fulfilled exactly all their individual promises to each other, the contract is deemed to be terminated or discharged by performance. Formerly, the common law demanded that only exact compliance with all the terms of the contract would suffice. However, if a performance is deemed to be as complete as a reasonable person would expect, the contract may be discharged. This is often called substantial performance. Furthermore, if a contract is divisible (capable of being divided into components), then the completion of a self-contained component amounts to a complete performance of that part, and would entitle the party providing it to sue in order to recover payment for the completed part.

## 2. Agreement

Since contracts are formed by agreement, it necessarily follows that they may be varied or terminated by agreement. If the parties wish to cancel their agreement or to enter into different terms, they are entitled to do so. Any agreement to discharge or vary a contract creates a new contract subject to the rules of consideration (see page 60).

## 3. Frustration

The parties to a valid contract are excused their obligations under it if the terms of the contract have become impossible to perform through no fault of either party. In these circumstances, the contract is deemed to be frustrated. The following are examples of frustration:

- where the subject of a contract is destroyed, as the destruction of a hotel by fire
- where an order of the Oireachtas makes the performance of the contract illegal, e.g. an order that hotels in a particular location must cease taking in guests because of an outbreak of infectious disease in the locality
- where the contract is for the personal service of an individual who has died
- where the contract depends on the occurrence of a special event and the event does not take place.

Any money paid over (for example, by way of deposit) may be so returned, but if expenses have already been incurred before the frustration, a deduction may be allowed to offset the costs incurred.

## 4. Breach

A breach of contract may arise if one of the parties to it indicates to the other that he is unable or unwilling to perform his side of the contract. This is known as an anticipatory breach. In such cases the innocent party may regard the contract as discharged and may sue for damages at once or, alternatively, he/she can treat the contract as still existing and await performance. In the latter case, the innocent party runs the risk that some event will occur that will discharge the agreement and thereby cause him/her to lose his/her right of action.

A breach of contract may also occur when one of the parties refuses to perform his/her agreement during the time it should be performed. The other party then has a right to sue for breach of contract.

If the conduct of one of the parties is such as to make performance of the contract impossible, or if one of the parties simply fails to perform its side of the bargain, the contract is discharged and the innocent party may sue.

When a breach of contract is sufficiently serious to entitle the innocent party to treat the contract as at an end, this is known as a fundamental breach and indicates that a vital term (called a condition) or indeed the whole contract has been broken. However, when a minor term (called a warranty) has been broken, the innocent party must continue to perform the agreement and is entitled to claim damages.

## Remedies for Breach of Contract

The common law remedy for a breach of contract is damages. This is a financial amount awarded to compensate an innocent party for the actual loss suffered. It is intended to put the innocent party in the position, as far as money can, that they would have been in if the contract had been fulfilled.

In addition to damages, other possible remedies for breach of contract include injunction, recision, rectification and specific performance:

(a) **Injunction** is an order of the court directing a party to do or refrain from doing a particular act.

(b) **Recision** is when an innocent party has the right to have the contract set aside and to be restored to his/her position before the contract was made.

(c) **Rectification.** The courts may rectify a later written document to bring it into accord with verbal terms agreed before the written document was prepared.

(d) **Specific performance.** This is an order of the court directing a party to perform his/her obligations under the contract, which may be granted at the discretion of the court.


## Statute of Limitations, 1957 and Contracts

An action for a breach of contract must be commenced within the time limits set down in the Statute of Limitations, 1957. In general, an action in contract is statute-barred after six years. However, in any action it is important to seek professional legal advice because certain actions can be barred after two years, i.e. an action against a deceased person's estate. In dealings between landlord and tenant, which, it should be borne in mind, is also a contractual relationship, there is a complex series of time limits, some of which can apply immediately on the termination of a lease.


## UNFAIR TERMS IN CONSUMER CONTRACTS

The European Communities (Unfair Terms in Consumer Contracts) Regulations, 1995, which give effect to Council Directive No. 93/13/EEC of 5 April 1993, were adopted by the then Minister for Enterprise and Employment on 1 February 1995. Regulation 1(2) states that 'these regulations shall apply to all contracts concluded after 31 December, 1994'. Therefore, the date of adoption of the regulations has the effect of making the prohibition on the use of unfair contractual terms retrospective to 1 January 1995, that is to say, one month before the regulations were adopted.

## Unfair Contract Terms Defined

For the purpose of these regulations, a contractual term will be regarded as unfair if, contrary to the requirement of good faith, it causes a significant imbalance in the parties' rights and obligations under the contract to the detriment of the consumer, taking into account the nature of the goods and services for which the contract was concluded. In making an assessment of good faith, as mentioned, particular regard will be had to:

- the strength of the bargaining positions of the parties
- whether or not the consumer had an inducement to agree to the term
- whether or not the goods or services were sold or supplied to the special order of the consumer, and
- the extent to which the seller or supplier has dealt fairly and equitably with the consumer whose legitimate interests he/she has to take into account.

## Application and Exclusions

In broad terms, these regulations apply to any clause in a contract concluded between a seller (a natural or legal person who, acting for purposes related to his/her business, sells goods) of goods or supplier (a natural or legal person who, acting for purposes related to his/her business, supplies services) of services and a consumer (a natural person who is acting for purposes which are outside his/her business) which has not been individually negotiated. These regulations do not, however, apply to:

- contracts of employment
- contracts relating to succession rights
- contracts relating to rights under family law
- contracts relating to the incorporation and organisation of companies or partnership
- any terms which reflect:
    - (i) mandatory, statutory or regulatory provisions of Ireland, or
    - (ii) the provisions or principles of international conventions to which the member states of the European Union are party.

The words 'individually negotiated' as used above are worthy of further elaboration. A contract term will always be regarded as having not been individually negotiated where it has been drafted in advance and the consumer has, therefore, not been able to influence its substance, and this is particularly so in the context of a pre-formulated standard contract.

The fact that a specific term or any aspect of a term has been individually negotiated will not exclude the application of these regulations to the rest of the contract if an individual assessment of the contract indicates that it is, nevertheless, a pre-formulated standard contract.

## Examples of Unfair Contract Terms

An indicative, though non-exhaustive, list of terms which may be regarded as unfair is as follows:

- Excluding or limiting the legal liability of a seller or supplier in the event of the death of a consumer or personal injury to the consumer resulting from an act or omission of the seller or supplier.

- Inappropriately excluding or limiting the legal rights of the consumer in the event of total or partial non-performance by the seller or supplier of any contractual obligations, including the option of offsetting a debt owed to the seller or supplier against any claim which the consumer may have against him/her.

- Making an agreement binding on the consumer, whereas the provision of services by the seller or supplier is subject to a condition whose realisation depends on the seller's or supplier's will alone.

- Permitting the seller or supplier to retain sums paid by the consumer where the consumer decides not to conclude or perform the contract, without providing corresponding compensation for the consumer in the event of the seller or supplier cancelling the contract.

- Requiring any consumer who fails to fulfil his/her obligations to pay a disproportionately high sum in compensation.

- Authorising the seller or supplier to dissolve the contract on a discretionary basis where the same facility is not granted to the consumer.

- Permitting the seller or supplier to retain sums paid for services not yet supplied by him/her where it is the seller or supplier who dissolves the contract.

- Enabling the seller or supplier to terminate a contract of indeterminate duration without reasonable notice, except where there are serious grounds for doing so; a supplier of financial services may terminate unilaterally such a contract where there is a valid reason, provided the supplier is required to inform the consumer immediately.

- Automatically extending a fixed-term contract where the consumer does not indicate otherwise, when a deadline fixed for the consumer to express the desire not to extend the contract is unreasonably early.

- Irrevocably binding the consumer to terms with which he/she had no real opportunity of becoming acquainted before the conclusion of the contract.

- Enabling the seller or supplier to alter the terms of the contract unilaterally without a valid reason which is specified in the contract. A supplier of financial services may reserve the right to alter the rate of interest payable by the consumer, or the amount of other charges for financial services without notice, where there is a valid reason. However, the supplier is required to inform the consumer at the earliest opportunity and the consumer is free to dissolve the contract immediately.

- Enabling the seller or supplier to alter unilaterally without valid reason any characteristics of the product or service to be provided.

- Providing for the price of goods to be determined at the time of delivery or allowing the seller of goods or supplier of services to increase their price without in both cases giving the consumer a corresponding right to cancel the contract if the final price is too high in relation to the price originally agreed; this will not apply to price indexation clauses, where lawful, provided that the method by which prices vary is explicitly described.

- Giving the seller or supplier the right to determine whether the goods or services supplied are in conformity with the contract or giving him/her exclusive right to interpret any term in the contract.

- Limiting the seller's or supplier's obligation to respect commitments by his/her agents or making his/her commitments subject to compliance with a particular formality.

- Obliging the consumer to fulfil all his/her obligations where the seller or supplier does not perform his/hers.

- Giving the seller or supplier the possibility of transferring his/her rights and obligations under the contract, where this may serve to reduce the guarantees for the consumer, without the latter's consent.

- Excluding or hindering the consumer's right to take legal action or to exercise any other legal remedy.

It should be noted that these regulations do not apply to transactions where the price is linked to fluctuations in a stock exchange quotation or financial market rate that the seller or supplier does not control. Neither do they apply to contracts for the purchase or sale of foreign currency, traveller's cheques or international money orders denominated in foreign currency.

## General Provisions

Where some or all of the terms of a contract offered to a consumer are in writing, the seller or supplier has an obligation to ensure that the terms are drafted in plain, intelligible language. If there is any doubt or ambiguity about the meaning of any particular term, the interpretation of the term most favourable to the consumer will prevail. If a contract contains an unfair term (or terms), such term will not be binding on the consumer, although the contract itself will continue to bind the parties, so long as it is capable of continuing in existence without the unfair term.

## Enforcement

The enforcement of these regulations is under the jurisdiction of the Director of Consumer Affairs. The Director has the power to apply to the High Court for an order prohibiting the use of any term in contracts concluded by sellers or suppliers adjudged by the Court to be an unfair term. The Director must, however, publish a notice of his/her intention to apply for such an order in *Iris Oifigiúil* and at least two national newspapers. Any person claiming to have an interest in the court application is entitled to appear before and be heard by the court. In any such application, it is not necessary for the Director of Consumer Affairs to prove

(a) actual loss or damage, or

(b) recklessness or negligence on the part of the seller or supplier.

The Minister for Enterprise, Trade and Employment or the Director of Consumer Affairs may appoint persons to be authorised officers for the purpose of these regulations. An authorised officer will be furnished with a warrant of appointment which will confer extensive powers, including

- the right to enter and inspect business premises
- the right to inspect any goods on the premises and, on paying or making tender of payment therefor, take any of the goods

- to require any person who carries on the business (or any employee) to produce any books, documents or records relating to the business which are in that person's control and to give the officer information in regard to any entries in the books, documents and records
- to inspect and take copies from the books, documents and records
- to require any person to give any information the officer may require.

A person who obstructs or impedes an authorised officer in the exercise of any power conferred under these regulations, or who does not comply with any requirements, will be guilty of an offence. A person guilty of an offence is liable on summary conviction to a fine not exceeding £1,500.

# Chapter 5

# THE LAW OF TORTS

Unlike many other words with a legal meaning, such as contract, evidence or crime, the word 'tort' does not immediately or easily yield up its meaning to someone who is not versed in the law. The word is Norman French and means 'a civil wrong'. This type of wrong, however, is generally regarded as not serious enough to be classed as a crime and thereby attract punishment by the state. Instead, when a tort is committed, the injured party must take the initiative and sue the wrongdoer. This type of legal action is usually taken to obtain compensation for the loss, injury or damage suffered. Tort is therefore concerned with civil liability, as distinct from criminal liability. It is important to stress that some torts — for example, trespass to the person and libel — give rise to both civil liability and criminal liability because they are at the same time torts and crimes. A person who assaults another may be prosecuted for the crime of assault and later may be sued by the injured party for damages.

## SPECIFIC TORTS

A number of individual torts are recognised in law, including

- negligence
- defamation (libel and slander)
- nuisance (both public and private)
- trespass (to goods, to land and to the person).

Each tort has its own particular rules governing liability, but in general a plaintiff must prove:

(a) that the defendant committed an act (or omitted to do something that he/she should have done)

(b) that he/she acted intentionally, or was negligent, or failed to comply with a strict duty imposed on him/her by law

(c) (in most cases) that the act (or omission) caused some injury, loss or damage to the plaintiff. Some torts (trespass and libel, for instance) are actionable without proof of loss.

## NEGLIGENCE

This is by far the most important tort and is of particular relevance to any person running a business. Negligence consists of a breach of a legal duty of care owed by the defendant to the plaintiff, whereby damage is caused to the plaintiff.

In order to succeed in an action for negligence, the plaintiff must prove

- that the defendant owed the plaintiff a legal duty of care
- that there was a breach of that duty of care
- that the plaintiff suffered damage, loss or injury.

Negligence is often explained as 'the doing of that which a reasonable person would not do or, failing to do that which a reasonable person would do'. It is clear, therefore, that negligence can arise as a result of an act or an omission.

### Duty of Care

This duty arises whenever a person should reasonably foresee that his or her conduct is likely to cause harm to someone else. It is important to stress the 'reasonable foreseeability' aspect. Questions relating to the existence of the duty of care are questions of law that must be decided by a court.

To help answer such questions, the courts have developed the test of the 'neighbour principle'. This states that reasonable care must be taken to avoid acts or omissions that can be reasonably foreseen as likely to injure a neighbour.

Who, then, is a neighbour? In law, a neighbour is defined as a person who is so closely and directly affected by the act (or omission) in question that the doer ought reasonably to have them in contemplation as being so affected when he/she directs his/her mind to the act (or omission).

## Breach of the Duty of Care

To establish negligence, the plaintiff has to prove that the defendant committed a breach of his or her legal duty of care. The law does not require the standard of absolute care, but instead requires reasonable care.

## Ensuing Damage (or Injury)

The final component to complete the essential elements necessary to sustain an action in negligence is damage or injury resulting from the breach of the duty of care.

## Contributory Negligence

In common law, it was formerly the case that a defendant could escape liability for negligence if it could be proved that the injury complained of would not have occurred if the plaintiff had not contributed to the harm by his or her own negligence.

The application of the Civil Liability Act, 1961 has made a significant change to the common law position. This now provides that, where a plaintiff suffers damage partly through his/her own fault and partly through the defendant's fault, he/she can still receive damages. However, the amount receivable will be reduced by the contribution that his or her negligence bears to the total cause of the loss or damage.

## Scope of Negligence

A duty under the law of negligence may arise in many and varied circumstances. New legal duties are recognised by the courts as the necessity arises. Amongst those already in place are duties owed by road users, producers of goods, carriers, occupiers of premises and employers. Because of their importance in the present context, the latter two — occupier's liability and employer's liability — must be examined.

## OCCUPIER'S LIABILITY

The liability for negligence in relation to persons who enter unsafe premises is generally directed at the occupier of the premises, since occupation of the premises, rather than ownership, is of primary importance. In cases where the premises are let to a tenant, and the landlord has a duty to carry out repairs under the tenancy agreement, then liability also may fall on the landlord.

Until recently the extent of the occupier's liability was determined by the status attached by the Common Law to the person who entered the premises. There were four possible categories into which the entrant could fall:

- contractual invitee
- invitee
- licensee
- trespasser.

The enactment of the Occupiers' Liability Act, 1995 has replaced the Common Law rules concerning occupier's liability and put in place a new set of rules in statutory form. Nevertheless, there remain, in places in the act, traces of the language of the old Common Law.

The 'occupier' is defined in the Act as a person exercising such control over the premises (which includes land, water and any fixed or moveable structures thereon and also includes vessels, vehicles, trains, aircraft and other means of transport) that it is reasonable to impose on that person a duty towards an entrant in respect of a particular danger existing on those premises. Where there is more than one occupier of the premises, the extent of the duty of each occupier towards an entrant will depend on the degree of control each occupier has over the state of the premises.

Under this Act, persons (entrants) who come onto another person's premises are now divided into three categories:

- Visitors
- Recreational users
- Trespassers

# 'Visitor' Defined

The Occupiers' Liability Act, 1995 defines a visitor as an entrant, other than a recreational user, who is on the premises:

- at the invitation or with the permission of the occupier or any member of the occupier's family who is ordinarily resident on the premises; or
- at the express invitation of the occupier or such family member; or
- with the permission of the occupier or such family member for social reasons connected with the occupier or such family member; or
- as an entrant, other than a recreational user, present on the premises by virtue of an express or implied term in a contract; or
- as an entrant as of right

provided that in each of the above cases the entrant is present

- for the purpose for which he or she was invited or permitted to be there; or
- for the purpose of the performance of the contract; or
- for the purpose of the exercise of the right; and
- includes any such entrant whose presence on the premises became unlawful after entry and who is taking reasonable steps to leave.

## Duty to Visitors

The occupier owes a duty of care ('the common duty of care') to a visitor. This duty is defined in the act as a duty 'to take such care as is reasonable, in all the circumstances (having regard to the care which a visitor may reasonably be expected to take for his or her own safety and, if the visitor is on the premises in the company of another person, the extent of the supervision and control the latter person may reasonably be expected to exercise over the visitor's activities) to ensure that a visitor to the premises does not suffer injury or damage by reason of any danger existing thereon'.

It can easily be seen that this duty of care resembles the standard of care in ordinary negligence and may therefore be affected by the visitor's own contributory negligence. It is also clear that the occupier's duty of care may be reduced when an injured visitor is on the premises in the company of another person who may be expected to supervise the visitor. A classic example of this would be where a child visitor is accompanied by a parent.

## 'Recreational User' and 'Trespasser' Defined

The Act defines a recreational, user as an entrant who, with or without the occupier's permission or, at the occupier's implied invitation, is present on the premises without a charge (other than a reasonable charge in respect of the cost of providing vehicle parking facilities) being imposed for the purpose of engaging in a recreational activity, including an entrant admitted without charge to a national monument.

Excluded from this definition of 'recreational user' are members of the occupier's family who are ordinarily resident on the premises, entrants who are expressly invited onto the premises, or entrants who are permitted onto the premises for social reasons connected with the occupier or a member of his or her family.

The recreational user must, therefore, be engaged in 'recreational activity' and this too is defined in the Act. Recreational activity means any such activity conducted, whether alone or with others, in the open air (including any sporting activity), scientific research and nature study so conducted, exploring caves and visiting sites and buildings of historical, architectural, traditional, artistic, archaeological or scientific importance.

A trespasser, for the purposes of the Act, is an entrant other than a recreational user or visitor. The Act groups recreational users with trespassers and accords them a much lower standard of care than visitors.

## Duty to Recreational Users and Trespassers

In respect of a danger existing on premises, an occupier owes a duty towards a recreational user of the premises or a trespasser:

- not to injure the person or damage the property of the person intentionally, and
- not to act with reckless disregard for the person or the property of the person.

In determining whether the occupier's conduct was reckless or not, all the circumstances must be taken into account, including:

(a) whether or not the occupier knew or had reasonable grounds for believing that a danger existed on the premises

(b) whether or not the occupier knew or had reasonable grounds for believing that the person and, in the case of damage, property of the person, was or was likely to be on the premises

(c) whether or not the occupier knew or had reasonable grounds for believing that the person or property of the person was in, or was likely to be in, the vicinity of the place where the danger existed

(d) whether or not the danger was one against which, in all the circumstances, the occupier might reasonably be expected to provide protection for the person and the property of the person

(e) the burden on the occupier of eliminating the danger or of protecting the person and property of the person from the danger, taking into account the difficulty, expense or impracticability, having regard to the character of the premises and the degree of the danger, of so doing

(f) the character of the premises, including, in relation to premises of such a character as to be likely to be used for recreational activity, the desirability of maintaining the tradition of open access to premises of such a character for such an activity

(g) the conduct of the person, and the care which he or she may reasonably be expected to take for his or her own safety, while on the premises, having regard to the extent of his or her knowledge thereof

(h) the nature of any warning given by the occupier or another person of the danger

(i) whether or not the person was on the premises in the company of another person and, if so the extent of the supervision and control the latter person might reasonably be expected to exercise over the other's activities.

The duty of the occupier not to injure intentionally or to be reckless is not owed to a person who enters the premises for the purpose of committing an offence or, while present on the premises, commits an offence. Such a person can recover from the occupier only when a court determines that recovery is 'in the interests of justice.'

As has already been stated, the general duty of an occupier to a recreational user or trespasser under this Act is not to injure them or be reckless in their regard. There is however, an exception to that rule and that is where a structure on premises is provided for use primarily by recreational users. In such an event, the occupier owes a duty towards such users 'to take reasonable care to maintain the structure in a safe condition'. In this case it can, therefore, be seen that the level of duty is raised. The emphasis must be laid on the fact that the structure on the premises is provided 'for use primarily by recreational users'. The Act goes on to make clear that where a stile, gate, footbridge or other similar structure is on the premises, but is not there for use 'primarily' by recreational users, the occupier's duty is not extended in the manner described.

## Modification of Duty to Entrants

The Act provides that the duty owed by the occupier to visitors, recreational users and trespassers may be extended by the occupier by express agreement. However, the occupier can only restrict, modify or exclude his or her duty towards visitors. Such restriction, modification or exclusion will not bind a visitor, unless

(i) it is reasonable in all the circumstances, and

(ii) in the case of an occupier restricting, modifying or excluding his or her duty, the occupier has taken reasonable steps to bring the notice to the attention of the visitor.

For the purpose of (ii) above, an occupier will be presumed, unless the contrary is shown, to have taken reasonable steps to bring a notice to the attention of a visitor if it is prominently displayed at the normal means of access to the premises.

In respect of a danger existing on premises, a restriction, modification or exclusion by an occupier will not be taken as allowing an occupier to injure a visitor or damage the property of a visitor intentionally or to act with reckless disregard for a visitor or the property of a visitor. Put another way, the restriction, modification or exclusion which an occupier attempts to impose on a visitor cannot fall below the standard due to the recreational user or trespasser. Therefore, the occupier may reduce the duty to take reasonable care of the visitor, but must not reduce it below the level due to recreational users and trespassers. So, even if an occupier has an effective and properly displayed notice curtailing liability, the occupier will still owe to the visitor the duty not to be reckless and not to intentionally injure him or her.

## General Provisions

The Act provides that, where the visitor has been warned of the existence of a danger by the occupier or another person, the warning cannot by itself be treated as absolving the occupier from liability, unless it was enough to enable the visitor to avoid injury or damage.

The occupier of premises will not be liable to an entrant for injury or damage caused by a danger existing on the premises owing to the negligence of an independent contractor employed by the occupier, provided the occupier has taken all reasonable care in the selection of the independent contractor (including such steps as to ascertain if the independent contractor was competent to do the work concerned) unless the occupier has or ought to have had knowledge that the work was not properly done.

The Act does not affect any enactment or any rule of law relating to self-defence, or the defence of property, or any liability imposed on an occupier in any other capacity, such as the hirer of transport, or carrier, employer or hotel proprietor. Finally the Act does not affect any liability under common law imposed on an occupier for a tort committed by another person in circumstances where the duty imposed on the occupier is of such a nature that its performance may not be delegated to another person.

## EMPLOYER'S LIABILITY

### Common Law Position

Under the common law of negligence, an employer owes a duty of care towards his employees. The extent of this duty is to take reasonable care for the safety of the employee, taking into account all the circumstances of the particular case. The courts have stressed, however, that the employer's duty is not unlimited and that the employer is not to be regarded as an insurer of his/her employees' safety. This means that the law does not require an employer in all circumstances to secure the safety of his/her employees. Furthermore, the duty may vary according to such considerations as the employee's age, work experience, knowledge and expertise.

The issue of employer liability is usually considered by the courts under four headings:

- the duty to provide competent staff
- the duty to provide a safe place of work
- the duty to provide proper equipment
- the duty to provide a safe system of work.

## Provision of competent staff

The employer has a duty to use due care in selecting competent fellow employees. Before an employer will be liable under this heading, it must be shown that the employer knew, or ought to have known, about an employee's incompetence. Evidence that the employer knew of previous acts of incompetence by the employee would establish this. It may also be proved by establishing a negligent system of employee selection. An employer will be liable in circumstances where he continues to employ a person of whose incompetence he is aware. It is possible, too, that a failure to provide competent staff may be regarded as a failure to provide a safe system of work, resulting from a poor standard of supervision.

## Provision of a safe place of work

Here, the employer must ensure that a reasonably safe place of work is provided and maintained for the benefit of the employee.

## Provision of proper equipment

The employer is under a duty to take reasonable care to provide proper equipment and to maintain such equipment so that an employee will not be exposed to unnecessary risk when using it.

As well as being liable for the supply of dangerous equipment, an employer may be liable for the failure to provide equipment essential to the safety of the employee, e.g. a safety guard for a slicing machine, safety glasses or shoes. Failure to maintain equipment in a safe condition will also incur liability.

## Provision of a safe system of work

If an accident causes injury to an employee and the accident is the result of an unsafe system of work, which the employer should have taken, but did not take, reasonable precautions to guard against, he or she will be held liable.

## Statutory position

Before 1 November 1989, when the Safety, Health and Welfare at Work Act, 1989 came into force, there were in existence some twenty other Acts of the Oireachtas which had a bearing on safety and welfare at work. These were supplemented by about two hundred regulations of one kind or another. In view of such an abundance of legislation, it is surprising that only 20 per cent of the workforce was covered by it. More surprising was the fact that no Act or regulation had any specific application to the hotel and catering industry.

While these statutes and regulations for the most part will remain in force, the Safety, Health and Welfare at Work Act, 1989 provides for their review and possible replacement in the future. This Act extends its provisions to cover all employers, employees and the self-employed.

In its references to the general duties of employers, the Act preserves the concepts and broad terminology of the common law and provides a framework for allowing the introduction of codes of practice and regulations. These codes and regulations will meet the needs, as they are identified, of particular work environments, dealing, in turn, with the factory or laboratory, hotel or corner shop, public house or supermarket.

Before examining certain aspects of the Act in some detail, it is necessary to focus on a number of definitions put forward in this legislation. The Act defines a 'place of work' very widely indeed and includes any place, land or location, premises, tent, temporary structure or moveable structure, vehicle, vessel or aircraft. The definition of 'employee' remains confined to persons employed under a contract of service. Thus the distinction between an employee and an independent contractor remains. However, the Act imposes a duty on the employer towards outside contractors who work on the premises. Furthermore, anyone undergoing training for employment or receiving work experience other than at school or university is regarded as an employee of the person who is providing the training or work experience. A 'self-employed person' is one who works for profit other than under a contract of employment, whether or not he or she employs other people.

## General Duties of Employers towards their Employees

The employer is required, as far as is reasonably practicable, to ensure the safety and health of all his employees. However, the interpretation of what is reasonable in any individual case is ultimately for the courts to decide. The Act identifies the particular duties for which the employer must take responsibility, but these obligations are limited by what is 'reasonably practicable'.

Such duties require of the employer that:

- the place of work is designed, provided and maintained in a condition that is safe and without risk to health
- the place of work has a safe means of entry and exit
- the design, provision and maintenance of plant and machinery are safe and without risk to health
- there is a safe system of work
- information, instruction, training and supervision are provided to ensure safety
- suitable safety equipment and protective clothing are provided
- there are adequate plans to deal with an emergency.

It can be seen that these duties embody in statutory form the existing common law duties referred to above.

Employers and the self-employed have a duty to conduct their business in such a way as to ensure that persons who are not their employees are not exposed to safety risks. Related to this duty is a further one whereby an employer is obligated to give to persons not employed by him, but who are on his premises, any information necessary for their safety.

## General Duties of Employees

While at work, it is the duty of every employee

- to take reasonable care for his/her own safety, health and welfare and that of any other person who may be affected by his/her conduct
- to cooperate with his/her employer
- to use as intended any safety equipment and protective clothing provided
- to report to his or her employer or supervisor, without unreasonable delay, any defects in plant, equipment, place of work or system of work of which he/she becomes aware.

## Duties of Designers, Manufacturers, Importers and Suppliers

There is an extensive range of duties on persons who design, manufacture, import or supply any article that is used in the workplace.

## Safety Statement

A very important requirement of the Act is that every employer and self-employed person is under a duty to prepare a written safety statement, specifying the manner in which the safety, health and welfare of employees is to be secured at work.

The statement must:

- identify the hazards faced by workers
- assess the risks involved
- set out the arrangements made and the resources provided for safeguarding employees
- state precisely how employees should cooperate
- set out the names and job titles of persons who are responsible for safety and health.

Where a safety inspector deems the safety statement inadequate or unsatisfactory, he or she can direct that it be revised. An employer has thirty days to make the revision.

When making their report to the Registrar of Companies under the Companies Acts, 1963-90, the company's directors must provide an evaluation of the extent to which the policy set out in the safety statement was fulfilled during the period covered by the report.

Each employer or self-employed person must bring the terms of the safety statement to the attention of employees and to any other person at the place of work who may be affected by it.

## Consultations between Employers and Employees

Every employer must consult his employees when making and main-taining arrangements for safety and, as far as practicable, must take into account representations made by employees. Employees may (but are not bound to) select from among themselves a person to represent them in consultations with their employer; he or she will be known as a safety representative. Among a range of rights, the safety repre-sentative is entitled to:

- make representations to the employer on any aspect of safety, health and welfare
- investigate accidents and dangerous occurrences
- make oral or written representations to inspectors
- receive information and advice from inspectors
- subject to prior notice, carry out inspections, at a frequency agreed with the employer, to consider the nature and extent of hazards
- subject to prior notice to the employer, investigate potential hazards and com-plaints made by an employee
- on request, accompany an inspector on a tour of inspection, other than a tour for the purpose of investigating an accident.

The employer must afford the safety representative reasonable time off from his/her normal work duties, without loss of pay, to discharge his functions.

## National Authority for Occupational Safety and Health

A National Authority for Occupational Safety and Health was estab-lished under the Safety, Health and Welfare at Work Act, 1989. The Authority consists of a chairman and ten members. Its main functions include the enforcement of the relevant statutory provisions (except to the extent that other bodies may be prescribed by regulations to enforce certain provisions); the provision of advice and information on safety, health and welfare at work; the promotion of schemes to encourage and foster the prevention of accidents and injury to health at work, and to undertake, promote and sponsor research relating to safety and health.

The Authority is also responsible for keeping under review the statutory provisions relating to safety, health and welfare at work and from time to time for submitting proposals to the relevant Minister for the introduction or review of regulations. With the consent of the Minister for Enterprise and Employment, the Authority is empowered to draw up and issue codes of practice; they will not be legal documents in themselves, but they may be used as evidence in court if legal requirements are contravened.

The Act provides for the appointment of what are called enforcing agencies. These may be used in lieu of the Authority for the purpose of enforcing the Act's statutory provisions. The Authority or an enforcing agency may appoint inspectors, who would have wide powers to ensure compliance with the Act's provisions.

## Inspectors
In the exercise of their powers, inspectors may enter premises at any time; require the production of any books, registers, documents or records, and examine and copy them as required; question and seek information from any person whom they believe can assist with inquiries; take possession of any article or substance in connection with their inquiries; take any measurements, photographs or tape recordings considered necessary; and exercise such other powers as may be necessary for carrying out their functions.

## Further Powers of an Inspector
An inspector may issue (a) an improvement direction, (b) an improvement notice, or (c) a prohibition notice.

(a) **Improvement direction.** An inspector may issue an improvement direction on a person in control of premises, where he or she is of the opinion that activities there involve, or are likely to involve, risk to the safety or health of any person. The direction requires the person in control to submit an improvement plan within a time specified by the inspector. The inspector may direct that the plan be revised if he or she is not satisfied with the remedial action proposed.

(b) **Improvement notice.** If the inspector is of the opinion that a person is contravening any of the Act's statutory provisions, or that such person has failed to submit an improvement plan or to implement an improvement direction, he or she may serve an improvement notice on that person. The improvement notice directs the person to remedy the contravention, but allows for 14 days in which he or she can appeal the notice to a judge of the District Court.

(c) **Prohibition notice.** Where the inspector is of the opinion that the activities carried out on the premises involve, or are likely to involve, a risk of serious personal injury, he or she may issue a prohibition notice that forbids the carrying on of the activities specified in the notice. In this case, the person served with the notice has 7 days in which to appeal to a judge of the District Court. Where a prohibition notice is issued and the contravention is allowed to continue, the inspector may apply for a High Court order to enforce the prohibition.

## Offences

An extensive range of offences is provided for, with penalties of up to £1,500 on summary conviction or, where conviction is obtained on indictment, an unlimited fine, or (at the discretion of the court) a term of imprisonment not exceeding two years, or both a fine and imprisonment.

## DEFAMATION

This is the law's answer to the need of an individual to protect his or her good name and reputation. Defamation is committed by the wrongful publication of a false statement about a person, which tends to lower that person in the eyes of right-thinking members of society or tends to hold that person up to hatred, ridicule or contempt, or causes that person to be shunned or avoided by right-thinking members of society.

There are two types of defamation. Libel consists of the communication of defamatory matter in a permanent form, such as writing, print or film, including video. This is actionable without proof of damage and is also a crime. Slander consists essentially of spoken words, but could include gestures or sign language. Slander is not a crime and is generally actionable only on proof of special damage, that is, actual loss. However, there are four instances where proof of damage in slander is not required:

1.  Words that impute unchastity or adultery to any female.

2. Words that impute the incompetence of a person in any office, trade, profession or business.

3. Words that impute criminal conduct.

4. Words that impute that a person is suffering from a contagious disease.

It is not a frequent occurrence for a libel action to originate in a hotel or catering environment. However, it could arise in a case where a food writer has given a critical review of a particular hotel or restaurant which the proprietor believes is untrue, unjustified and damaging. In such a case, the proprietor may pursue legal redress.

Slander, on the other hand, could occur in practically any situation, at any time: heated exchanges between a receptionist and an irate prospective guest who has been refused accommodation; between the proprietor and an employee who is being reprimanded for some misdeed; and even amongst guests.

## NUISANCE

In legal terms, a nuisance is an unlawful annoyance caused to others. It consists of the unreasonable interference with another person in the exercise of his or her rights. There are two types of nuisance: private nuisance and public nuisance.

### Private Nuisance

A private nuisance is a substantial interference with another person's comfort or enjoyment of his/her land or premises. A substantial interference is established by repetitive or continuous acts of nuisance.

A person in lawful occupation of land or premises is entitled to take a civil action in private nuisance. However, since it is not necessary to be the owner of the property, a tenant can sue in private nuisance.

Nuisance encompasses such things as noise, dust, smells, heat, smoke, vibrations and fumes, but a mere inconvenience does not constitute a private nuisance. To sustain an action in private nuisance, it is necessary to show proof of damage. An injunction or damages may be awarded against an individual or business causing a nuisance.

As can readily be appreciated from the foregoing, there is ample scope for hotel and catering enterprises to be faced with a legal action in nuisance. Rowdy guests, late-night revelling, and loud singing and shouting all could contribute to a nuisance in a residential area over a period of time.

## Public Nuisance

A public nuisance is a crime, and a private individual may sue in public nuisance only if it can be proved that he or she has suffered damage over and above that suffered by the public at large.

A public nuisance is an unlawful act or omission that causes a public obstruction or that endangers the health, safety or comfort of the general public or a section of it.

## TRESPASS

Trespass is the direct interference with the person, land or goods of another. Liability for trespass is actionable without proof of damage.

## Trespass to the Person

This may occur in three ways:

1. **Assault.** This is an act that puts a person either directly or indirectly in reasonable apprehension of immediate violence. For example, shaking a fist or brandishing a stick from a short distance constitutes assault. Words alone may not constitute assault, but if the words used suggest the imminent use of force, this may amount to assault.

2. **Battery.** This amounts to a physical contact with another person which is contrary to that person's will. To punch or kick a person are examples of a direct battery; to throw water over a person is an indirect battery. It is important to stress here that a person employed on premises as a 'bouncer' enjoys no special licence or immunity and is subject to the same requirements of the civil and criminal law as any other person.

3. **False Imprisonment.** This is the unlawful and total restraint of the personal liberty of another.

## Trespass to Land

This occurs when there is a direct and forcible interference with the land or premises of another. Where a person enters, or remains, or places objects on the land or premises of another, this constitutes a trespass. In these cases, it is not necessary for the plaintiff to prove damage. Trespass is similar to private nuisance in as much as it seeks to protect the occupier, making it unnecessary to own the land or premises in question.

The owner of the land is entitled to use reasonable force to remove a trespasser who will not voluntarily leave his or her property. The force used should be no more than is necessary to eject the trespasser. Where the entry to the property has been peaceful, it is necessary to request the trespasser to leave before any force can be used.

## Trespass to Goods

Trespass to goods involves a direct interference with the possession of goods, and may take one of three forms: (a) taking goods, (b) damaging goods, or altering their physical condition, (c) interfering with goods, by moving them about, for example. The interference must be direct, although in rare cases physical contact is not necessary. For example, to chase cattle amounts to a trespass to goods.

It is not necessary to prove actual loss or damage in order to sustain an action of this kind. Furthermore, the action is brought by the person in possession of the goods at the time of the trespass, although he or she may not necessarily be the owner.

### INTENTION IN TORT

As a general rule, the intention to do, or omit from doing, a particular act is necessary before liability arises in tort. However, it should be stressed that what is necessary is not the intention to cause injury but the intention to do the act that causes the injury. For example, while demonstrating a stroke, a golfer swings his club, hits a bystander in the face and causes an injury. While he did not intend to injure the bystander, he nevertheless intended to swing his club.

## DEFENCES IN TORT

When a person is sued in tort, and depending on the particular tort in question, there are a number of general defences that might be considered in reply:

1. **Consent.** The general rule is that a person has no remedy for harm done to her/him if she/he has expressly or impliedly consented to suffer the actual harm inflicted, or if she/he has consented to run the risk of it. However, mere knowledge does not necessarily imply consent. The plaintiff must both appreciate the nature of the risk or injury and consent to run such risk.

2. **Necessity.** This amounts to the deliberate doing of a particular act, but with the intention of avoiding a greater harm. For example, the demolition of a building to prevent the spread of fire.

3. **Inevitable Accident.** This arises where the consequences of an act are not foreseen, are unintended, and are unavoidable, in spite of the defendant's reasonable care.

4. **Act of God.** This defence may be put forward to meet circumstances that no human being could have foreseen or protected against.

5. **Statutory Authority.** Where an Act of the Oireachtas has expressly authorised the thing complained of, this amounts to a complete defence, provided that the defendant used all proper care in the matter.

In addition to those defences, the special nature and individual characteristics of the specific torts identified above (page 73) allow for further defences particular to each tort. Where a court action in tort is contemplated, it is essential to ensure that the action is commenced in the time permitted by the Statute of Limitations, 1957. Where the case involves personal injury or damage arising out of negligence, nuisance or slander, the time allowed is three years. In all other torts, the time limit is six years.

## REMEDIES IN TORT

These may be judicial or extra-judicial. Extra-judicial remedies can be used by the aggrieved party without going to court. For example, one may use force to defend a person, goods or property, and where a nuisance occurs it may be abated by the person affected.

Judicial remedies, namely damages and injunctions, must be

pursued through the courts. The measure of damages is the amount of money that will compensate the plaintiff for the damage caused. An injunction is an order of the court that directs a person to do or refrain from doing a particular act. When the court grants an injunction and it is disobeyed, it is enforced by committal to prison.

## TORT DISTINGUISHED FROM BREACH OF CONTRACT

A breach of contract is the breach of a duty created by the parties themselves, whereas tort results from the breach of some duty imposed by law.

However, a wrongful act may be both a tort and a breach of contract; for example, where a surgeon, who has been engaged to perform an operation, performs his work negligently and causes damage, he may be sued either for a breach of contract or for the tort of negligence.

## TORT DISTINGUISHED FROM CRIME

A crime is an injury to the community as a whole, whereas a tort is an injury to an individual.

A crime gives rise to punishment, whereas a tort usually gives rise to a right to compensation.

A crime involves an action brought in the name of the state, whereas a tort involves an action brought in the name of an aggrieved individual.

# Chapter 6

# LAW FOR THE IRISH HOTEL AND CATERING INDUSTRY

## THE HOTEL PROPRIETORS ACT, 1963

The Hotel Proprietors Act, 1963 would not be out of place if it was included with legislation referred to generally as 'consumer protection law'. In situations where it applies, this Act weighs considerably in favour of consumers of hotel services, while at the same time making demands of the hotel proprietor. However, since this statute arguably represents the single most directly applicable legislation for the day-to-day operation and management of a hotel, it deserves to be extracted from the generality of consumer protection law.

### Coming into Force

The Act came into force on 1 May 1963 and repealed the previous legislation, some of it dating from as long ago as 1652. The repealed legislation used the now outmoded terms of 'inn' and 'innkeeper'. These have been replaced by the more appropriate expressions 'hotel' and 'hotel proprietor', each of which is defined in the statute.

### Definitions

A hotel is defined as 'An establishment which provides or holds itself out as providing sleeping accommodation, food and drink for reward for all comers without special contract and includes every establishment registered in the register of hotels kept under Part III of the Tourist Traffic Act, 1939'. Although this definition is not exhaustive, it is clear that an establishment is a hotel if it has been registered as such with Tourism Quality Services (Ireland) Ltd., on behalf of Bord Fáilte Éireann. Merely appending the word 'hotel' to the name of an establishment does not automatically bring the establishment within the statutory definition. On the other hand, the omission of the word 'hotel' from the name does not of itself deny recognition of the establishment as a hotel. It is generally accepted that guesthouses, boarding houses, restaurants, cafés and public houses are not included in the definition.

The term 'proprietor' in relation to a hotel means 'the person carrying on the business of the hotel' and, in the case of a hotel registered in the register of hotels kept under Part III of the Tourist Traffic Act, 1939, 'includes the person entered in the register as the proprietor thereof'.

### Duties Imposed by the Act

The Act identifies and imposes three duties upon the hotel proprietor:

- a duty to receive all-comers
- a duty regarding the safety of the guests and the safety of the hotel premises
- a duty to receive the guests' property.

### Duty to Receive All-Comers

A hotel proprietor is under a duty to receive as guests all persons who, whether or not under special contract (e.g. by a prior booking), present themselves and require sleeping accommodation, food or drink and to provide them with such unless he or she has reasonable grounds for refusal. The interpretation of what are 'reasonable grounds for refusal' will depend largely on the particular circumstances and will be for the court to determine.

However, reasonable grounds for refusal may exist where

(a) the prospective guest is in an unfit state to be received; for example, as a result of intoxication, or

(b) all the bedrooms in the hotel are sold, or

(c) the prospective guest is unable to pay, though this may be ascertained by the simple expedient of requesting payment in advance.

If a proprietor unreasonably refuses accommodation, he or she risks exposing himself/herself to both civil and criminal liability.

Subject to the terms of any special contract entered into in advance between the proprietor and the guest, the proprietor is under a duty to provide accommodation, food and drink at the hotel's current charges.

## Duty Regarding the Safety of Guests and Premises

Where a person is received as a guest at a hotel, whether or not under special contract, the duties arising therefrom are twofold. Firstly, the proprietor is under a duty to take reasonable care of the guest's person. The standard here is one of reasonable and not absolute care; the proprietor cannot be regarded as an insurer of the personal safety of the guest. Secondly, the proprietor must ensure that, for the purpose of the personal use of the guest, the premises are as safe as reasonable care and skill can make them. The duty of a proprietor appears to be extended in circumstances where a guest receives personal injury because of the dangerous state of the hotel.

It is interesting to note that Section 4 of the Hotel Proprietors Act, 1963 states 'where a person is received as a guest at a hotel, whether or not under special contract, the proprietor of the hotel is under a duty to take reasonable care of the person of the guest and to ensure that for purposes of personal use by the guest, the premises are as safe as reasonable skill and care can make them'. It seems, therefore, that the guest's statutory right against a hotel proprietor is wider than an invitee's right against an invitor. From the phrasing of the statute, it seems that the hotel proprietor is also liable for the acts of his or her independent contractor. Furthermore, in Section 4(2) the duty is independent of any liability of the proprietor as occupier of the premises.

## Duty to Receive the Property of Guests

Where sleeping accommodation is engaged for a person as a guest at a hotel, the proprietor is under a duty to receive any property brought to the hotel by or on behalf of that person and for which the proprietor has suitable accommodation. It is worth noting that this duty appears to be qualified in two respects:

(a) that sleeping accommodation has been engaged

(b) that the proprietor has suitable accommodation for the guest's property.

It seems that in order to impose the duty to receive the guest's property, it is a prerequisite that sleeping accommodation has been engaged. The use of the word 'engaged' is noteworthy because it means that the proprietor could be held liable for the property of a guest who 'engages' sleeping accommodation but never occupies it. Furthermore, the proprietor has a duty to accept the normal baggage and possessions of a guest, while at the same time reserving the right to refuse, for example, dangerous or excessively cumbersome property.

The duty to receive property where sleeping accommodation has been engaged applies not only during the time for which the guest is entitled to use the accommodation, but extends to a reasonable period before and after that time. It seems that this includes liability for property sent in advance of the guest's arrival or held for a period after the guest's departure. What is a 'reasonable period' depends on the particular circumstances and, in cases of dispute, would be for the court to resolve.

In addition to civil liability, a proprietor who is in breach of his or her duty to receive a guest's property is guilty of an offence and is liable to a fine not exceeding £100.

## Liability for Guest's Property

As with the duty to receive the property of a guest, liability for such property extends only to the property of a guest who has engaged sleeping accommodation. The hotel proprietor is liable for any damage to, or loss or destruction of, property received by him or her from or on behalf of a person who has engaged sleeping accommodation. This liability extends to property of which the proprietor takes charge, whether at the hotel or outside it, and could arise, for example, where a hotel employee is despatched to collect a guest's property from a bus terminal or railway station.

A motor vehicle is deemed to have been received by the proprietor where it has been placed within the precincts of the hotel or in any garage, car park or other premises provided by the proprietor. However, the proprietor will not incur liability unless he or she, or a servant of his or hers authorised, or appearing to be authorised, for the purpose, has been previously notified that the vehicle has been brought to the hotel. Here the question of what constitutes notification arises. It has been held, albeit at Circuit Court level, that notification is effected when a hotel guest drives his or her car into the hotel's car park.

The proprietor's liability for a guest's property arises not only during the period for which sleeping accommodation has been engaged, but also during a reasonable period before or after that time. However, the proprietor is exempt from liability if the damage, loss or destruction suffered is due to

- an unforeseeable and irresistible act of nature
- an act of war
- the guest himself or herself
- any person accompanying the guest
- any person in the employment of the guest
- any person visiting the guest.

## Limiting Liability

The Hotel Proprietors Act, 1963 provides the means whereby the proprietor may limit his or her liability for the property of any one person to a maximum of £100. In order to effect this, it is a prerequisite that the proprietor conspicuously displays a notice where it can be conveniently read by guests at or near the reception office or desk, or near the main entrance to the hotel. The content of the notice is prescribed in the first schedule to the statute. It is important to stress that the Act expressly states that the limitation of liability does not apply to motor vehicles.

Furthermore, the Act identifies a series of situations where liability is not limited and where display of the notice as previously explained will be of no avail. These are:

- where the property was damaged, lost, stolen or destroyed through the wrongful act, default or omission of the proprietor or of some servant of his, or
- where the property was deposited by or on behalf of the guest expressly for safe custody with the proprietor or some servant of his authorised, or appearing to be authorised, for that purpose and, if so required by the proprietor or that servant, in a container fastened or sealed by the depositor, or

- where either the property was offered for deposit as aforesaid and the proprietor or his servant refused to accept it, or the guest or some person acting on his or her behalf wished so to offer the property but, through the default of the proprietor or a servant of his, was unable to do so.

It is very important to note that the reason for requiring the conspicuous display of the statutory notice limiting liability at or near the reception area or entrance to the hotel is because a fundamental principle of contract law dictates that any exclusion clauses relating to a contractual agreement must be clearly brought to the notice of the person affected by the clause before he or she accepts the contract.

## Rights of the Proprietor

It will be readily appreciated from the foregoing that the obligations and liabilities imposed on the proprietor amount to a considerable burden. Some effort to redress the balance is attempted by affording the proprietor in certain circumstances

(a) a right to a lien on property (i.e. a right to seize and hold property), and

(b) a right to sell such property.

## Right of Lien

A proprietor has a lien on property for a debt due from the guest for sleeping accommodation, or for food or drink supplied by the proprietor. The lien extends to property that does not belong to the guest, but only if the proprietor was unaware of that fact when he or she received the property at the hotel. Furthermore, this right may be exercised in circumstances where a guest has had only a meal or a drink and is unable or unwilling to pay.

In the absence of a provision expressly excluding the right of lien in the case of motor vehicles and their contents, it is presumed that the lien extends to these in the same way as any other property.

## Right of Sale

A proprietor may sell by public auction any property to which his lien extends if, after six weeks, the debt remains unpaid. The proprietor is entitled to deduct the amount of the debt, together with the costs and expenses of the sale, from the proceeds of the auction. Any surplus remaining must be surrendered to the person by or on behalf of whom the property was brought to the hotel. A purchaser of goods from a hotel proprietor who exercises his right of sale at a public auction gets a good title to the goods as provided for under the Sale of Goods Act, 1893.

## General Provisions

A proprietor is prohibited from contracting out of any liability that arises under this Act, and any notice or agreement that purports to exclude or limit such liability is therefore void. For example, a notice that is placed in a hotel car park with the words 'The proprietor is not liable for loss or damage to guests' cars' will have no effect if the car of a guest who has engaged sleeping accommodation is damaged or stolen from the car park. On the other hand, such notice may be effective if a customer has not engaged sleeping accommodation and is calling at the hotel for a meal.

The Accidental Fires Act, 1943 does not apply in relation to any claim for damages under the Hotel Proprietors Act, 1963. The Accidental Fires Act, 1943 provides that no legal proceedings can be instituted by a person who has suffered damage by reason of a fire accidentally occurring in the building or on the land of another. The effect of this is that, where damage is suffered as a result of a fire accidentally occurring on hotel premises, proceedings are not inhibited by the Accidental Fires Act, 1943.

The duties and liabilities of a hotel proprietor may be enforced by means of a civil action. In this regard, the District Court has jurisdiction to deal with claims for damages under this Act where the amount claimed does not exceed £5,000. The jurisdiction of the Circuit Court, which is normally limited to £30,000, may be extended to that of the High Court (which has unlimited jurisdiction), provided that both parties to the litigation consent to the case being tried in the Circuit Court (such mechanism is provided for under the Courts (Supplemental Provisions) Act, 1961).

Where there is a breach of the duty to receive all-comers, or to receive a guest's property at a hotel, without prejudice to his or her civil liability, a hotel proprietor is guilty of a criminal offence and is liable on summary conviction to a fine not exceeding £100.

## KEEPING A REGISTER OF HOTEL GUESTS

The proprietors of hotels and guesthouses are required under the Aliens Order, 1946 to keep a register in the premises of all residents and to preserve the register for a period of two years from the date on which the last entry in it was recorded.

The order does not specify whether the register is to be kept as a book, on cards, or otherwise and, therefore, it appears to allow the proprietor discretion to decide the method that best suits the hotel's administrative procedures. However, it does specify the information that must be recorded in relation to each guest, on arrival:

- date of arrival of guest
- guest's name
- place of ordinary residence
- place of residence immediately before arrival at premises
- nationality

and on departure:

- date of departure
- address to which the guest is proceeding.

While it is the duty of the guest to furnish these particulars, his or her duty to enter the particulars in the register arises only if he/she is required to do so by the proprietor or the receptionist.

Any member of the Garda Síochána or authorised officer of the Minister for Justice has the power to enter hotel premises at any reasonable time to inspect the register; the proprietor is under a duty to facilitate the inspection and produce the register.

# THE RETAIL PRICES
## (FOOD IN CATERING ESTABLISHMENTS)
## DISPLAY ORDER, 1984

This order, which came into operation on 1 September 1984, requires that every person who carries on the business of selling foods by retail for consumption on the premises must display a detailed price list at the premises. The order is specific in extending the meaning of 'premises' to include vehicles and vessels. Examples of such premises, therefore, include a ship's restaurant and dining cars on trains.

## Foods Defined

While there is a general inclusion of all food and beverages sold to the public for consumption on the premises, the order makes some notable exclusions from its scope:

- foods sold in conjunction with accommodation, e.g. bed and breakfast
- alcoholic beverages
- biscuits not made at the premises where they are on sale
- foods that are prepacked elsewhere than on the premises where they are on sale, except the following prepacked foods: bread, sandwiches, rolls, salads, meats, carbonated or aerated waters (whether coloured or not and whether flavoured or not), fruit juices or similar beverages.

## Prices and Charges to be Displayed

The price charged for each item of food on sale at the premises, and covered by the order, must be displayed on a notice or menu. If there is a minimum price, or a service charge, cover charge, entry charge, entertainment charge or any similar charge, the notice must specify the amount of any such price or charge, inclusive of value-added tax, and at the same time identify the matter to which it relates. If the particular charges are included already in the price of the food, the fact of such inclusion must be stated.

Where a group of foods are intended to be sold together at a single inclusive price, as, for example, in a table d'hôte menu, the foods covered by the menu must be specified, together with the single inclusive price. If any of the foods provided as part of the table d'hôte menu are not on sale separately, it is not necessary for the notice to specify their prices separately. Where there is a range of foods on sale, only the highest and lowest prices charged for each range need be given, e.g. the notice may state 'soups 75p-£1.40' or 'pastries 65p-£1.65'. The groups of foods provided for in this way by the order are: soups, ice creams, cakes, pastries, sandwiches, sandwich rolls, or similar foods made mainly of flour, carbonated or aerated waters (whether coloured or not and whether flavoured or not), fruit juices or similar beverages. If foods are sold at different prices at different times or on different days, the notice must display the different prices and must explain the circumstances in which they are chargeable.

## Manner in which Notices must be Displayed

In laying down the manner in which price notices are to be displayed, the order distinguishes between

(a) premises that are used solely as a catering establishment, e.g. a restaurant, in which case the notice must be displayed immediately outside or immediately inside each entrance to the premises open to the public, and

(b) premises that are used for other purposes besides that of a catering establishment, e.g. a department store, in which case the notice must be displayed either immediately outside or immediately inside each entrance to the catering area, and

(c) where the premises is a hotel or public house, the notice may be displayed either at each entrance to the premises or at each entrance to the catering area.

In all cases, the notices must be displayed in such a position as to be clearly visible, easily accessible and in such form and manner as to be capable of being easily read by all persons using the entrances.

## Defence to Proceedings

In any proceedings for offences committed under this order, it is a defence for the person charged to prove:

(a) that the commission of the offence was due to the act or default of another person or some other cause beyond his or her control, and

(b) that he or she took all reasonable precautions and exercised all due diligence to avoid the commission of such an offence by himself/herself or by any other person under his/her control.

## Penalties

A fine on summary conviction not exceeding £100 may be imposed for failing to comply with this order.

## THE RETAIL PRICES (BEVERAGES IN LICENSED PREMISES) DISPLAY ORDER, 1976

This order provides mainly for the display in licensed premises of the tax-inclusive prices at which intoxicating liquor and non-alcoholic beverages are sold for consumption on the premises.

## Requirements of the Order

The order requires that every person carrying on the business of selling intoxicating liquor by retail, for consumption on the premises, must display two types of notice inside the premises.

*The First Notice*. This must specify each kind of beverage on sale (whether alcoholic or non-alcoholic) and the quantities, measures or units by which they are sold, together with the price charged for each. Where different prices are charged in different parts of the premises (e.g. a public bar and a lounge bar), a separate notice providing this information must be displayed in each part. Where wine is sold for consumption on the premises and the notice as described, or a wine list, specifies the price of wine by reference to a container (other than an unopened bottle), such must specify the metric or imperial measure of the quantity of wine in the container.

The letters and figures on this notice must be at least 3 millimetres (one-eighth of an inch approximately) high and of a proportionate width.

*The Second Notice*. This must specify:

(a) The price per pint charged at the premises for at least one kind of draught stout.

(b) The price per pint charged at the premises for at least one kind of draught ale.

(c) The price per half-pint bottle charged at the premises for at least one kind of stout.

(d) The price per half-pint bottle charged at the premises for at least one kind of ale.

(e) The price per half-glass (quarter-gill) charged at the premises for at least one kind of Irish whiskey.

(f) The price per half-glass charged at the premises for at least one kind of Irish-made vodka.

(g) The price per half-glass charged at the premises for at least one kind of Irish-made gin.

(h) The price per bottle (6 fl. ozs) charged at the premises for at least one kind of aerated beverage having an orange base.

(i) The price per bottle (6 fl. ozs) charged at the premises for at least one kind of aerated beverage having a cola base.

If none of the beverages specified above are for sale in the premises, the requirement to display this notice will not apply. However, if some of the beverages are for sale, a notice specifying such beverages must be displayed.

Here again, where different prices are charged in different parts of the premises, a separate notice must be displayed in each part.

The notice in this case must be at least 2.5 centimetres (one inch) high and of a proportionate width.

## Display of Notices

Every notice required to be displayed by this order must be in such a position as to be clearly visible and capable of being easily read by all persons in the area of the premises to which the notice relates. Where a single notice cannot be displayed in such a position to comply with these requirements, such number of notices as may be necessary to secure compliance must be displayed.

## References to Prices Charged

References made to the price charged for any beverages on sale in the premises are references to the retail price (stated as a single amount and inclusive of any charge made for any tax payable in respect of the beverage) charged in the premises for that beverage for consumption on the premises.

## Refund of Deposit on Bottles

Where any beverage is sold by retail in any premises for consumption off the premises, and it is a condition of the sale that if the bottle in which the beverage is sold is returned, the seller will give a specified sum of money to the person returning the bottle, the seller must display a notice (at least 3 millimetres high — one-eighth of an inch — and of a proportionate width) inside the premises, specifying

(a) the price of the beverage, including the amount of the deposit, stated as a single amount, and

b) the price of the beverage, excluding the amount of the deposit, stated as a single amount.

## Penalties

A fine on summary conviction not exceeding £100 may be imposed under this order.

## CONSUMER INFORMATION AND PROTECTION

A considerable body of legislation is broadly directed for the protection of the general public in its dealings with the suppliers of goods and services. Reference has already been made to the Hotel Proprietors Act, 1963 and to menu and drink price display orders. Other statutes — for example, the Merchandise Marks Acts, 1887-1972, the Sale of Goods Act, 1893, the Consumer Information Act, 1978, the Sale of Goods and Supply of Services Act, 1980 and the Package Holidays and Travel Trade Act, 1995— are all aimed at consumer protection.

For present purposes, it is intended to examine aspects of the latter three Acts.

## CONSUMER INFORMATION ACT, 1978

The effect of this Act is to increase the level of accuracy required of information that is given in relation to the supply of goods and services. Since the offences that may be created by the Act can be committed by persons only in the conduct of their business, trade or profession, an individual who is selling goods or providing a service on a once-off basis is not burdened by the Act's provisions. For example, a householder who wishes to sell a fridge or washing machine, and who advertises the sale in a local newspaper, would not be affected by the Act.

The Act provides for a range of offences dealing with the false description of goods, services, accommodation and facilities; false or misleading indications of prices or charges; misleading advertisements; the contravention of ministerial orders, and a number of other offences.

## False Statements relating to Services, Accommodation or Facilities

In the course of, or for the purposes of, a trade, business or profession, it is an offence to make a false statement relating to services, accommodation or facilities. The offence arises where the person making the statement knows it to be false or recklessly makes a statement that is false. The term false as used here means false to a material degree.

Possible offences in the hotel trade occur where the proprietor exercises a degree of 'poetic licence' in advertising the hotel's facilities and services. For example, 'en suite bathroom and colour television in every room' when the reality is shared bathroom facilities on each floor and a communal television room. Or, 'extensive recreational facilities, including pony trekking, mini–golf, tennis and both indoor and outdoor heated swimming pools', when the most that is provided is a dilapidated outbuilding for table tennis. Menu items such as 'Baked Limerick Ham' or 'Roast Antrim Turkey' which do not originate from the places specified are also in contravention of the Act.

## False or Misleading Indication of Prices or Charges

In circumstances where the prices or charges relating to goods, services or accommodation are marked down — as, for example, in a sale or so-called 'special offer' — specific provisions are laid down in the Act. Any reference to a former price or charge is automatically taken to mean that the goods or services in question were openly available at that price at the same place within the preceding three months for not less than twenty-eight consecutive days. If this is not the case, the supplier of the goods or services must state so. The hotelier who advertises 'a cut price weekend', indicating the 'normal' price and the more attractive 'cut price', must comply with these requirements.

It is an offence to publish or cause to be published a misleading advertisement in relation to the promotion of goods, services or facilities.

## Prosecutions

Prosecutions for offences under this Act may be brought by the Minister for Enterprise, Trade and Employment, by the Director of Consumer Affairs, or by the local authority within whose functional area the offence is alleged to have been committed.

## Defences available under the Act

A person charged with any offence under the Act may prove:

(a) that the offence was due to a mistake, or to a reliance on information supplied to him, or to the act or default of another person, to an accident or to some other cause beyond his control, and

(b) that he took all reasonable precautions and exercised all due diligence to avoid the commission of the offence by himself or by any person under his control.

Where a false description has been applied to goods, the person charged can show that he or she had neither actual nor constructive knowledge of either the fact that the goods did not conform to the description provided or the fact that the description had been applied to the goods.

The Act also provides a defence for the proprietors of newspapers and magazines in connection with the publication of advertisements, if they can show that they did not know and had no reason to suspect that publication would amount to an offence under the Consumer Information Act, 1978.

## Penalties

On summary conviction, the maximum penalty is a fine of £500 and/or six months' imprisonment. On indictment, the maximum penalty is a fine of £10,000 and/or two years' imprisonment. It is noteworthy that where an offence has been prosecuted to a summary conviction, the court has discretion to award as compensation all or part of the fine to the person who has suffered loss as a result of the offence. In order to benefit from this provision, such a person must have been called to give evidence in the prosecution of the case.

## SALE OF GOODS AND SUPPLY OF SERVICES ACT, 1980

The terms implied by the above Act are of special concern to those such as hoteliers and restaurateurs who, in the course of a business, provide a service. Every contract for the supply of a service is implied to contain the following terms:

- that the supplier has the necessary skill to render the service

- that he or she will supply the service with due skill, care and diligence

- that, where materials are used, they will be sound and reasonably fit for the purpose for which they are required

- that, where goods are supplied under the contract, they are of merchantable quality.

It is possible to avoid any of these implied terms by expressly stating that it is excluded. However, where the recipient of the service is a consumer, it must be shown that the express term is fair and reasonable and has been specifically brought to his or her attention.

## PACKAGE HOLIDAYS AND TRAVEL TRADE ACT, 1995

As with a considerable amount of Irish legislation in recent times, the impetus for the introduction of the Package Holidays and Travel Trade Act, 1995 lies in the necessity to fulfil obligations imposed by the European Union. This Act, therefore, gives effect to Council Directive No.90/314/EEC of 13 June 1990, on package travel, package holidays and package tours. The main thrust of the Act is to afford greater protection to consumers who take package holidays and has, as a result, important implications for holiday-makers, tour operators and travel agents alike. The Act came into operation on 1 October 1995.

The most significant aspect of the Act is the imposition of direct liability on the holiday organiser for the non-performance and/or improper performance of the holiday contract, irrespective of whether such obligations are to be performed by the organiser, the retailer, or other suppliers of services. Holiday organisers are primarily responsible for anything that goes wrong in connection with the package holiday. For example, if a hotel fails or improperly performs its part of a holiday contract, the package organiser or tour operator may be liable for damages. This does not affect any claim the organisers may independently have against a retailer or other supplier of services, but means that the consumer can sue the organiser for breach of contract, even if the problem is caused by a hotel or other service provider.

The amount of compensation payable to the consumer for damage arising from failure to perform the package correctly (other than death, personal injury or damage caused by the wilful misconduct or gross negligence of the organiser) may be limited by the contract, but liability cannot be excluded.

## Limitation of Liability

The consumer's compensation for death or personal injury, defamation, or damage caused by the wilful misconduct or gross negligence of the organiser cannot be limited by the contract. Otherwise, the amount recoverable may be limited by the terms of the contract subject to the Sale of Goods and Supply of Services Act, 1980 and any International Conventions applicable, but does not affect the Hotel Proprietors Act, 1963. The compensation cannot be limited to less than double the inclusive price of the package for an adult or, for a minor, the inclusive price of the package to the minor concerned.

## What is a Package Holiday?

The 1995 Act defines 'package' to mean a combination of at least two of the following components prearranged by the organiser when sold or offered for sale in Ireland at an inclusive price and when the service covers a period of more than 24 hours or includes overnight accommodation:

- transport

- accommodation

- other tourist services, not ancillary to transport or accommodation, accounting for a significant proportion of the package

   (In the case of the last, other tourist services could include golf, fishing, horse riding and suchlike.)

It makes no difference if the consumer is required to pay separately for each of the elements of the package holiday; the holiday is nevertheless regarded as a package under the Act. It should be emphasised, however, that arrangements made by a tour operator or travel agent to cater specifically for an individual consumer's requirements are not regarded as a package holiday.

A package holiday may be taken at home in Ireland or abroad and the Act covers both holidays sold or offered for sale in Ireland and holidays sold in Ireland by companies established outside the country.

## Who is an 'Organiser'?

In the Act 'organiser' means 'a person, who other than occasionally, organises packages and sells or offers them for sale to a consumer, whether directly or through a retailer'. This definition of organiser allows an exemption from the provisions of the Act for an 'occasional' organiser. The Act goes on to state that 'a person shall not be regarded as organising packages occasionally unless that person is a member of a class specified in regulations made by the Minister (for Public Enterprise)'. Regulations under S.I. No. 271 of 1995 were put in place on 29 September 1995 (just in time for the operation of the Act on 1 October 1995). This instrument sets out who may be classed as an 'occasional organiser' and includes professional, medical, scientific, cultural or trade associations or societies, social and sporting clubs, voluntary organisations, schools and educational institutions, religious groups and charities. (While the above groups are mentioned in the statutory instrument, they could fall outside its protective ambit should the exact wording of the statutory instrument not be observed.)

It is very clear, therefore, that the 1995 Act applies not just to tour operators but to all package organisers. For example, a coach company that organises overnight accommodation could be a package organiser, as could a guest house or hotel that organises local tours or the recently popular 'Murder Mystery Weekend'!

## Holiday Brochure Content

The Act prohibits an organiser or retailer from making a brochure available to a potential consumer unless it indicates in a legible, comprehensible and accurate manner the following information:

- the price of the holiday

- the holiday destination and the means, characteristics and categories of transport used to get there

- the type of accommodation, its location, category or degree of comfort and its main features (e.g. pent-house suite), and the approval or tourist classification by the relevant authority

- the meal plan

- the itinerary

- passport and visa requirements and health formalities required for both the journey and the stay

- either the monetary amount or the percentage of the price to be paid as a deposit and the timetable for payment of the balance

- whether or not a minimum number of persons is required for the package to take place, and, if so, the latest time for informing the consumer in the event of a cancellation

- any tax or compulsory charge

- in the case of packages offered by an organiser who has no place of business in the state, a nominated agent in the State who will accept service on behalf of and represent the organiser in any proceedings (including criminal proceedings) brought in connection with any provision of this Act

- in the event of insolvency of the organiser, the arrangements for security for money paid over and (where applicable) for the repatriation of the consumer.

Organisers and retailers must not supply to a consumer any information concerning a package which is false or misleading. In any proceedings taken against a retailer in this respect, it will be a defence for the retailer to show that he/she did not know and had no reason to suspect that the brochure or other descriptive matter contained information which was false or misleading. Organisers and retailers are liable to compensate the consumer for any damage caused to the consumer as a direct consequence of his/her reliance on false or misleading information in a brochure.

When mentioning compensation, it is important to point out that a claim for compensation could include consequential loss for disappointment at the quality of the holiday package, as well as financial loss.

## Pre-contractual Requirements

Before a contract is made, the organiser (whether directly or through a retailer) must provide the intending consumer with the following information in writing or in some other appropriate form:

- general information about passport and visa requirements which apply to the purchase of the package, including information about the length of time it is likely to take to obtain these.

- information about health formalities required by national administrations for the journey and the stay.

- where the consumer is required as a term of the contract to take out insurance to cover cancellation and assistance (including repatriation) in the event of accident or illness, the minimum level of cover needed. The consumer cannot be forced to take out the organiser's or retailer's insurance.

- where insurance is optional, the tour operator must, if he/she has information which would help the consumer to decide to insure or not, give it to the consumer.

These obligations may be fulfilled by referring the intending consumer to such information contained in a brochure supplied to him or her and to which no relevant alterations have been made since the brochure was published.

## Pre-holiday Information

In good time before the package holiday is due to start, the organiser (or retailer) must make sure that the consumer is given in writing the following information:

- where the package includes transport, the times and places of intermediate stops and connections and details of the place to be occupied by the traveller, including cabin or berth on a ship, sleeper compartment on a train

- the name, address and telephone number of the representative (or agent) of the organiser in the locality where the consumer is to stay

- if there is no representative or agent, such information as will enable the consumer to contact the organiser or retailer

- in the case of a journey or stay outside the State by a minor, information enabling direct contact to be made with the minor or with the person responsible at the minor's place of stay.

## Essential Terms of the Contract

With the exception of a package which is booked 14 days or less before departure, all the terms of the contract must be set out in writing and communicated to the consumer before the contract is completed. Regardless of when the booking is made, every consumer must be given a written copy of the contract. Depending on the nature of the package, each contract must contain, where relevant, at least the following:

- the travel destination or destinations, the period of stay, with dates

- the means of transport to be used, including dates, times and places of departure and return

- the location of the accommodation, its tourist category, and its compliance with the law of the state if in the European Union

- the meal plan

- whether a minimum number of persons is required for the package to take place, and, if so, the latest time for informing the consumer in the event of cancellation

- the itinerary

- visits, excursions or other services which are included in the total price agreed for the package

- the name and address of the organiser, retailer and, if appropriate, the insurer

- in the case of a package sold by an organiser who has no place of business in the State, the name of an agent with an address in the State who will accept service on behalf of the organiser in any proceedings (including criminal proceedings)

- the price of the package and the payment schedule, including any price revisions which may be made and an indication of any taxes, dues or fees which may be incurred and which are not included in the cost of the package

- any special requirements which the consumer has requested and which are accepted by both parties to the contract

- arrangements for complaints by the consumer about the failure or inadequate performance of the contract. The consumer must be given at least 28 days from the date of completion of the package in which to lodge a complaint.

## Transfer of Booking

In circumstances where the consumer who booked the package is not able to travel, the Act implies a term in the contract to allow the consumer to transfer the booking to another person, so long as that person satisfies all the conditions attached to the package. To transfer to another person, the consumer must give reasonable notice to the organiser or retailer of their intention to transfer the package to someone else. It is important to note that where a transfer is made, both the original purchaser of the package and the person to whom it is transferred are both liable to the organiser for payment of the package (or for the balance of the payment, as the case may be) and for any other reasonably incurred incidental costs.

## Contract Price Revision

Price revisions may be allowed but only under strictly observed conditions and only where there is provision for price reductions as well as price increases. These conditions are:

- that the manner in which the price revision will be calculated will be described precisely in a contract term

- that the circumstances in which the price may be revised must be described in a contract term and must be such as to provide that price revisions may be made only to allow for variations in:

  - transport costs, including the cost of fuel

  - dues, taxes or fees chargeable for services such as landing taxes or embarkation or disembarkation fees at ports and airports, or

  - the exchange rates which apply to the particular package.

However, no price increase may be made within the twenty-one days before the departure date of the consumer.

## Alteration or Cancellation by Organiser

Where an organiser significantly alters a term of the contract, such as price, or cancels the contract altogether, the consumer must be notified of this as soon as possible in order to enable him or her to take appropriate decisions. In such circumstances the consumer is entitled

- to take a replacement package of equivalent or superior quality if the organiser is able to offer such a replacement, or

- to take a replacement package of lower quality and to recover the difference in price between the two packages from the organiser, or

- to have a full refund.

Instead of any of the above forms of redress, the consumer can sue for breach of contract. There are two situations in which the organiser can cancel a package holiday without incurring liability for compensation to the consumer. These are:

- where the package is cancelled because the minimum number of persons for the package is not reached and the consumer is given the required notice of this in writing

- where the package is cancelled by *force majeure*, that is to say, by reason of unusual and unforeseeable circumstances beyond the control of the organiser, retailer or other supplier of services, the consequences of which could not have been avoided even if all due care had been exercised. (However, overbooking can never be considered as coming into this category).

## Failure of the Package

If, after the start of the holiday, something serious goes wrong and the organiser is unable to provide a significant proportion of the services contracted for, the organiser must

- make suitable alternative arrangements, at no extra cost, for the continuation of the package holiday
- pay compensation for any shortfall in the services actually supplied
- if it is impossible to make suitable alternative arrangements, provide transport home.

## Protection against Insolvency

Travel agents and tour operators have for some time been required to enter into a bond for the protection of consumers travelling abroad only. Providers of domestic package holidays are also now required to enter into security arrangements (a bond or insurance policy) for the refund of money and the repatriation of consumers. This extends protection against insolvency to holidays at home and abroad.

## Complaints

Holiday-makers are required to communicate complaints 'at the earliest opportunity', in writing or any other appropriate form (this could include oral communication, provided written details of the complaint are confirmed to the organiser or local representative if the consumer fails to obtain a satisfactory response to the oral complaint) to the supplier of services concerned, and to the organiser or local representative, any failure which the consumer perceives at the place where the services are supplied.

There is also an obligation on the organiser or local representative that when a complaint is made by a consumer, it receives prompt attention to find an appropriate solution.

## Offences and Penalties

Contravention of any of the provisions of this Act carries, on summary conviction, a maximum fine of £1,500, while conviction for an indictable offence is punishable by a fine of up to £50,000 and/or a two-year imprisonment.

## Prosecutions

Prosecutions for offences under this Act may be brought in the case of summary offences by the Director of Consumer Affairs and, in limited circumstances, by the Minister for Public Enterprise. Indictable offences are prosecuted by the Director of Public Prosecutions.

### FIRE SAFETY LEGISLATION

The horror and potential for devastation of fire should need little by way of reminder to anyone, much less to anyone responsible for the safety of others. Regrettably, it is so often with hindsight, and almost invariably after a disaster of considerable magnitude, that the need for adequate fire safety measures is brought sharply into focus.

It is not generally appreciated that there is a statutory duty on every person who has control over scheduled premises to which members of the public have access, to take all reasonable measures to guard against the outbreak of fire on the premises and, furthermore, if there is an outbreak, to ensure, as far as is reasonably practicable, the safety of anyone on the premises.

This general obligation, which arises under the Fire Services Act, 1981 (the principal fire safety legislation in Ireland and supplemented to date with the Fire Safety in Places of Assembly (Ease of Escape) Regulations, 1985, The Fire Authorities (Emergency Operations) Regulations, 1987 and the Fire Services Act, 1981 (Prescribed Premises) Regulations, 1987) applies to premises put to any of the following uses:

- for any purpose involving the provision of sleeping accommodation (but excluding premises consisting of a dwelling house occupied as a single dwelling)

- as, or as part of, an institution providing treatment or care
- for the purpose of entertainment, recreation or instruction
- for the purpose of any club, society or association
- for purposes of teaching, training or research
- for any purpose involving access to the premises by members of the public, whether on payment or otherwise
- for any other purpose that may be prescribed.

Even a cursory reading of the foregoing will assist in identifying a wide range of premises in respect of which the obligation applies: hotel, guesthouse, hospital, cinema, restaurant, public house, sports stadium, gymnasium, bingo hall, disco/dance hall, church, school, college, university, club. This list is not exhaustive.

Almost equally important is the fact that the Act imposes a duty on every person present in these premises to conduct himself/herself in such a way as to ensure that, as far as is reasonably practicable, any person on the premises is not exposed to danger from fire through any act or omission.

A fire authority may give advice in relation to fire safety to the owner or occupier of any premises or to any person having control over any premises.

## Potentially Dangerous Building

The expression 'potentially dangerous building' conjures up an image of a building in an advanced stage of dereliction and perhaps about to collapse. If this was a common interpretation of the term, many owners, occupiers and persons having control of premises could be forgiven for thinking that their premises were exempt from such description or classification. However, after reading the meaning ascribed to this term by the Fire Services Act, 1981, these people are likely to be jolted out of their complacency.

The Act defines a 'potentially dangerous building' as any building that would, in the event of a fire occurring in it, constitute a serious danger to life for any of the following reasons:

(a) The fact that large numbers of people enter the building or are accommodated there.

(b) The absence or inadequacy of appliances or fittings for:

- extinguishing fires
- enabling the occupants to escape on the occurrence of fire
- the automatic detection of an outbreak of fire
- giving fire warning
- ensuring that the means of escape can be safely and effectively used at all times.

(c) The flammable nature of the materials of which the building is made.

(d) The flammable nature of the furniture, furnishings and fittings in the building.

(e) The absence of adequate means of escape from the building.

(f) The absence or inadequacy of notices on the procedure to be followed in the event of fire.

(g) The flammable, explosive or potentially explosive nature of anything used, stored or deposited in the building.

(h) The fact that a fire in the building would be likely to spread rapidly within the building or to other premises.

(i) The fact that any power supply or lighting system with which the building is provided is defective, inadequate or inadequately maintained.

(j) The fact that any heating or ventilating system with which the building is provided is defective or inadequately maintained, or presents a fire hazard.

(k) Any similar reason.

## Fire Safety Notices

A fire authority may serve a notice on the owner or occupier of any building that appears to it to be potentially dangerous. This 'fire safety notice' may

(a) prohibit the use of the entire building or a specified part of it for any purpose or purposes set down in the notice.

(b) prohibit the use of the building or a specified part of it for any purpose(s) specified in the notice, unless or until specified precautions are taken to the satisfaction of the fire authority. Such precautions might include the provision of appliances or fittings, the execution of structural alterations or additions to the building, the removal of furniture, furnishings or fittings or, in short, anything that the fire authority considers necessary.

A fire safety notice may impose obligations on the owner or occupier of a building in relation to a number of matters, as follows:

1. Provision and maintenance of exit signs, emergency lighting and notices regarding the procedure to be followed in the event of a fire.

2. Provision and maintenance of equipment and fittings for fire detection, fire prevention, the extinguishing of fire, and giving warning of fire.

3. Installation, maintenance and use of power, lighting, heating and ventilation systems.

4. Arrangements to be made for the safe storage of flammable, explosive or potentially explosive articles or materials stored, used, or deposited in the building.

5. Measures to be taken for securing that persons employed in the building receive appropriate instruction or training in fire safety, and what to do in the event of fire, and that records are kept of such instruction or training.

6. The holding of fire safety evacuation drills at specified intervals and keeping records of such drills.

7. The nomination of an appropriate person or persons employed in the building to have responsibility for fire safety measures in that building.

8. Limiting the number of persons who may be in the building at any one time.

Where a fire safety notice is issued under provisions contained at (b) above, for the taking of precautions by the fire authority, it is not possible for the fire safety notice to specify a time limit in respect of taking such precautions. This means that the use of the building (or a specified part of it) for a specified purpose is prohibited once the notice takes effect in accordance with the rules outlined. It is not possible, therefore, to delay the prohibition of use beyond the date on which the notice takes effect. However, where a notice imposes requirements of the type outlined in points 1–8 above, it is possible to impose a time limit for compliance with those requirements (see the Department of Environment Circular Letter Ref.4/82). Each fire authority is required to keep at its offices a register of fire safety notices served by it and the register must be open to inspection by any person at all reasonable times.

Where a fire safety notice requires the carrying out of any work, and the owner or occupier alleges that the whole or part of the expense of the work should be borne by the occupier or owner, he or she may apply to the District Court for an order concerning the expenses or their apportionment, and the court shall have jurisdiction to make such order as it thinks fit.

## Appealing against a Fire Safety Notice

Any person on whom a fire safety notice has been served may, within fourteen days from the date of service, appeal against the notice to the District Court on any one or more of the following grounds:

(a) That he or she is not the owner or occupier of the building or land.

(b) That the building is not a potentially dangerous building.

(c) That the notice is unreasonable because of the improbability of a fire occurring in the building or because of the improbability of serious danger to life arising from fire.

(d) That the compliance with the requirements of the notice would involve unreasonable expense or an unreasonable interference with the use of the building or land.

(e) That the notice specified an unreasonably short time for complying with any of its requirements.

Notice of the appeal must be given to the fire authority, which is entitled to appear, be heard and adduce evidence at the hearing of the appeal.

On hearing the appeal, the District Court may, as it considers proper,

(a) confirm the notice unconditionally, or

(b) confirm the notice subject to such modifications, alterations or additions as the court thinks reasonable, or

(c) annul the notice.

Where the court confirms the notice, subject to modifications, alterations or additions, the notice will have effect subject to these changes.

A fire safety notice will not have effect until

(a) the expiration of fourteen days from the date of service of the notice, or

(b) if an appeal is taken and the notice is confirmed, with or without modification, on the date on which the decision of the court is pronounced.

The decision of the District Court in relation to appeals against fire safety notices cannot be further appealed to the Circuit Court.

## Powers of Inspection

A person authorised for the purpose by the fire authority is entitled to enter at all reasonable times and inspect any land or building (other than a dwelling house occupied as a single dwelling). Such person is entitled to:

- inspect any water supply in a building or on any land
- inspect all records required to be kept by a fire safety notice or by regulation
- require to be informed by the owner or occupier of any land or building or by any person in his employment of the following:
  - the purpose for which the land or building is used
  - the number of persons habitually employed or accommodated on the premises
  - the number of persons who frequent the premises
  - the substance of which any building is made
  - the method of construction of any building
  - any other matter that the authorised person considers relevant.

A fire authority, by giving notice in writing, may require an owner or occupier to provide the authority (within such period as it may specify) with plans of the land or building and any other information in writing as it may require. The owner or occupier is under a statutory duty to comply with these demands. Furthermore, a person authorised by the fire authority is entitled to take with him/her such persons and equipment considered necessary to assist in the examination and testing of any ventilation, heating, power or lighting system, and any materials or substances used.

An offence is committed by any person who:

(a) refuses to allow an authorised person to enter any land or building or to take any person or equipment with him/her in the exercise of his/her authority, or

(b) obstructs or impedes an authorised person in the exercise of any of his/her powers, or

(c) fails or refuses to give to an authorised person on demand, or to the fire authority following a notice in writing, any plan or information that the authorised person or fire authority is entitled to require, or

(d) wilfully or recklessly gives to an authorised person or to a fire authority information that is false or misleading in a material respect, or

(e) fails to comply with any requirement relating to the powers of inspection by authorised persons.

Where an authorised person is refused entry to land or a building in the exercise of his or her powers, the fire authority may apply to the District Court for a warrant that authorises entry. If a fire authority considers that the risk to persons in the event of a fire is so serious that the use of land or a building should be restricted or immediately prohibited until specified measures have been taken to reduce the risk to a reasonable level, it may apply to the High Court for an order restricting or prohibiting the use of the land or building.

## FIRE SAFETY IN PLACES OF ASSEMBLY (EASE OF ESCAPE) REGULATIONS, 1985

The Fire Services Act, 1981 makes provision for the introduction of orders and regulations concerning fire safety and related matters. In exercise of this authority, the Fire Safety in Places of Assembly (Ease of Escape) Regulations, 1985 came into operation on 1 September 1985.

The regulations define a 'place of assembly' as a 'building or any part of a building' put to any of the following uses:

> amusement arcade, bingo hall, casino, cinema, concert hall, dance hall, discothèque, theatre, bus or train passenger station, ecclesiastical building, exhibition hall, funfair building, grandstand, gymnasium, indoor bowling alley, indoor games court, non-residential club, café, restaurant, canteen, premises licensed for the sale of intoxicating liquor (other than an off-licence), radio or television studio to which the public is admitted, riding school, skating rink, sports pavilion, stadium, swimming baths (including any swimming pool, changing room, or similar facility), tent or marquee to which the public is admitted.

### Duties of Persons having Control over a Place of Assembly

Every person having control over a place of assembly must ensure that, while the place is in actual use as a place of assembly:

- all escape routes are kept unobstructed and immediately available for use.

- doors, gates and other barriers across escape routes are not secured in such a manner that they cannot be easily and immediately opened by anyone in the place.

- all chains, padlocks and other removable fastenings for securing doors, gates or barriers are removed and kept in a place where they may be readily inspected by a person authorised under the Fire Services Act, 1981.

- no hanging or drape is placed across or along an escape route in a manner that would impede or obstruct escape.

- no mirrors are placed across or along an escape route or adjacent to an exit in such a way as to confuse the direction of escape.

## Duty of Persons in a Place of Assembly

A person who is in a place of assembly must not prevent or obstruct the person having control over the place from complying with the regulations.

## DEPARTMENT OF THE ENVIRONMENT CODES OF PRACTICE

The Department of the Environment has published a series of codes of practice dealing with

- furnishings and fittings in places of public assembly
- the management of fire safety in places of public assembly
- fire safety in hotels and guesthouses
- fire safety in flats.

(Other codes are in the course of preparation.)

The importance of these codes and the necessity that they be read and understood by those with responsibility for places of assembly cannot be overstated. Furthermore, it is likely that regulations will be introduced in due course to make compliance with the codes mandatory.

## THE FIRE SERVICES ACT, 1981 AND LICENSING UNDER OTHER STATUTES

The Fire Services Act, 1981 requires that applicants for certain specified licences and certificates must give one month's notice in writing of the application to the fire authority in whose functional area the premises are situated. In special circumstances, the fire authority may agree to a shorter period of notice than one month. At the hearing of the application, the fire authority is entitled to appear, be heard and adduce evidence in respect of the application. The licences and certificates concerned are as follows:

(a) A certificate for the grant or renewal of a licence (other than an off-licence) under the Licensing Acts, 1833-1995.

(b) The grant or renewal of a certificate of registration under the Registration of Clubs Acts, 1904-86.

(c) A licence in respect of premises under
    (i)   The Public Dance Halls Act, 1935, or
    (ii)  Part IV of the Public Health Acts Amendment Act, 1890

(d) A certificate in respect of premises under the Gaming and Lotteries Acts, 1956-79.

## FOOD HYGIENE REGULATIONS, 1950-89

There are always some grounds for argument when a definitive assertion is made that one source of danger is more perilous than another. It is, therefore, with a little trepidation that the suggestion is made that the importance of a strict regime of hygienic practices to avoid serious health risk is second only on the scale of importance to fire safety and achieves this ranking only because of the immediacy of fire.

The health boards are charged with the responsibility of enforcing food legislation. Environmental health officers are empowered to enter and inspect all types of food premises to ensure that an acceptable standard of food hygiene is achieved and maintained. Their powers derive from the Food Hygiene Regulations, 1950-89; it is under these regulations that proceedings for contravention are instigated by the health boards.

The intention of the Food Hygiene Regulations is to afford protection to the public and to lay down minimum standards of hygiene. The burden of compliance with the regulations is largely on the proprietor of the food outlet, but the food worker is not exempt from responsibility on his/her own account.

## Regulations Governing Food Premises

The proprietor of a food premises must comply with the following provisions:

1. The walls, ceilings, floors, doors, windows and all parts of the premises must be kept in a proper state of repair and in a clean and hygienic condition.

2. A suitable and sufficient means of ventilation and lighting must be provided and maintained.

3. A suitable and sufficient supply of potable water to the premises from a public water supply must be maintained.

4. A suitable and sufficient supply of potable water, soap and clean towels (or other suitable means of drying) must be provided, together with a sufficient number of wash basins.

5. Lavatories and waste bins must not be located within or be adjacent to any food room.

6. A cistern for the supply of water to any food room must not be connected with a sanitary convenience or a drain in such a way as to make it possible for the water in the cistern to be contaminated.

7. There must not be any outlet in a food room for the ventilation of a drain or, except with the approval of the health authority, an inlet into any drain containing sewerage or foul water.

8. A sufficient number of lavatories must be provided for the use of food workers, either in the premises or in some other suitable adjacent place and, where required by the health board, notices must be displayed in lavatories, instructing food workers to wash their hands after using the toilet.

9. Food rooms must not be used as sleeping accommodation.

10. Machinery must not be put in contact with foodstuffs unless it has been constructed so as to prevent the contamination of food by dirt from the mechanism.

11. All equipment, including machinery, utensils, containers and tables, that has been in contact with foodstuffs must be readily cleanable, free from corrosion and kept in a clean and hygienic condition.

12. Chipped or cracked containers or utensils must not be used for food or served for use in the consumption of food. A single service utensil must be used on one occasion only.

13. Suitable and sufficient facilities must be provided and maintained for the washing and cleaning of the premises and equipment. A suitable and sufficient supply of hot and cold water must be provided for cleaning purposes.

14. Refuse must not be allowed to accumulate in any food room.

15. All waste and garbage must, until it is destroyed or removed from the premises, be kept in suitable containers. The proprietor must provide a sufficient number of the containers for this purpose.

16. Adequate measures must be taken to prevent the contamination of food by foreign matter, unnecessary handling, vermin, pests, or otherwise.

17. Unprotected food must not be placed or kept where it would be likely to be contaminated by animals or otherwise.

18. Foodstuffs that might be adversely affected by heat must be kept in a cool place. Where it is necessary to wrap food, only clean paper or other suitable material must be used.

19. Ice used in connection with any food business must be made of potable water and must be kept clean.

20. Animals must not be allowed to come into contact with foodstuffs.

21. Clothes, other than overalls or other clothing worn specially while at work in the food business, must not be stored in a room where food is prepared or stored.

22. Where meals are sold to the public or where intoxicating liquor is sold for consumption on the premises, a sufficient number of appropriate lavatories inside the premises or in some suitable adjacent place must be provided for the public's use. Proper wash basins adjacent to the lavatories, with a sufficient supply of water, soap and clean towels (or other suitable means of drying), must also be provided.

In addition to the foregoing regulations, the proprietor of the food premises must take every other reasonable precaution to prevent danger to public health arising from the food business and to prevent the contamination of food on the premises.

## Regulations Governing Food Stalls

Where a food business is carried on from a food stall, the stall-holder must comply with the following requirements:

1. The food stall must be soundly constructed of suitable materials and must be kept in a proper state of repair and in a clean and hygienic condition.

2. When it is not in use, the stall must be stored in a clean place.

3. The food business must not be carried on in any place near a lavatory, an accumulation of refuse or where animals are kept.

4. The food stall must not be used as sleeping accommodation.

5. Machinery must not be put in contact with foodstuffs unless it has been constructed so as to prevent the contamination of food by dirt from the mechanism.

6. All equipment — machinery, utensils, containers and tables — that has been in contact with foodstuffs must be readily cleanable, free from corrosion and kept in a clean and hygienic condition.

7. Chipped or cracked containers or utensils must not be used for food or served for use in the consumption of food. A single service utensil must be used once only.

8. All waste and garbage must be kept in suitable containers until they are destroyed or removed from the vicinity of the stall. The stall-holder must provide a sufficient number of the containers for this purpose.

9. Adequate measures must be taken to prevent the contamination of food by foreign matter, unnecessary handling, vermin or pests, or otherwise.

10. Unprotected food must not be exposed for sale at the food stall unless the stall is so constructed as to prevent contamination of food exposed for sale.

11. The food stall must contain proper facilities for cooling foodstuffs adversely affected by heat. Only wrappers made of clean paper or other suitable material must be used to wrap food.

12. Ice used in or in connection with the food business must be made of potable water and must be kept clean.

13. Where meat is offered for sale from a food stall, the stall must be suitably covered over and screened at the sides and back.

14. The food stall must contain suitable and sufficient facilities for keeping any machinery, utensils and equipment in a clean and hygienic condition.

As with the proprietor of a food premises, the stall-holder has a general duty to take every reasonable precaution to prevent danger to public health or the contamination of food.

The Food Hygiene (Amendment) Regulations, 1989, which came into effect on 1 May 1989, added to the foregoing provisions and introduced a system of licensing for food stalls.

Where meat or meat products (other than fish or fish products) are sold, or where food is prepared, cooked or heated for sale directly to the public in a form ready for consumption, the stall-holder must comply with the following provisions:

- Display his or her name and address in letters at least 7.5cm in height in a conspicuous position on the food stall.

- Ensure that suitable and sufficient facilities are available, at or adjacent to the food stall, for hand-washing and hand-drying.

- Ensure that the food stall is adequately lit.

- Ensure that a supply of waterproof dressings and antiseptics is provided at the stall.

- Ensure that meat and meat products, milk and milk products and all other food-stuffs susceptible to rapid bacterial growth are kept at a temperature of 3°C or less, except when heated or cooked for sale as hot food.

- Ensure that hot food is kept at a temperature of at least 63°C.

- Ensure that cooked meats and uncooked meats are stored and handled separately.

- Ensure that when the food stall is also a mechanically propelled vehicle or trailer, the driving compartment of the vehicle is suitably separated from the food area.

## Licensing Procedure for Food Stalls

Since 1 May 1989 it has been mandatory for every health board in the state to keep a register of licensed food stalls. Every person who proposes to commence a food business at a licensable food stall must, before starting the business, apply to the health board (in whose functional area the stall will be normally kept) for a licence, using form F.H.G.

A stall-holder whose food stall is normally kept outside the state, but who wishes to trade in the state, must apply for a licence to the health board whose functional area is nearest to where the stall normally will be kept.

Within two months of the date of receipt of an application for a licence, a health board must either

(a) licence the food stall for a period of one year and enter details of the licence in the register of licensed food stalls and notify the applicant accordingly, or

(b) refuse to license the food stall and notify the applicant of the decision specifying in reasonable detail the grounds for the refusal.

## General Provisions Relating to Food Stall Licences

- A food stall licence is not transferable.

- The stall-holder must display in a conspicuous place on the food stall a licence badge (form F.H.H.) which is supplied by the health board.

- Every applicant for a licence must pay the health board a fee of £100 in respect of each application.

- A licensed stall-holder must immediately inform the health board of any change of the address at which the stall is normally kept, or of his home address.

- In granting a licence for a food stall, the health board must have due regard to the nature and extent of the food business, and the health board accordingly may specify conditions under which the licence is granted.

- A food business must not be carried on from a food stall that is subject to the licensing requirements of these regulations unless there is in force a licence issued by a health board.

## Regulations Governing Food Vehicles

The proprietor of a food business that uses a food vehicle for the conveyance of food and food materials must comply with the following provisions:

- Ensure that the food vehicle is so constructed as to prevent the contamination of food carried in it and is made of suitable materials which are smooth, durable and free from all internal rust and corrosion.

- Ensure that the food vehicle is readily washable and cleanable and is kept in a proper state of repair and in a sound, clean and hygienic condition.

- Ensure that the food vehicle is weather-proof and pest-proof.

- Ensure that where the food vehicle is not fully insulated or refrigerated, the food compartment is suitably ventilated.

- Ensure that meat, meat products (other than fish or fish products), chilled food, chilled food materials, ice cream and all foods susceptible to rapid bacterial growth are transported at an internal temperature of

  - not more than 7°C in the case of meat in carcasses, half-carcasses or quarters

  - not more than minus 12°C in the case of frozen meat

  - not more than minus 17°C in the case of ice cream

  - not more than 3°C in the case of all other such foods, food products or materials.

  These requirements will not apply to carcass meat or offal transported between an abattoir and a butcher's shop over a distance of not greater than five miles or to foods to which regulations under the International Carriage of Perishable Foodstuffs Act, 1987 apply.

- Ensure that where cooked and uncooked meals are transported in the same food vehicle, care is taken to avoid cross-contamination.

- Ensure that adequate measures are taken for the prevention of the contamination of food by foreign matter in or on the food vehicle, or by unnecessary handling, or by rats, mice, insects or otherwise.

- Ensure that the part of the food vehicle in which food is carried or is intended to be carried is not used as sleeping accommodation.

- Ensure that articles, goods or materials that could cause contamination of foodstuffs are not carried in the food compartment of the food vehicle.

- Ensure that a food vehicle is not used at any time to carry farm animals or offensive toxic materials of any kind.

- Ensure that every other reasonable precaution is taken to prevent contamination of the food carried in the food vehicle.

A number of additional provisions, relating mainly to the meat trade, are also included in the regulations.

## Other Food Businesses

Any box, basket or container used in connection with a food business must be soundly constructed of suitable materials and must be kept in a proper state of repair and in a clean and hygienic condition. Such a container, when not in use, must be stored in a suitable place. Any food that is unwrapped and customarily eaten without being cooked or cleaned must be kept in a covered container.

## Regulations Governing Food Workers

A food worker engaged in any work in connection with a food business is required to keep himself/herself clean and adhere in particular to the following regulations:

- Wash hands immediately after using a sanitary convenience.

- Wash hands and (if they are uncovered while engaged in the work) forearms as often as may be necessary to keep them clean.

- Wear clean outer clothing.

- Keep all machinery, apparatus, utensils, tables or other equipment that is in contact with foodstuffs in a clean and hygienic condition.

- Avoid handling foodstuffs unnecessarily.

- Do not spit or engage in any other unhygienic practice in such proximity to food as to be liable to cause contamination or infection.

- Do not cause any contravention of the Food Hygiene Regulations.

- In addition to the foregoing matters, take every other reasonable precaution to prevent the contamination of food and to prevent danger to the public health arising from his or her work in the food business and presence in the place where the food business is carried on.

## Employment of Infected Persons

Any person who is a probable source of infection with a scheduled infectious disease, which includes acute anterior poliomyelitis, diphtheria, dysentery, paratyphoid A and B, salmonella infection, scarlet fever, streptococcal sore throat, tuberculosis, typhoid, or who is suffering from any boil, septic sore or other skin ailment on the hand or forearm which could contaminate or infect food, must not perform any work in connection with a food business, except with the permission of the local Director of Community Care and Medical Officer of Health. An employer must not permit such a person to work in connection with food unless the local Director of Community Care and Medical Officer of Health permits it. (For a complete schedule of notifiable diseases, see the Infectious Diseases Regulations, 1981.)

When a person proposes to take up employment in connection with a food business, the proprietor must require him or her to state (in writing if necessary) whether or not he or she is suffering from or is a probable source of infection from a scheduled disease, and whether or not he or she has ever suffered typhoid or paratyphoid. Such a person must to the best of his/her knowledge comply with the request.

## Power of Health Board Chief Executive Officer

If a Chief Executive Officer of a health board has evidence in relation to a food premises, food stall or food vehicle that there is a 'grave and immediate danger that food intended for human consumption may become so diseased, contaminated or otherwise unfit for human consumption as to be liable to cause serious illness if consumed', he may apply to a District Judge for a closure order. The application must be made to the Judge of the District Court in the court area in which the premises, stall or vehicle is situated.

The Judge may grant or refuse the order as he or she thinks fit. If granted, the effect of the closure order is to prohibit the operation of the food business from the premises, stall or vehicle as the case may be.

The health board Chief Executive Officer must give written notice of his or her intention to seek a closure order to the proprietor of the food business before the date of the court hearing.

The proprietor of a food business in respect of which a closure order is in force may apply at any time to the Judge of the District Court for an annulment of the order. The District Judge may confirm or annul the order as he or she thinks fit.

A food business must not be carried on at any premises, stall or vehicle in respect of which a closure order is in force.

## Penalties

Violation of the Food Hygiene Regulations carries for each offence a maximum penalty of £1,000, plus £10 per day for each day the offence continues and/or a term of imprisonment not exceeding six months. It is important to bear in mind that costs may be added to the financial penalties.

## Further Regulations

The Hygiene Regulations, 1950–1989 have been augmented by the introduction in April 1998 of two further sets of Regulations. These are:

- the European Communities (Official Control of Foodstuffs) Regulations, 1998 (S.I. No. 85 of 1998)
- the European Communities (Hygiene of Foodstuffs) Regulations, 1998. (S.I. No. 86 of 1998).

Also introduced in April 1998 was the European Communities (Official Control of Foodstuffs) (Approved Laboratories) Order, 1998, (S.I. No.95 of 1998.) This order simply specifies the list of laboratories, located countrywide, approved for the analysis of food samples taken by authorised officers. While this order merely requires mention, the previously referred to sets of Regulations require to be dealt with in more detail.

## European Communities (Official Control of Foodstuffs) Regulations, 1998

These Regulations, which came into effect on 1 April 1998, give effect to Council Directives 89/397/EEC and 93/99/EEC, both concerning the official control of foodstuffs.

The term 'foodstuffs' as used in the Regulations includes any substance used for food or drink by humans and which enters into or is used in the composition or preparation of food for use by humans. These Regulations extend control over not just foodstuffs but food additives, vitamins, mineral salts and trace elements, as well as materials and articles intended to come into contact with foodstuffs (known as controlled items). All these are subject to control by authorised officers (persons authorised in writing by the Minister for Health and Children or by the Chief Executive Officer of a health board). The exercise of this control may be by inspection; sampling and analysis; inspection of staff hygiene; examination of written and documentary material; and examination of any verification systems set up by the undertaking and of the results obtained.

As a general rule, inspections will be carried out without warning and will cover all stages of production, manufacture, import, processing, storage, transport, distribution and trade. The Regulations identify the following as being subject to inspection by authorised officers:

- the condition and use to which is put the site, premises, offices, plant and plant surroundings, means of transport, machinery and equipment
- raw materials, ingredients, technological aids and other products used for the preparation and production of foodstuffs
- semi-finished products
- finished products
- materials and articles intended to come into contact with foodstuffs
- cleaning and maintenance products, processes and pesticides
- processes used for the manufacture or processing of foodstuffs
- labelling and presentation of foodstuffs
- preserving methods.

The inspection may be supplemented by:

- interviews with the head of the inspected undertaking and with persons working for that undertaking
- the reading of values recorded by measuring instruments installed by the undertaking
- inspections carried out by the health board, with its own instruments, of measurements taken with instruments installed by the undertaking.

## Powers of Authorised Officers

An authorised officer may, at all reasonable times, enter

- any premises in which he/she has reasonable grounds for believing that any controlled item is being produced, manufactured, imported, processed, stored, transported, distributed or traded
- any railway wagon, vehicle, ship, vessel, aircraft or container in which he/she has reasonable grounds for believing that a controlled item is being transported for sale,

and there or at any other place carry out any or all the following:

- interview the head of the undertaking or any person working for that undertaking
- take note of written and documentary material
- inspect and take copies of, or extracts from, any books, records, computerised data or other information submitted to him/her for examination
- take the reading of values recorded by measuring instruments installed by the undertaking
- inspect with his/her own instruments measurements taken with instruments installed by the undertaking
- make such other examinations, tests and inspections, including the opening of any receptacle, as may be necessary.

## Sampling

An authorised officer may, for the purposes of these Regulations purchase or take without payment a sample of any controlled item. Where a sample is taken with the intention of having it examined by an approved examiner, the authorised officer must notify the seller, owner or person in apparent charge or control* of the controlled item of his/her intention of having the sample analysed.

Where the division of the sample is reasonably practicable, the authorised officer may divide the sample into not more than three approximately equal parts, each of which he/she must mark in such a way as to identify it as a part of the sample taken by him/her. The authorised officer must mark, seal and fasten each part of the sample in such a manner as its nature will permit, forward one part to the approved examiner in an official laboratory for analysis, give or send one part to the seller, owner or person in apparent charge or control of the item (as the case may be) and retain the third part.

*(NOTE: Any reference in these Regulations to a seller, owner or to a person in apparent charge or control of a controlled item will in the case of a sample pur-

chased from a vending machine be construed as a reference:

- where the name and address of such proprietor is stated on the machine and such address is in the state, to the proprietor of the machine,
- in other cases, to the occupier of the premises at or which the machine stands or to which it is affixed.)

Where an authorised officer takes a sample of a controlled item in unopened containers and its division into parts is not reasonably practicable or might affect the composition or impede the proper analysis of the sample, the Regulations will be deemed to be complied with if the officer divides the containers into three lots, with each lot as if it were a sample as described above.

The approved examiner or a person under his/her direction must analyse the sample as soon as possible and certify to the person who submitted it the result of the analysis.

The seller, owner or person in charge of the sample of the controlled item is, upon request in writing, entitled to the results of the analysis.

It is important to note that in proceedings for an offence under these Regulations, the results of any test, examination or analysis of, or report on a sample of a controlled item taken pursuant to these Regulations will not be cited as proof unless before the proceedings were instituted the sample was divided as described above. The part, package or container of the sample retained by the authorised officer must be produced at the hearing.

**Enforcement**

An authorised officer may seize, remove, detain and/or direct the withdrawal from the market of any controlled item intended for sale for human consumption which is:

- suspected by him/her to be diseased, contaminated or otherwise unfit for human consumption, and/or
- suspected by him/her to fail to comply with the provisions of any other Regulations applicable to such a controlled item

An authorised officer may also, with the written consent of the owner or person in charge of a controlled item or with an order of a judge of the District Court, destroy or otherwise dispose of such item so as to prevent it being used for human consumption.

## Co-operation and Assistance
Under these Regulations the health boards are required to co-operate with the officials designated by the Commission of the European Union in accordance with Council Directive 93/99/EEC and to give the officials all the necessary assistance to enable them to accomplish their tasks.

The health boards must also permit the officials of the Commission to accompany authorised officers while carrying out the controls referred to on page 136. The officials of the Commission are entitled to the same powers of entry as authorised officers.

## Offences and Penalties
Any person who contravenes these Regulations shall be guilty of an offence and liable on summary conviction to a fine not exceeding £1,000 or, at the discretion of the Court, to imprisonment for a term not exceeding 6 months or to both.

Where an offence under these Regulations is committed by a body corporate and is proved to have been committed with the consent, connivance or neglect of any director, secretary or officer of the body, he/she, as well as the body corporate, shall be guilty of such offence.

An offence under these Regulations may be prosecuted by the Minister for Health and Children or the health board in whose functional area the offence is committed.

Notwithstanding Section 10(4) of the Petty Sessions (Ireland) Act, 1851, proceedings for an offence under these Regulations may be instituted within twelve months from the date of the offence or any time within twelve months from the date on which knowledge of the commission of the offence came to the attention of an authorised officer.

# European Communities (Hygiene of Foodstuffs) Regulations, 1998

These Regulations give effect to Council Directive 93/43/EEC concerning the hygiene of foodstuffs. They set down and in many cases restate from the earlier Hygiene Regulations, the legal obligations on proprietors of food businesses. The Regulations cover requirements for business premises, rooms where food is prepared, foodstuffs, transportation, equipment, food waste, water supply, personal hygiene and training.

For the purpose of these Regulations, 'food business' means 'any undertaking, whether or not for profit and whether public or private, carrying out any or all of the following: preparation, processing, manufacturing, packaging, storing, transportation, distribution, handling or offering for sale or supply of foodstuffs'. The Regulations also define 'food hygiene', which means, 'all measures necessary to ensure the safety and wholesomeness of foodstuffs. The measures shall cover all stages after primary production (including, for example, harvesting, slaughtering and milking) during preparation, processing, manufacturing, packaging, storing, transportation, distribution, handling and offering for sale or supply to the consumer.'

## Hazard Analysis and Critical Control Points (HACCP)

The Regulations impose on the proprietor of a food business the obligation to ensure that any step in the activities of the food business, which is critical to food safety, is identified. Furthermore, that adequate safety procedures are identified, implemented, maintained and reviewed on the basis of the following principles used to develop the system of HACCP (Hazard Analysis and Critical Control Points):

- analysing the potential food hazards in a food business operation
- identifying the points in those operations where food hazards may occur
- deciding which of the points identified are critical to food safety (known as critical points)
- identifying and implementing effective control and monitoring procedures at those critical points
- reviewing the analysis of food hazards, the critical points and the control and monitoring procedures periodically and whenever the food business operations change.

## General Provisions

The following provisions must be complied with by the proprietor of a food business:

- The food premises must be kept clean and maintained in good repair and condition.
- The layout, design, construction and size of the food premises must permit adequate cleaning and/or disinfection, and be such as to protect against the accumulation of dirt, contact with toxic materials, the shedding of particles into food and the formation of condensation or undesirable mould on surfaces.
- The layout, design, construction and size of the food premises must permit good hygiene practices, including protection against cross-contamination and provide, where necessary, suitable temperature conditions for the hygienic processing and storage of products.
- An adequate number of flush lavatories with proper natural or mechanical ventilation must be available and connected to an effective drainage system but such lavatories must not lead directly into rooms in which food is handled.
- An adequate number of washbasins must be available, suitably located and designated, provided with hot and cold running water and with suitable materials for cleaning and hygienically drying hands. The provisions for washing food must be separate from the hand-washing facility.
- There must be suitable and sufficient means of natural or mechanical ventilation. Mechanical air flow from a contaminated area to a clean area must be avoided and ventilation systems must be so constructed as to enable filters and other parts requiring cleaning and replacement to be readily accessible.
- Food premises must have adequate natural and/or artificial lighting.
- Drainage facilities must be adequate for the purpose intended and must be designed and constructed to avoid the risk of contamination to foodstuffs.
- Adequate changing facilities for personnel must be provided where necessary.

## Food Rooms

The regulations make very specific and detailed provisions to be complied with in relation to rooms where food is prepared, treated or processed and pay particular attention to floor surfaces, wall surfaces, ceilings and overhead fixtures, windows and other openings, doors and work surfaces including surfaces of all equipment. Where necessary, adequate facilities must be provided for the cleaning and disinfecting of work tools and equipment. These facilities must be constructed of materials resistant to corrosion and must be easy to clean and have an adequate supply of hot and cold water. When appropriate, adequate provision must be made for any necessary washing of food.

## Movable and Other Premises

Specific provisions also apply to the proprietor of a food business which is carried on from a movable and/or temporary premises (such as a marquee, market stall or mobile sales vehicle), premises used primarily as a private dwelling house, premises used occasionally for catering purposes or from a vending machine.

## Vehicles and Containers

Vehicles and/or containers used for transporting foodstuffs must be kept clean and maintained in good repair and condition in order to protect foodstuffs from contamination and must, where necessary, be designed and constructed to permit adequate cleaning and/or disinfection.

Receptacles in vehicles and/or containers must not be used for transporting anything other than foodstuffs where this may result in contamination of foodstuffs. Where vehicles and/or containers are used for transporting anything in addition to foodstuffs or for transporting different foodstuffs at the same time, there must be effective separation of products and, where necessary, effective cleaning between loads, to protect against risk of contamination. Foodstuffs must be maintained at appropriate temperatures and in such a way as to allow temperatures to be monitored.

## Food Waste

Food waste and other refuse must not be allowed to accumulate in food rooms, except so far as is unavoidable for the proper functioning of the business. Refuse must be deposited in closable containers unless the food business operator can satisfy the health board that other types of containers are appropriate. All containers must be of an appropriate construction, kept in good condition and easy to clean and disinfect. Adequate provision must be made for the removal and storage of all food waste and other refuse. Refuse stores must be designed and managed in such a way as to enable them to be kept clean and free of pests.

## Water, Ice and Steam

The proprietor of a food business must ensure that there is an adequate supply of potable water and that when required ice must be made from potable water. Ice must be made and stored under conditions that protect it from all contamination.

Steam used directly in contact with food must not contain any substance that presents a hazard to health or is likely to contaminate the product. Water that is unfit for drinking and used for the generation of steam, refrigeration, fire control and other similar purposes not relating to food, must be conducted in separate systems, readily identifiable and having no connection whatsoever with the potable water systems.

## Personal Hygiene

Every person working in a food-handling area must maintain a high degree of personal cleanliness and hygiene and must wear suitable, clean and, where appropriate, protective clothing. It is the responsibility of the proprietor to ensure that no person known or suspected to be suffering from, or to be a carrier of, a disease likely to be transmitted through food, is permitted to work in any food-handling area.

## Hygiene Training and Supervision

The proprietor of a food business must ensure that food handlers are trained and/or instructed and supervised in food hygiene matters commensurate with their work activity.

## Guides to Good Hygiene Practice

These Regulations provide that the Minister for Health and Children has the power to approve certain guides to good hygiene practice to be used by the proprietor of a food business, as a guide to compliance with the Regulations.

The Regulations state that the guides are to be developed as follows:

- by food business sectors or by organisations representative of food business sectors or other interested parties
- in consultations with interests substantially affected, including the health boards, and
- where appropriate, having regard to the Recommended International Code of Practice, General Principles of Food Hygiene of the Codex Alimentarius.

Guides to good hygiene practice may also be developed under the aegis of a national standards institute that, currently, is the National Standards Authority of Ireland.

The Minister has the power to withdraw any approval given to a guide to good hygiene practice.

A health board, when determining compliance with these Regulations, shall have due regard to any relevant guide to good hygiene practice that has been

- approved by the Minister for Health and Children in accordance with these Regulations and forwarded to the Commission pursuant to Article 5.5 of Council Directive 93/43/EEC, or
- developed, in accordance with Article 5.6 and 5.7 and published in accordance with Article 5.8 of Council Directive 93/43/EEC.

## Offences and Penalties

The prosecution of offences and imposition of penalties under these Regulations are the same as those identified in the European Communities (Official Control of Foodstuffs) Regulations, at page 139.

## PROHIBITION AND RESTRICTION ON SMOKING IN PUBLIC AREAS AND FACILITIES

The Tobacco (Health Promotion and Protection) Act, 1988 made provision for the introduction of regulations to prohibit and restrict the consumption of tobacco products in certain designated areas and facilities. On 1 May 1990, the first set of regulations to address this issue came into force, but these have now been replaced by the

Tobacco (Health Promotion and Protection) Regulations, 1995. The most recent regulations extend and enlarge the provisions contained in the 1990 regulations. Since the 1990 regulations were revoked in their entirety, no useful purpose is served here in referring to them at all. The current regulations came into operation on 1 January 1996, with the exception of the specification of the minimum non-smoking proportion of seating in restaurants, canteens, cafés and snack bars, which came into effect on 1 May 1996.

## Prohibition on Smoking

Smoking is prohibited:

- In the circulation space (this includes stairways, escalators, lifts, corridors, landings, concourses and foyers) of all state buildings (government departments, state-sponsored bodies, health boards and local authorities). Hotels owned by the state or by a state-sponsored body are excluded.
- In offices to which the public has access in state and semi-state buildings (e.g. post offices, employment exchanges and ESB offices).
- In any part of a pre-school, crèche, playgroup, day nursery or other service which caters for pre-school children; in any part of a primary or secondary school (including the school yard), although a smoking facility may be provided for teachers, so long as it is not a classroom or a room used by schoolchildren for recreation.
- The buildings of third-level colleges, with the exception of (a) any licensed premises within the institution, (b) specific facilities that are provided for staff and students to smoke, (c) the smoking sections of restaurants, canteens, cafés and snack bars.
- In the kitchens and food preparation areas in hotels, restaurants, cafés, snack bars, retail and licensed premises in which food is stored or prepared for human consumption.
- In the retail, storage and food preparation areas in supermarkets, grocery stores and butchers' premises.
- In waiting rooms in railway stations and bus stations.
- In the auditoria of cinemas, theatres and concert halls.
- In the indoor spectator and games areas in sports centres.
- In the games areas in ten-pin bowling centres.
- In the playing areas and circulation space in premises used for playing bingo and bridge.
- In state-owned art galleries and museums and in public libraries, except for staff rooms and 'smoking areas' in restaurants, canteens, cafés and snack bars.
- In childcare centres (except where specific facilities are provided for staff to

smoke).

- In hospitals, nursing homes, long-stay geriatric homes, maternity homes, centres for the mentally handicapped and centres for the physically handicapped (except where specific facilities are provided for staff to smoke).
- In waiting rooms on the premises of doctors' and dentists' practices.
- In health premises (other than those already listed) and psychiatric hospitals which provide health services to the public and which include health centres and retail pharmacies (except where specific facilities are provided for staff to smoke).
- In the areas to which the public has access in banks, building societies and other retail financial agencies.
- In the areas to which the public has access in hairdressing salons and barbers' shops.

## Restriction on Smoking

Smoking is restricted in certain designated areas and facilities as follows:

- psychiatric hospitals
- restaurants, canteens, cafés and snack bars — in these areas at least one-half of the seating area must be identified as a no-smoking area or, alternatively, where the chief executive officer of the relevant health board has confirmed in writing that he or she is satisfied that the ventilation system is adequate to prevent, as far as practicable, the circulation of tobacco smoke into the area where smoking is prohibited, at least one-quarter of the seating area
- the seating accommodation in the concourse area in the arrivals and departure lounges of airports and harbours; at least two-thirds of the seating area must be clearly identified as an area in which smoking is prohibited
- trains; at least two-thirds of the seating must be designated as a no-smoking area (except the Dublin Area Rapid Transit (DART) and Arrow Train Systems operated by Iarnród Éireann, where smoking is totally prohibited).
- aircraft and passenger ferries; at least two-thirds of the seating area must be identified as an area in which smoking is prohibited.

Designated no smoking areas in these places should be identified clearly by an appropriate notice. It is a matter for the owner or manager of the premises or facility to decide on the extent to which the restriction on smoking should apply, subject to a minimum restriction appropriate to the particular area or facility.

## Enforcement

The regulations are enforced by officers of the Minister for Health and Children and by officers of the health boards. In practice, the environmental health officers of the health boards are the officers authorised for the purposes of the regulations.

The 1988 Act also places an important responsibility for the enforcement of the regulations on the owner, manager, or person in charge of an area or facility designated to be a 'no smoking area'. In the exercise of his or her responsibility, an owner or manager is expected to liaise with the local environmental health officer in regard to infringements of the regulations.

## Penalties

Any person who contravenes a provision of the regulations shall be guilty of an offence and shall be liable on summary conviction to a fine not exceeding £100.

The owner, manager or other person in charge of a designated facility or area who fails, neglects or refuses to ensure that the prohibitions and restrictions that apply to that facility or area are complied with, shall be guilty of an offence and shall be liable on summary conviction to a fine not exceeding £500, or to imprisonment for a term not exceeding six months or, at the discretion of the court, to both a fine and imprisonment.

## Defence to a Prosecution

It shall be a defence to establish that the owner, manager or other person in charge had taken all reasonable steps to ensure that the restrictions and prohibitions had been complied with fully.

# Chapter 7

# INTOXICATING LIQUOR LICENSING — PART I

## INTRODUCTION AND GENERAL PROVISIONS

Before 1902, there existed a very liberal approach to the granting of retail licences for the sale of intoxicating liquor. Any person had the common law right to apply for such a licence, and the licensing authorities were required to issue them. However, the enactment of the Licensing (Ireland) Act, 1902, the main purpose of which was to limit the growth in numbers of both on-licences and off-licences, introduced a stricter approach, which remains in force with perhaps even greater rigour today.

The law relating to the sale of intoxicating liquor in Ireland is as voluminous as it is complex. The relevant body of law is a combination of rules emanating from decided cases and a series of Acts of the Oireachtas, referred to collectively as the Intoxicating Liquor Acts, 1833-1995. Given the volume and complexity of the liquor licensing law, its treatment here must be confined, of necessity, to a summary of those aspects considered immediately relevant.

## CATEGORIES OF LICENCE

To be legally entitled to sell intoxicating liquor, it is necessary to be the holder of an appropriate licence issued by the Collector of Customs and Excise in the name of the Revenue Commissioners. What is an appropriate licence is determined largely by the requirements of the law governing the type of business being conducted, the liquor to be sold, and the circumstances of the sale.

Liquor licences may be categorised in different ways for different purposes. For example, they can be studied under the twin headings of 'on-licences' and 'off-licences'. The expression on-licence is slightly misleading since it embraces the sale of intoxicating liquor for consumption either on or off the licensed premises. An off-licence, however, permits the sale of liquor for consumption off the licensed premises only. Alternatively, licences may be examined in relation to those that require the production of a court certificate before they can be issued by the Revenue Commissioners and those that can be issued by the Revenue Commissioners without a court certificate. For present purposes, it is not intended to follow slavishly either of these methods of licence categorisation, but instead to adopt a more flexible approach, paying particular attention to retail on-licences. It seems that these play the greater part in the livelihood of the caterer, hotelier, publican or restaurateur.

## TAX CLEARANCE CERTIFICATES

Section 242 of the Finance Act, 1992 requires applicants for certain liquor licences to have a tax clearance certificate. This document certifies that on the date on which the application is received, the taxpayer concerned has complied with all his/her obligations under the Tax Acts with regard to the payment of tax, interest, penalties and the submission of tax returns. The liquor licences affected by this provision include:

- spirits retailers' on-licences (this embraces publicans' licences, hotel licences, publicans' six-day licences, publicans' early closing licences, publicans' combined six-day and early closing licences, special restaurant licences, theatre licences, railway refreshment room licences)
- spirits retailers' off-licences
- wine retailers' on-licences.

In circumstances where a tax clearance certificate has been refused by the Revenue Commissioners on the date of the renewal of licences (see page 156) and an appeal has been lodged, and where a licence has been granted in respect of the previous licensing year, such licence would continue in force beyond its expiry date pending the outcome of the appeal. Where a tax clearance certificate has been refused, the applicant has thirty days within which to appeal against the refusal.

Where a licence has not been granted in the previous licensing year, a temporary licence will be issued. This will remain in force until the determination of the appeal, provided the licence could have been issued but for the requirements relating to the tax clearance certificate and provided that the amount of duty that would have been payable on the granting of the licence has been lodged with the Customs and Excise authority. Where an appeal fails, the temporary licence will expire not later than seven days after the determination of the appeal. In such circumstances, any excess duty paid will be refunded to the applicant.

In certain circumstances where a licence is being transferred, a tax clearance certificate will not be issued unless the tax affairs of the applicant and those of the previous holder of the licence, in so far as they relate to the activities conducted under the licence, are up to date. The circumstances which require tax clearance of the previous licence-holder are:

- where the transfer took place after 24 April 1992 (but not if the transfer was contracted for before 24 April 1992) and
- the transfer was one of the following:

  (a) a company to an individual

  (b) a company to a company

  (c) a company to a partnership

  (d) a partnership to a company

  and
- there is a connection between the parties.

Those applying for a tax clearance certificate in these circumstances should give details of the connection between the parties to the Revenue Commissioners. The Revenue Commissioners — tax clearance section (licensing) — will provide information on the types of connection that are relevant.

The tax clearance certificate provisions became law on 1 October 1992.

# PROHIBITION ON THE SALE OF INTOXICATING LIQUOR TO PERSONS UNDER 18 YEARS

It is an offence for the holder of any licence for the sale of intoxicating liquor to

- sell or deliver, or permit any person to sell or deliver, intoxicating liquor to a person under the age of 18 years

- sell or deliver, or permit any person to sell or deliver, intoxicating liquor to any person for consumption on his/her licensed premises by a person under the age of 18 years

- permit a person under the age of 18 years to consume intoxicating liquor on his/her licensed premises

- permit any person to supply a person under the age of 18 years with intoxicating liquor on his/her licensed premises

- sell or deliver, or permit any person to sell or deliver, intoxicating liquor to any person for consumption outside his/her licensed premises by a person under the age of 18 years in any place other than a private residence.

A person is liable on summary conviction for any of these offences to a fine not exceeding:

(a) £300 in the case of a first offence, or

(b) £500 in the case of a second or subsequent offence.

Such a conviction is endorsed and recorded on the licence.


# CHILDREN ON LICENSED PREMISES

For licensing purposes, a child is defined as a person under the age of 15 years. Children are prohibited from being on licensed premises unless they are accompanied by a parent or guardian. However, exceptions to this rule, as set out in Section 34, Subsection 3(i) of the Intoxicating Liquor Act, 1988, apply in the case of a child who is:

- a child of the licence-holder, or

- a resident in the licensed premises, or

- in the bar of licensed premises solely for the purpose of passing through to gain access to another part of the premises.

The licence-holder is obliged to display in a conspicuous place in

---

**INTOXICATING LIQUOR ACT, 1988**
SECTION 34
*Exclusion of Children from Bars of Licensed Premises*
Subject to the provisions of Section 34, Subsection 3(i) of the
Intoxicating Liquor Act, 1988, it is an offence to allow a child, being a
person under 15 years of age, to be in a bar at any time during which
the sale of intoxicating liquor is permitted, unless accompanied by a
parent or guardian.
Where any child is found in a bar unaccompanied by a parent or
guardian, the parent or guardian shall be guilty of an offence.
**N.B. Section 34 requires that the above notice shall be displayed in a
conspicuous place in a bar of the licensed premises.**

---

the bar of the licensed premises a notice stating that it is an offence to
allow a child to be in a bar at any time during which the sale of
intoxicating liquor is permitted unless accompanied by his/her parent
or guardian. For an example of the notice, see above.

Offences in relation to children being on licensed premises are
punishable by a fine not exceeding:

(a)  £100 in the case of a first offence, or
(b)  £250 in the case of a second or subsequent offence.

For failure to display the notice prohibiting children (except where
accompanied by the parent or guardian) from being on licensed
premises, a licence-holder is liable to a fine not exceeding:

(a)  £20, in the case of a first offence, or
(b)  £50, in the case of a second or subsequent offence.

Such convictions are not subject to an endorsement on the
licence.

Where a prosecution has been brought, it is a defence for the
licence-holder to prove that

- he or she used all due diligence to prevent the child being admitted to the bar,
  or

- he or she had reasonable grounds for believing that the person in respect of
  whom he or she is alleged to have committed the offence was not a child.

## EMPLOYMENT OF PERSONS UNDER THE AGE OF 18 YEARS ON LICENSED PREMISES

It is an offence for the holder of a licence to employ any person under the age of 18 years on licensed premises, with the following exceptions:

(a) A sister, step-sister, daughter, step-daughter or sister-in-law of the licence holder, who resides with him and is over 16 years.

(b) A brother, step-brother, son, step-son or brother-in-law of the licence-holder, who resides with him and is over 16 years.

(c) A person who is apprenticed to the licensee and is over 16 years.

The penalty for a violation of these requirements is a fine not exceeding:

(a) £50 for a first offence, or

(b) £100 for a second or subsequent offence.

A conviction is endorsed on the licence.

## OBTAINING A DECLARATION RELATING TO PROPOSED LICENSED PREMISES

For anyone contemplating entry to the licensed trade, there is a very useful mechanism which, in effect, amounts to an approval in principle to the granting of a new licence and which could go some considerable distance in saving the prospective licensee unnecessary expense and disappointment. It is known as a 'Declaration as to the fitness and convenience of proposed licensed premises' and works in this way. Where a person proposes either to acquire, construct or alter premises for the purpose of conducting a licensed business, he or she may apply in advance to the appropriate court —

(a) The District Court in the case of an off-licence

(b) The Circuit Court in the case of an on-licence

— for a declaration that such premises would be fit and convenient to be so licensed. If the court is satisfied, it may grant the application on such terms as it thinks fit.

## PROCEDURE FOR OBTAINING
## A DECLARATION

An applicant for a declaration must

- insert a notice of intention to make an application in a newspaper circulating in the area where it is proposed to have the premises at least 21 days before making the application.

- give the superintendent of the Garda Síochána within whose district it is proposed to have the premises at least 21 days' notice in writing of the intention to make the application, and deposit with the superintendent a copy of the plans of the premises.

*NOTE: The chief fire officer in whose functional area it is proposed to have the premises is not required by legislation to be notified where a declaration is sought. However, it would be a wise precaution to notify him or her.*

## OBJECTIONS TO THE GRANTING
## OF A DECLARATION

Anyone entitled to object to the granting of a certificate to obtain a licence is in the same manner entitled to object to the granting of a declaration (see page 168). Such declaration, if granted, in effect removes all grounds for objection other than the character of the applicant, provided the premises are constructed or altered in substantial accordance with the plans submitted.

## PROCEDURE FOR THE RENEWAL OF
## INTOXICATING LIQUOR LICENCES

A simplified procedure for the renewal of intoxicating liquor licences was introduced following the activation, by ministerial order on 22 July 1988, of relevant sections of the Courts (No. 2) Act, 1986. Where the premises for which the renewal is required have been licensed in the immediately preceding year, it will not now be necessary to produce a certificate of the District Court to the Collector of Customs and Excise. It is necessary, however, to serve a notice of renewal on the local fire authority, one month before the date of the Annual Licensing District Court. Special circumstances still remain where it will be necessary to obtain a certificate from the District Court. These are:

- where a notice of objection to the renewal of the licence has been lodged within the time limits prescribed (see page 157)
- where the holder of a licence ceases to be resident in the state or cannot be found, and an application for renewal is made by another person within one year after the expiry of the licence
- where it is proposed to insert a condition in the licence to convert it to either a six-day or an early closing licence.

The Annual Licensing District Court will take place as normal to deal with the exceptions indicated above. Otherwise, the licensee will apply for the licence renewal directly to the Collector of Customs and Excise. The Annual Licensing District Court sitting is held on the day of the last sitting of the court for the hearing of cases of summary jurisdiction in September, except in the case of the Dublin Metropolitan District Court, which is held on the last Thursday of September.

## OBJECTIONS TO THE RENEWAL OF A LICENCE

It is expressly provided for in the Courts (No. 2) Act, 1986 that an objection to the renewal of a licence may be made by any person who, but for the change in the law relating to licence renewal procedures, would have been authorised to object to the granting of a certificate for the renewal of a licence.

Amongst those who may lodge an objection to the renewal of a licence are:

- any member of the community
- the superintendent of the Garda Síochána for the licensing area
- the District Court Judge for the licensing area
- the health authority in whose functional area the premises are situated
- the fire authority in whose functional area the premises are situated.

# PROCEDURE FOR MAKING AN OBJECTION TO THE RENEWAL OF LICENCES

An objection to the renewal of an on-licence for the sale of intoxicating liquor must be made at the Annual Licensing District Court for the court area in which the premises objected to are situated.

The objection must be preceded by the service of a notice in the prescribed form (for form, see schedule to Statutory Instrument Number 145 of 1988) signed by the objector or his/her solicitor. The notice must be served on the licence-holder at least 21 days, or where the objector is a fire authority at least 7 days, before the date of the next Annual Licensing District Court. The original of the notice must be lodged with the District Court clerk at least 10 days, or where the objector is a fire authority at least 4 days, before the date of the next Annual Licensing District Court.

Immediately on receipt of the notice of objection, the District Court clerk must send notification of its lodgment to the Collector of Customs and Excise for the district in which the premises are situated and, where the objector is not a member of the Garda Síochána, the clerk must also send notification to the superintendent for the area.

Where the court allows the objection and no notice of appeal has been lodged with the District Court clerk within 14 days from the date of the court order, the clerk must send to the Collector of Customs and Excise a certified copy of the court order. Where the court disallows an objection and no notice of appeal has been lodged with the clerk within 14 days, the clerk must forthwith send a certificate for the renewal of the licence to the Collector of Customs and Excise. The Collector of Customs and Excise in due course will send out a demand to the licence-holder for the duty payable in respect of the renewed licence.

If an appeal against an order of the court is lodged at any time with the District Court clerk, he or she must immediately send a notice to this effect to the Collector of Customs and Excise.

**NOTE: Documents that are required to be sent to the Collector of Customs and Excise should be sent by registered post.**

# HOURS OF TRADING IN
# LICENSED PREMISES

## Prohibited Hours Generally (applies to Public Houses)

Except as may be provided otherwise by the Intoxicating Liquor Acts, it will not be lawful for any person to sell or expose for sale any intoxicating liquor, or to open or keep open any premises for the sale of intoxicating liquor, or to permit any intoxicating liquor to be consumed on licensed premises:

(a) on any weekday, before 10.30 in the morning, or

    (i) during a period of summer time,★ after 11.30 in the evening, or

    (ii)during a period that is not summer time, after 11.00 in the evening, or

(b) on any Sunday before 12.30 in the afternoon or between 2.00 and 4.00 in the afternoon or after 11.00 in the evening, or

(c) on St Patrick's Day, where that day falls on a weekday, before 12.30 in the afternoon or after 11.00 in the evening.

(d) at any time on Christmas Day or Good Friday.

(e) on a Sunday which falls on December 23 or 24 in any year, before 10.30 in the morning or after 11.00 in the evening.

## ★ Summer Time Defined for Licensing Purposes

The expressions 'summer time' and 'a period that is not summer time' are used in the Licensing Acts. The Standard Time Act, 1968 provides the formula for defining 'summer time' for the purposes of the Licensing Acts. The formula is as follows:

> *'Summer time'* commences at 3 a.m. on the Sunday following the 3rd Saturday in April, or if that day is Easter Sunday, at 3 a.m. on the Sunday following the 2nd Saturday in April and, in either case, ending at 3 a.m. on the Sunday following the 1st Saturday in October. Accordingly, the hours of trading for licensed premises are not affected by the extended or curtailed times until the following Monday.

It follows, therefore, that 'a period that is not summer time' is that period which is not referred to in the formula above.

## Drinking-up Time

After the ordinary closing time has been reached, a period of thirty minutes is permitted for the finishing of drinks and the clearing of the premises. No orders may be taken or served during this period.

## Exemptions for Hotels and Restaurants

The hours outlined above may be extended by the holder of an on-licence relating to a hotel or restaurant to permit the consumption of intoxicating liquor as follows:

(a) During a period of summer time, between the hours of 11.30 in the evening on any weekday and 12.30 in the morning on the following day, or

(b) During a period that is not summer time, between 11.00 in the evening on any weekday and 12.30 in the morning of the following day, or

(c) Unless the licence is a six-day licence, on any Sunday between 2.00 and 3.00 in the afternoon, or

(d) On Christmas Day, between 1.00 and 3.00 in the afternoon or between 7.00 and 10.00 in the evening.

(e) On a Sunday which falls on 23 or 24 December in any year, between 11.00 in the evening and 12.30 on the morning of the following day (Monday).

To benefit from the foregoing extended hours, the intoxicating liquor must be:

(i) ordered by the customer at the same time as a substantial meal★ is ordered by him/her.

(ii) consumed at the same time as, and with, the meal.

(iii) supplied and consumed in a portion of the premises usually set apart for the supply of meals, and

(iv) paid for at the same time as the meal is paid for.

## ★ Substantial Meal Defined for Licensing Purposes

A meal shall not be deemed to be a 'substantial' meal unless:

(a) The meal is such as might be expected to be served as a main midday or main evening meal or as a main course at either such meal, and

(b) The meal is of a kind for which

(i) having regard to the prices charged for meals in the premises at times other than prohibited hours, or

(ii) if meals are not normally served in the premises, having regard to all the circumstances,

it would be reasonable to charge a sum that is not less than £2.

It should be noted that this does not mean that it is necessary to charge anything for the meal. Furthermore, it is useful to note that the High Court has held that waiter or waitress service is not required and that the meal can be served by being laid out on a buffet table.

## Drinking-up Time

The 30-minute drinking-up time does not apply after periods during which drink may be served only with a meal in hotels and restaurants.

# GENERAL LICENSING CONSIDERATIONS AND OFFENCES

## Custody of the Licence

A licence-holder is required to exercise such custody of and control over his or her licence as to be able to produce it when required for any purpose or requirement of the Licensing Acts. The licence is a personal authority to the licensee to conduct business in the designated premises and cannot be assigned to any other person without proper authority.

## Sale of a Licence

A publican's licence may, at the discretion of the Court, be transferred to the new owner of a licensed premises. However, a licence cannot be 'sold' in the ordinary sense of the word. A licence-holder who no longer wishes to continue trading may consent to his or her licence being extinguished to facilitate an applicant for a new licence for a different premises. The procedure of requiring the extinguishment of one or more licences as a condition for granting a new one may be responsible for the commonly held, but mistaken, belief that licences can be sold. This fallacy may be further compounded when substantial sums of money change hands for the extinguishment of a licence. This is a particular aspect of licensing where no venture should be embarked upon by the intending licence-holder without legal advice.

## Holding a Licence

A licence may be held by the following:

- an individual
- a partnership
- the nominee of a body corporate
- a body corporate, e.g. a limited company.

## Intoxicated Persons on the Premises

A licensee is entitled to refuse to admit any person who is drunk, violent or disorderly and is required by law to refuse to sell intoxicating liquor to any drunken person. Furthermore, it is an offence to sell intoxicating liquor to a sober person for use by himself and a drunken companion.

## Prostitutes on the Premises

While it is an offence for a licensee to permit his/her premises to be the habitual resort or meeting place for reputed prostitutes, it is not an offence to sell liquor to a prostitute and to allow a reasonable time for its consumption.

## Premises used as a Brothel

If a licensed premises is used as a brothel, a licensee convicted of this offence will forfeit his or her licence and be disqualified for life from holding a licence.

## Harbouring a Garda

An offence is committed where the licensee harbours or knowingly allows to remain on his or her premises any Garda on duty, unless in the exercise of his/her duty. The supply of any liquor or refreshment, whether by way of gift or sale, to any Garda on duty is also an offence, unless authorised by a superior.

## Bribing a Garda

It is an offence to bribe or to attempt to bribe a Garda.

## Obstructing Entry of a Garda

Any person, whether the licensee or not, who obstructs the entry to licensed premises of a Garda in the execution of his or her duty of preventing or detecting licensing violations, commits an offence.

## Betting and Gaming on Licensed Premises

There are particular statutory provisions relating to betting, gaming and lotteries which should be consulted for detailed information. However, all these activities generally are prohibited on licensed premises.

## Obligation to Serve

A licensee is under no obligation to serve intoxicating liquor to anyone. He/she is entitled to refuse any customer without explanation. Furthermore, he/she may require any person to leave the premises and may exert such force as is reasonably necessary to achieve this end.

## Sale of Liquor on Credit

It is an offence to sell intoxicating liquor on credit, although liquor ordered and consumed with a meal, and paid for at the same time as the meal, is permitted. A licensee who sells drink on credit has no legal right to recover the debt nor the right to retain anything left as security for the debt. In England it has been held by a court that purchase by credit card is not a 'sale on credit', i.e. a credit card sale is by 'plastic money', rather than a sale on credit.

Subject to the exception concerning drink served with meals, a drink must be paid for before or at the time of consumption. This means that, for example, bars that serve drink and await payment by the customer until the time he or she is leaving the premises do not have any recourse to law if the customer manages to leave without paying. This is because the initial supply of drink was, technically speaking, unlawful.

## Endorsements

In cases where a conviction carries an endorsement on the licence, the following rules apply to the retention of the endorsement on the licence:

1. A first endorsement remains recorded on the licence for two years from the date of conviction.

2. A second endorsement remains recorded on the licence for four years from the date of conviction.

3. A third and every subsequent endorsement remains recorded on the licence for six years from the date of conviction.

## Forfeiture of the Licence

The Licensing Acts lay down the offences for which the penalty is forfeiture of the licence, but the imposition of the penalty varies. For serious offences, such as permitting the premises to be used as a brothel or having possession of or selling illicitly distilled spirits, the penalty is forfeiture and permanent disqualification from holding a licence. Some offences, while carrying a fine for a first offence, incur forfeiture of the licence for a subsequent offence; for example, allowing consumption of liquor on premises licensed for off sales only. Another variation is to impose a fine for a first offence and forfeiture for a second offence, with disqualification for a stated period of two years, as in the offence of knowingly harbouring thieves. Finally, a range of offences carry endorsements, the accumulation of which, usually three, incurs forfeiture. When a licence has been ordered to be forfeited by a court, having had three current endorsements, it is important to stress that no licence can ever afterwards be obtained in respect of the premises to which the licence applied.

## Leasing of Licensed Premises

The owner of licensed premises cannot lease or hand over control of his/her premises or part of his/her premises to any person without either delicensing that portion of the premises or arranging for a transfer of the licence.

## Clearing of Premises

A hotel is entitled to carry on its licensed business twenty-four hours a day and does not have to clear its premises after drinking-up time, as is the case for publicans. The only necessity in the case of hotels, in this respect, is not to allow on its premises the consumption of alcoholic beverages by non-residents outside of permitted hours.

## Extension or Alteration of Premises

If a licence-holder wants to extend or substantially alter his or her premises, even if that extension is only by a few feet, he or she must apply to the Circuit Court for a new licence to cover the entire premises, including the part that has been added. It must be shown to the Court that the granting of the new licence will render the licensed premises more suitable for the business carried on in it.

# Chapter 8

# INTOXICATING LIQUOR LICENSING — PART II

## SPECIFIED PURPOSE LICENCES, CERTIFICATES AND ORDERS

### SPIRITS RETAILER'S ON-LICENCE

A spirits retailer's on-licence, more popularly known as a publican's licence, is generally regarded as the premier intoxicating liquor licence and is highly sought after by anyone contemplating the licensed trade as a means of livelihood. Its importance is underlined by the fact that, when granted, it authorises the sale of the full range of intoxicating liquor—spirits, beers, wines, cider and home-made wines.

A spirits retailer's on-licence, in its more usual form, is a seven-day licence. However, it may contain:

- a Sunday closing condition (such licence is then commonly referred to as a 'six-day' licence), or
- an early closing condition (under which the licence-holder is required to close an hour earlier than normal closing time), or
- both the foregoing conditions.

Reference has already been made to the difficulty, since 1902, of obtaining a new licence and, in particular, of obtaining a full publican's licence. Nowadays, there are two circumstances in which a publican's licence may be sought:

- where the application is in respect of premises situated in a rural area, or
- where the application is in respect of premises situated in a town or city.

## Licence in a Rural Area

Where an application is being made under this heading for a licence in respect of premises to which no licence is attached, the applicant must show:

- that he or she can extinguish two existing licences of the same character as the licence being sought
- that the new premises to be licensed are not situated in a county or other borough, an urban district or a town
- that the new premises are not within a mile of an existing licensed premises (whose licence was granted on or before 4 July 1960)
- that the rateable valuation of the new premises is not less than £10.

## Licence in a Town or City

Where there has been a growth or extension in any town or city, the licensing authority may consent to a relaxation of the restrictions imposed by the Licensing Acts in respect of the granting of a new licence. However, in order to benefit from this provision, the following rules must be adhered to:

(a) There must have been an actual growth or extension in the city or town in question, and

(b) there must have been an increase of not less than 25 per cent in the population in the civil parish within which the premises sought to be licensed are situated. Such growth in population is calculated by reference to the population census taken in 1901 and the most recently held census, and

(c) the applicant must extinguish an existing licence held in respect of premises situated in the town or city where the growth or extension has occurred.

## Procedure for Obtaining a New On-Licence

The Circuit Court has jurisdiction in all cases of applications for new on-licences; this jurisdiction is exercised by the Judge of the Circuit Court for the area in which the premises are situated. The procedure is in two distinct phases:

**Phase 1** - Obtaining a certificate from the Circuit Court.
**Phase 2** - Obtaining the on-licence from the proper officer of Customs and Excise upon handing over the court certificate.

## Procedure for Obtaining the Court Certificate

1. The application must be made at a sitting of the Circuit Court held in the town nearest the premises but in the same county.

2. The application must be preceded by a notice signed by the applicant and stating:

   - his/her intention to apply to the court for a certificate
   - the precise location of the premises
   - the address of the person applying
   - the court sitting at which the application is to be made
   - the act and section under which the application is intended to be made.

3. The notice containing the foregoing information must then be served on the following:

   (a)  The officer in charge of the Garda Síochána of the district

       (i) in which the applicant resides, and

       (ii) in which the premises are located

   (b)  The District Judge of the district in which the premises are located

   (c)  The county registrar for the county in which the premises are located

   (d)  The fire authority in the functional area in which the premises are located.

4. The notice must be served on each of the above, with the exception of the fire authority, at least twenty-one days before the first day of the sitting of the court at which the application is to be made. Where the application is made in the Dublin Circuit Court, notice must be given at least twenty-one days before the day on which it is intended to make the application. In the case of the fire authority, one month's notice is required, or such shorter period as the fire authority is prepared to accept.

5. The notice must be advertised in a newspaper circulating in the place in which the premises are situated, not more than four and not less than two weeks before the court sitting.

6. A copy of the newspaper must be lodged with the county registrar immediately on publication.

7. The applicant must produce a plan of the premises.

## Procedure for Obtaining the On-Licence

When the court has granted a certificate and this, in turn, is surrendered to the proper officer of Customs and Excise, together with the appropriate fee, the officer is obliged to issue the on-licence. The Customs and Excise authority has no discretion in this matter and its function is purely administrative.

## Objections to the Granting of a New On-Licence

The following are entitled to lodge an objection to the granting of a new licence:

- the District Judge for the district in which the premises are situated
- any inhabitant of the parish in which the premises are situated
- the health authority in whose functional area the premises are situated
- the superintendent of the Garda Síochána for the district in which the premises are situated and/or in which the applicant resides
- the fire authority in whose functional area the premises are situated.

## Grounds for Objections

The law permits either a written objection sent in beforehand or an oral objection presented to the court in session.

Objections may be based on the following:

- the character, misconduct, or unfitness of the applicant
- the unfitness or inconvenience of the premises or location
- the number of previously licensed premises in the neighbourhood.

The provision under which the licence is sought will also impose requirements which must be met. For example, the court must be satisfied in the case of a new 'rural licence' that the granting of a new licence would not be unreasonably detrimental to the business then carried on in some licensed premises in the neighbourhood. The applicant must satisfy the court that he or she is able to comply with all the requirements of the relevant section of the Intoxicating Liquor Acts and that his or her application, if granted, would not fall foul of any of the safeguards included for existing licensees. Furthermore, in considering the grounds of objection, the court has very wide discretionary power, particularly in relation to ground No. 3, the number of already existing licensed premises.

## Right of Appeal

The right to appeal a decision of the Circuit Court extends to an objector as well as to an applicant. Accordingly, the decision of a Circuit Court judge to grant or to refuse to grant a certificate for the issue of a new on-licence may be appealed to the High Court.

## Notifying the County Registrar

When an on-licence is issued by the Customs and Excise authority, the holder is required to complete a notice in writing which sets out his/her full name and address and the full name and address of the owner, together with the description and location of the licensed premises. This notification is then forwarded by the Customs and Excise authority to the county registrar, who is responsible for keeping a register of all on-licences. From time to time a copy of this register is sent to each District Court clerk within the county registrar's jurisdiction.

In practice, it is very often the case that the Customs and Excise authority notifies the District Court clerk directly.

## Excise Duty for a Publican's Licence

Where the annual turnover of a business is not yet established, the duty payable is equal to the amount paid when the premises was last licensed, subject to a minimum duty of £200. Where a licence is granted in respect of premises not previously licensed, the duty payable is £200. Otherwise, the appropriate rate of excise duty is in accordance with the level of annual turnover of the licensed business.

Where the annual turnover of the licensed business is under £150,000, the excise duty is £200. The following table shows the excise duty payable where turnover exceeds £150,000:

- £150,000, but under £300,000, the excise duty is £400
- £300,000, but under £500,000, the excise duty is £900
- £500,000, but under £750,000, the excise duty is £1,400
- £750,000, but under £1,000,000, the excise duty is £2,000
- £1,000,000, or more, of turnover, the excise duty is £3,000.

## HOTEL LICENCES

A hotel is defined for licensing purposes as a 'house containing at least ten or, if situated in a county borough, at least twenty apartments set apart and used exclusively for the sleeping accommodation of travellers, and having no public bar for the sale of intoxicating liquor'.

Between 1902 and 1960 there were only two ways in which a hotel in Ireland could operate a public bar. These were:

- that a publican's licence was held in respect of the particular hotel premises, or
- that the hotel licence was granted before 1902.

The enactment of the Intoxicating Liquor Act, 1960 redressed this anomalous position and permitted hotels that sold intoxicating liquor under a hotel licence granted since 1902 to acquire the right to have a public bar, as long as an already existing seven-day publican's licence was extinguished.

However, if the premises cease to comply with the statutory definition of a hotel — for example, by not having sleeping accommodation set apart and exclusively used as sleeping accommodation — the licensee cannot sell intoxicating liquor to anyone. It follows, therefore, that a hotel licence exists only for as long as the premises functions as a hotel, and the granting of an order under Section 19 of the 1960 Act permitting a public bar on hotel premises does not alter this situation. Licences granted in respect of hotel premises prior to the passing of the Licensing (Ireland) Act, 1902 are not so restricted, being in effect publican's licences.

The holder of a licence in respect of hotel premises may:

- carry on non-licensed business at any time
- apply for special exemption orders (see page 182)
- supply intoxicating liquor with meals at the times and under the conditions outlined on page 159.

Furthermore, intoxicating liquor may be served by the licensee to a hotel resident at any hour except on Good Friday, when it may be sold only for consumption with a meal. However, during prohibited hours, liquor cannot be sold for consumption by a resident and a guest of his/hers who is non-resident.

## Excise Duty for Hotels

Hotel licences are spirit retailer's on-licences and as such attract the same rate of excise duty as an ordinary publican's licence (see excise duty for a publican's licence, above).

## SPECIAL RESTAURANT LICENCE

The most recent addition to the already existing array of licences available for the sale of intoxicating liquor is the special restaurant licence, the provisions relating to which were brought into operation on 1 July 1988. A special restaurant licence may be granted, subject to a formal procedure, to a person in respect of a restaurant of which he/she is owner and occupier, authorising:

(a) the supply of intoxicating liquor for consumption on those premises, and (b) the consumption of intoxicating liquor on those premises if, in each case, the intoxicating liquor is

    (i) ordered by or on behalf of a person for whom a substantial meal has been ordered

    (ii) supplied in the restaurant's waiting area or dining area

    (iii) consumed in the waiting area before the meal by the person for whom the meal has been ordered, or consumed by that person in the dining area of the restaurant either during the meal or at any time not later than thirty minutes after the meal has ended, and

    (iv) paid for at the same time as the meal.

Suitable beverages, including drinking water, must also be available for consumption. It should be noted that this licence does not permit the sale of intoxicating liquor for consumption off the premises.

The Act defines a restaurant as a premises that is structurally adapted and used for the purpose of supplying substantial meals to the public for consumption on the premises and in which any other business carried on is ancillary and subsidiary to the provision of meals. The Act also stipulates that the waiting area in the restaurant must be used only for the accommodation of persons waiting to enter the dining area. Furthermore, the floor area of the waiting section must not exceed 20 per cent of the floor area of the dining section.

## Procedure for Obtaining a Special Restaurant Licence

Before the Circuit Court procedure, which is a necessary step in the process of obtaining a special restaurant licence, the applicant must first satisfy Tourism Quality Services (Ireland) Ltd. (see page 36) that the premises for which the licence is sought comply with the Special Restaurant Licence (Standards) Regulations, 1988. These regulations require that an applicant must obtain a Tourism Quality Services (Ireland) Ltd. certificate and also specify the procedure to be followed to acquire it. The application for this certificate, which has to be made by the owner and occupier of the restaurant, must be in writing and in a form provided for by the regulations. It must be accompanied by:

- survey drawings of the restaurant
- evidence that the restaurant is registered by the health board in whose functional area it is situated and that the health board is satisfied that the requirements of the Food Hygiene Regulations, 1950-89 will not be interfered with
- evidence that the restaurant complies with the Local Government (Planning and Development) Acts 1963-93 and with any building bylaws that may be in force
- particulars of any requirements of the local fire authority made under the Fire Services Act, 1981 and evidence that these requirements have been or are being complied with
- the application and inspection fee of £325.

Upon receipt of the application, the restaurant will be inspected by a representative of Tourism Quality Services (Ireland) Ltd., in accordance with the detailed standards set out in the regulations. When the inspection has been carried out, Tourism Quality Services (Ireland) Ltd. will notify the applicant, not later than 21 days after making its decision:

(a) that it is satisfied that the restaurant complies with the regulations, in which case, on payment of the certification fee (£75), the applicant will be granted a Tourism Quality Services (Ireland) Ltd. certificate, or

(b) that it is not satisfied that the restaurant complies with the regulations.

Where the holder of a special restaurant licence wishes to renew his/her licence at the next annual renewal, he/she may apply to Tourism Quality Services (Ireland) Ltd. at any time after 1 May and before 30 June for the renewal of the Tourism Quality Services (Ireland) Ltd. certificate.

At the Circuit Court proceedings, the court will be concerned mainly about three matters:

- That the applicant is the holder of a Tourism Quality Services (Ireland) Ltd. certificate.

- That the applicant is the owner and occupier of the restaurant for which the licence is sought. The owner, in relation to a restaurant, is so defined in the Act as to include 'any person having any estate or interest in the restaurant'.

- That there are no objections; any inhabitant of the parish can object on the grounds of the character, misconduct or unfitness of the applicant or the unfitness or inconvenience of the premises.

If the court is satisfied that the requirements have been met and that there are no objections, it will issue a certificate. This certificate entitles the applicant, on payment of the prescribed fee of £3,000, to a special restaurant licence from the Revenue Commissioners.

When a special restaurant licence has been granted, any licence and any existing restaurant certificate held in respect of the restaurant will cease to have effect, and no other licence or restaurant certificate can be granted in respect of those premises while the special restaurant licence is in force.

It is worth noting that an applicant for a special restaurant licence cannot avail of the declaratory order provisions (see page 154). Therefore the restaurant already must comply with the regulations before the Circuit Court application.

## Renewal of a Special Restaurant Licence

A special restaurant licence may be renewed annually, at the end of September, by the Customs and Excise authority. A Tourism Quality Services (Ireland) Ltd. certificate is required to be produced to the Customs and Excise authority at each renewal. A District Court certificate for the renewal of a special restaurant licence is required only if an objection to the renewal has been lodged. Where an application is made for the renewal of the licence, an objection can be made by:

- any inhabitant of the parish
- the superintendent of the Garda Síochána for the district in which the restaurant is situated
- the health board in whose functional area the restaurant is situated.

Without prejudice to any other grounds of objection available under the Intoxicating Liquor Acts, an objector may contend that the premises concerned have not been bona fide and solely used as a restaurant within the meaning of the Act since the granting or latest renewal of the licence. If the District Court upholds the objection, the Revenue Commissioners cannot renew the licence.

## Powers of Tourism Quality Services (Ireland) Ltd.

Where it appears to Tourism Quality Services (Ireland) Ltd. that a restaurant, in respect of which a Tourism Quality Services (Ireland) Ltd. certificate is in force, no longer complies with the standards laid down in the Special Restaurant Licence (Standards) Regulations, 1988, Tourism Quality Services (Ireland) Ltd. will send a notification to the licence-holder to that effect.

The notice will direct the licence-holder to take specific steps within a specified time limit to bring the restaurant into compliance with the required standards; it also will inform the licence-holder that failure to comply with the standards will result in the cancellation of the certificate.

If the certificate is cancelled, Tourism Quality Services (Ireland) Ltd. will give notice that the certificate is no longer in force to:

(a) the holder of the special restaurant licence

(b) the District Court clerk for the area in which the restaurant premises are situated

(c) the Revenue Commissioners

(d) the superintendent of the Garda Síochána for the district in which the premises are situated.

## Hours of Trading under a Special Restaurant Licence

The permitted hours of trading for a restaurant for which a special restaurant licence is in force are as follows:

- On any weekday, from 12.30 p.m. to 12.30 a.m. on the following morning
- On a Sunday, from 12.30 p.m. to 3.00 p.m. and from 6 p.m. to 11.00 p.m.
- On Christmas Day, between 1.00 p.m. and 3.00 p.m. and from 7.00 p.m. to 10.00 p.m.
- Intoxicating liquor cannot be served at any time on Good Friday or between the hours of midnight and 12.30 on the next day, Holy Saturday.
- On a Sunday which falls on December 23 or 24 in any year, between 12.30 in the afternoon and 12.30 on the morning of the following day.

## Offences

Outside of the hours permitted, it is an offence for any person, in any premises to which a special restaurant licence applies, to

(a) sell or expose for sale, or

(b) open or keep open the premises for the sale of, or

(c) permit the consumption on the premises of, any intoxicating liquor.

Any person who contravenes the terms of a special restaurant licence is liable on summary conviction to a fine not exceeding £500. Such an offence will be endorsed on the licence.

Since a restaurant that operates under a special restaurant licence must not contain a bar, violation of this directive carries a fine not exceeding

(a) £150 for a first offence, or

(b) £350 for a second or subsequent offence. Such an offence is endorsable on the licence.

## Further Provisions relating to Special Restaurant Licences

- The holder must display prominently in the premises both the special restaurant licence and the Tourism Quality Services (Ireland) Ltd. certificate. Failure to do so in either case is an offence which, on conviction, carries a fine not exceeding £100. It is also an offence (carrying a maximum fine of £100) to display a Tourism Quality Services (Ireland) Ltd. certificate that has been cancelled.

- The holder of a special restaurant licence is not entitled to obtain either an occasional licence (see page 186) or special exemption orders (see page 182).

- A special restaurant licence cannot be surrendered for extinguishment in connection with any application that requires the extinguishment of an intoxicating liquor licence to facilitate the granting of a new licence.

## Excise Duty for Special Restaurant Licence

As already referred to above, a fee of £3,000 is payable to the Revenue Commissioners on the initial grant of a special restaurant licence. The rate of excise duty on renewal is £200.

## WINE RETAILER'S ON-LICENCE

This licence authorises the sale of wine or sweets★ (in any quantity not exceeding two gallons, or not exceeding twelve quart bottles) for consumption either on or off the premises.

★ Sweets means any liquor made from fruit and sugar that has undergone fermentation. It includes Irish wines and mead.

## Application Procedure

Application for a wine retailer's on-licence may be made directly to the Customs and Excise authority.

The application must be made in triplicate and should provide the following information:

- name and address of applicant
- description and location of premises
- the rateable valuation of the premises for which the licence is required.

The Customs and Excise authority then forwards a copy of the requisition to the Garda superintendent for the district in which the premises are located, and to the District Court clerk for the district in which the premises are located.

Unless an objection in writing is received from the District Judge, the licence applied for will be issued after the expiry of 30 days from the date of notification to the Garda superintendent and the District Court clerk.

It should be noted that this licence cannot be granted to any refreshment house with a rateable valuation of less than £15 if it is situated in a location with a population exceeding 10,000 people or, if located elsewhere, the rateable valuation is less than £8.

## Objections to the Granting of a Licence

The only person entitled to object to the granting of a wine retailer's on-licence is the officer in charge of the Garda Síochána for the district in which the premises are situated.

The grounds for objection are confined to the following:

- The house for which the licence is required is not a confectionery shop or an eating house within the meaning of the Refreshment Houses (Ireland) Act, 1860.

- The premises do not meet the rateable valuation requirements of the Act.
- The premises are disorderly, or frequented by prostitutes or disorderly persons.
- The premises are disqualified for the sale of wine.
- The applicant is a member of an unlawful society.
- The applicant is disqualified from selling wine under the Act, and the grounds of such are specified.
- The applicant has been convicted within three years of an offence punishable by imprisonment.
- The applicant, having within three years held a licence to keep a common inn, alehouse or victualling house, or being licensed as a spirit grocer, has forfeited or been refused a renewal of such licence.

If an objection has been lodged, the applicant must be summoned to a sitting of the District Court in the district in which the premises are situated and given an opportunity to rebut the objection. The summons must specify the grounds of the objection. If the objection is upheld, the applicant may appeal the refusal to grant the licence to the Circuit Court.

Such licences expire on 30 September each year and may be renewed on payment of the appropriate excise duty. A court certificate is not required.

**Transfer of the Licence**

Where a wine on-licence is to be transferred — for example, on the sale or transfer of the premises — the assignee may apply to the District Court for a 'certificate of no objection'. This will entitle him or her to carry on the licensed business until he/she qualifies for the issue of a licence in his/her own name (see procedure above).

**Hours of Trading**

The holder of a wine retailer's on-licence must adhere to the normal opening hours permitted by the Licensing Acts (see page 158). However, the holder of this licence may apply to the District Court to certify that the premises to which the licence is attached are a restaurant. If the court recognises the premises as a restaurant, refreshment house or a place where substantial meals are served to the public, it will grant a restaurant certificate, and this confers two additional and valuable benefits upon the licensee:

- an entitlement to apply for special exemption orders (see page 182) but only to sell wine.

- an entitlement to serve wine with meals during certain prescribed times after normal hours (see page 159).

## Excise Duty

The excise duty payable in respect of a wine-retailers' on-licence is £200.

## RESTAURANT CERTIFICATE

A restaurant certificate (as distinct from a special restaurant licence) may be granted by the Circuit Court at the time of granting a certificate for a new on-licence, or at any time following an application for the renewal of the liquor licence to the Revenue Commissioners. The holder of a wine retailer's on-licence may also apply at any time for a restaurant certificate.

N.B. The premises must be structurally adapted for use and bona fide run as a restaurant, refreshment house or place for supplying substantial meals to the public. In recent years the District Court at the Annual Licensing District Court has sought evidence of bona fide use, e.g. an accountant's report showing that the principal turnover is from food and not from drink.

## Application Procedure

Notification by the applicant of his/her intention to apply for a restaurant certificate must be given, in writing, to

(a) the officer in charge of the Garda Síochána for the licensing area, not less than ten days before the proposed date of application, and

(b) the clerk of the District Court at which the application is to be made, not less than 48 hours before making the application.

Application for a restaurant certificate is confined to the holders of ordinary on-licences and wine on-licences. The holders of special restaurant licences or premises that are hotels within the meaning of

Section 1 of the Intoxicating Liquor Act, 1927 (i.e. at least 10 bedrooms for guests, irrespective of whether in a borough or elsewhere) do not need a restaurant certificate.

## Benefits of Obtaining a Restaurant Certificate

A licensee who provides meals is not compelled to obtain a restaurant certificate but, having done so, benefits by being able to serve intoxicating liquor with meals at certain prescribed times after normal licensing hours and by being able to apply for special exemption orders.

## Permitted Hours

The holder of a restaurant certificate is entitled to serve intoxicating liquor (confined to wine only, if the holder of the restaurant certificate is the holder of a wine retailer's on-licence) with meals at times additional to those normally permitted, as follows:

- during a period of summer time, between the hours of 11.30 in the evening on any weekday and 12.30 in the morning on the following day, or
- during a period that is not summer time, between the hours of 11.00 in the evening on any weekday and 12.30 in the morning on the following day, or
- unless the licence is a six-day licence, on any Sunday between the hours of 2.00 and 3.00 in the afternoon, or
- on Christmas Day, between the hours of 1.00 and 3.00 in the afternoon and the hours of 7.00 and 10.00 in the evening.

For the licence-holder to qualify for these extended drinking times, it is essential that the intoxicating liquor is:

- ordered at the same time as a substantial meal is ordered
- consumed at the same time as, and with, the meal
- supplied and consumed in a portion of the premises set apart for the supply of meals, and
- paid for at the same time as the meal.

## Restaurant Certificate Granted

Once granted, the restaurant certificate remains in force (unless it is revoked) until the next Annual Licensing District Court. The holder is required to display the certificate in a prominent place on the premises.

The officer in charge of the Garda Síochána for the district may apply at any time to the District Court to revoke a restaurant certificate on the grounds that the premises have ceased to be structurally adapted for use, or to be bona fide and mainly used, as a restaurant.

## LIMITED RESTAURANT CERTIFICATE

This certificate permits the holder to serve intoxicating liquor with meals in a specially nominated part of the licensed premises set aside for the provision of meals, as if the area were a restaurant. However, this part of the premises must not contain a public bar, nor must there be public access to it through a public bar.

While the holder of a limited restaurant certificate is entitled to serve intoxicating liquor during the same hours as those permitted to the holder of a restaurant certificate, there is no entitlement to apply for a special exemption order.

### Court Jurisdiction

The Circuit Court has jurisdiction to grant a limited restaurant certificate at the same time as it grants a certificate for a new on-licence. At any other time, the application may be made by the holder of an on-licence at any sitting of the District Court in the court area in which the premises are situated.

### Application Procedure

Notification by the applicant of his/her intention to apply for a limited restaurant certificate must be given, in writing, to both

(a) the officer in charge of the Garda Síochána for the licensing area, not less than ten days before the proposed date of application, and

(b) the clerk of the District Court at which the application is to be made, not less than 48 hours before making the application.

## Limited Restaurant Certificate Granted

As with a restaurant certificate, a limited restaurant certificate remains in force (unless it is revoked) until the next Annual Licensing District Court; here, too, the holder must display the certificate prominently on the premises.

## GENERAL EXEMPTION ORDER

A general exemption order may be obtained

(a) for the accommodation of any considerable number of people attending a public market or fair, or

(b) for the accommodation of any considerable number of people following any lawful trade or calling.

The applicant must be the holder of an on-licence and must satisfy the Judge of the District Court that such an order is necessary and desirable. When granted, the order has the effect of exempting the holder from those provisions of the licensing acts relating to prohibited hours, on such days and at such times as are specified in the order. A general exemption order is often referred to as an 'early morning exemption', to distinguish it. This is the type of licence held by 'early morning' public houses in dock or market areas.

## Application Procedure

Notification by the applicant of his/her intention to apply for an order must be served, in writing, to

(a) the Garda superintendent for the appropriate licensing area, not less than one week before making the application, and

(b) the clerk of the District Court at which the application is to be made, not less than 48 hours before the application is made.

## Permitted Hours

### 1. Public Market or Fair

A general exemption order for the accommodation of people attending a public market or fair cannot be granted for any time before 5.00 a.m. or for any time

(a) during summer time, after 11.30 p.m., or

(b) during a period that is not summer time, after 11.00 p.m.

## 2. Lawful Trade or Calling

A general exemption order for the accommodation of people following any lawful trade or calling cannot be granted for any time before 7.00 a.m. or for any time

(a) during summer time, after 11.30 p.m., or

(b) during a period that is not summer time, after 11.00 p.m.

A general exemption order cannot be granted for any time on a Sunday or for St Patrick's Day, Christmas Day or Good Friday. Licensed premises situated in the County Borough of Dublin are prohibited from holding such an order, unless one was in force in respect of the premises on 19 April 1962 or at some time during the two years preceding that date. The Judge of the District Court may withdraw or alter a general exemption order at any time. Normally an order will remain in force until the next Annual Licensing District Court, unless it is withdrawn or is expressed to expire sooner.

Every general exemption order must contain as one of its terms a condition that the holder must, during every period of exemption, supply on the premises food and non-alcoholic drink at reasonable prices to any person requiring such refreshment.

Unless the order is expressly limited to certain classes of person (and the court may, if it desires, so limit the operation of a general exemption order), the licensee can sell intoxicating liquor to any member of the public.

Finally, the holder of a general exemption order must affix a notice in a conspicuous place outside the premises, stating the periods of exemption. Failure to comply with this provision is an offence. It is also an offence for a person to represent falsely that he or she is the holder of a general exemption order or to state falsely the periods of exemption.

## SPECIAL EXEMPTION ORDER

A special exemption order may be applied for by the holder of an on-licence (but not by the holder of a special restaurant licence) for premises that are a hotel, restaurant, licensed holiday camp, licensed aerodrome or licensed omnibus station. The effect of a special exemption order is to permit the licence-holder, on any 'special occasion', to be exempt from normal licensing hours to the extent specified in the order by the District Court Judge.

## Application Procedure

Notification by the applicant of his/her intention to apply for a special exemption order must be given, in writing, at least 48 hours before making the application, to

(a) the officer in charge of the Garda Síochána for the licensing area, setting out the applicant's name and address, and the place, occasion and time for which the special exemption order is required, and

(b) the clerk of the court at which the application is to be made.

## Meaning of 'Special Occasion'

For the purpose of obtaining a special exemption order, the Intoxicating Liquor Acts have defined the expression 'special occasion' to mean

(a) (i) the occasion of a special event that is organised for the entertainment of the members of a particular association, organisation or other similar group, or

(ii) the occasion of a private function in the premises in relation to which the special exemption order is sought and at which a substantial meal (the price, if any, of which is included in the price, if any, of admission to the event) is served to the persons attending the event. (For the definition of a substantial meal, see page 159.)

(b) the occasion of a dance that is held in a ballroom licensed under the Public Dance Halls Act, 1935, and forming part of the premises in relation to which the special exemption order is sought and being a dance at which a substantial meal (the price, if any, of which is included in the price, if any, of admission to the dance) is served to persons attending the dance, or

(c) the occasion of a dance that is held in such a ballroom on a day that, in the opinion of the court, is a day of special festivity generally or in the locality in which the premises are situated.

**NOTE: Special exemption orders will not be granted for more than six days in any year in category (c).**

## Conditions Relating to Special Exemption Orders

1. Intoxicating liquor must not be sold during the hours of the order to persons other than those attending the event.

2. Members of the public, other than those attending the event, must not be admitted to the part of the premises in which intoxicating liquor is being supplied or consumed.

3. A special exemption order cannot be granted for any time on a Sunday or for any time between 1 a.m. and 10.30 a.m. on a Monday morning (it should be noted also that no special exemption order can be granted for any time on a Sunday morning following a Saturday night function).

4. Notwithstanding the previous rule, a special exemption order may be granted for a Sunday that is New Year's Eve, New Year's Day, or St Patrick's Day.

5. Where a special exemption order is in force, a person under the age of 18 years is prohibited from being on any part of the premises to which the order relates (other than a person under that age whose employment in the licensed premises is not prohibited).

6. Where a special exemption order is in force, the licensee must display in a conspicuous place in the licensed premises a notice stating that it is an offence for a person who is under the age of 18 years to be on the premises to which the order relates at any time during the period in respect of which the exemption order was granted. (For an example of the notice, see page 185.) Where offences are committed in relation to permitting persons under the age of 18 years to be on licensed premises to which a special exemption order is in force, it will be a defence for the licence-holder to state:

   - that he/she used all due diligence to prevent the person under 18 years being admitted to the premises, or

   - that the person produced proof of age, or

   - that the licence-holder had reasonable grounds for believing that the person was over the age of 18 years.

Where the prescribed notice is not so displayed, the licence-holder is liable to a fine not exceeding:

(a) £20 for a first offence, or

(b) £50 for a second or subsequent offence.

A licence-holder convicted of the offence of having a person under 18 years on his premises while a special exemption order is in force is liable to a fine not exceeding:

(a) £100 for a first offence, or

(b) £250 for a second or subsequent offence.

This offence is endorsed on the licence.

---

### INTOXICATING LIQUOR ACT, 1988

#### SECTION 35

*Restriction on persons under the age of 18 years being on licensed premises during extended hours.*

It is an offence for a person who is under the age of 18 years to be on that part of the premises in respect of which an exemption order under sections 4 or 5 of the Intoxicating Liquor Act, 1927, or section 10 of the Intoxicating Liquor Act, 1962 is in force, at any time during the period in respect of which the exemption order has been granted.

**N.B. Section 35 requires that the above notice shall be displayed in a conspicuous place in the part of the licenced premises which is used on foot of an exemption order.**

---

In practice, the District Court usually grants a special exemption order up to 1.30 a.m., although this is sometimes extended to 2.00 a.m. and, very rarely, later.

A special exemption order must be applied for in respect of every separate special occasion to be held on the premises. This means that if a number of different functions are taking place simultaneously, a special exemption order is required for each individual function.

### EXEMPTION FOR SPECIAL EVENTS

An application for an exemption for a special event or special events, commonly known as an 'area exemption', can be made by the holder of an on-licence in any locality except the County Borough of Dublin. If, after hearing the officer in charge of the Garda Síochána for the locality, the Judge of the District Court is satisfied that the application has the approval of the majority of licence-holders in the locality (such may be attested by their signature to a statement of approval), and that the event and the period during which it is to be held will attract a considerable number of people, he may make an order exempting the holders of licences in or near the locality from normal licensing hours at such times and on such days as he thinks fit. This type of licence can be obtained by a number of publicans in the same area. They can all sign the notice of application. This is the type of licence that is held during a music festival, strawberry festival or the Rose of Tralee festival, for instance.

Exemptions for special events cannot be granted for more than nine days in any year in relation to the one locality. It is permissible, however, for the nine days to be divided into not more than three periods in combinations of full days, so as not to exceed nine days in total.

## Application Procedure

Notification by the applicant of his/her intention to apply for an exemption for a special event must be served, in writing, to:

(a) the officer in charge of the Garda Síochána for the locality, not less than seven days before the date of intended application, and to

(b) the clerk of the court at which the application is to be made, at least 48 hours before making the application.

Furthermore, a notice of the applicant's intention to apply for an exemption for a special event must be published in a newspaper circulating in the locality, not less than seven days before the date on which it is proposed to make the application.

NOTE: *Where an exemption for a special event has been granted, the holder of a six-day licence is required to adhere to the provisions relating to prohibited hours on Sundays.*

## OCCASIONAL LICENCE

Where the District Court is satisfied that a special event is being held at a place that is not already licensed, it may grant an occasional licence on the application of the holder of an on-licence. The effect of the occasional licence is to permit the holder to sell intoxicating liquor at the place of the special event during such times and on such days (not exceeding six) as may be specified in the occasional licence.

The licensee is confined to selling such liquor as is authorised by his or her original on-licence.

## Procedure for Obtaining an Occasional Licence

Notification by the applicant of his/her intention to apply for an occasional licence must be given, in writing, at least 48 hours before making the application, to

(a) the officer in charge of the Garda Síochána for the locality to which the application relates, stating the applicant's name and address, and the place, occasion and time for which the occasional licence is required, and to

(b) the clerk of the court at which the application is to be made.

*NOTE: It is not a statutory requirement to notify the chief fire officer for the area of the intention to apply for an occasional licence, though it may be prudent to do so.*

## Rules Applying to Occasional Licences

- An occasional licence will not be granted for a dinner unless it is organised as a special function for the entertainment of members of a particular association or group.

- An occasional licence will not be granted for a dance, unless

  (a) it is held elsewhere than in the open air, a tent, marquee or other such structure, and

  (b) (i) it is organised as a special function for the entertainment of a particular association or group, and a substantial meal (the price, if any, of which is included in the price of admission, if any, to the dance) is served to persons attending the dance,

  (ii) it is held wholly or partly on a day that, in the opinion of the court, is a day of special festivity generally or in the locality. (In this category, an occasional licence cannot be granted for more than six days in any year.)

- Where the occasional licence is granted for a dinner or dance, the sale of intoxicating liquor must be confined to those attending that dinner or dance.

- An occasional licence cannot be granted for any Sunday, Christmas Day or Good Friday.

- An occasional licence cannot be granted for any time after ten o'clock in the evening or before eight o'clock in the morning, unless the event is a dinner or dance.

- A member of the Garda Síochána at all times may enter the premises where an occasional licence is in force.

- The granting of an occasional licence does not affect the applicant's on-licence.

## FESTIVAL CLUBS

An occasional licence or a special exemption order can be granted in respect of a function held for members of a club and organised in connection with a festival consisting wholly or mainly of the presentation or performance of music, dancing, plays, films, or any combination of these, even if a substantial meal is not served to those attending the event.

The function may be held either:

- at a place to which no licence is attached, in which case appropriate application will be for an occasional licence (see above), or
- at an hotel or licensed premises that has a full restaurant certificate, in which case the appropriate application will be for a special exemption order (see page 182).

The sale of intoxicating liquor in these circumstances is confined to:

- members of the club holding the function
- persons holding written invitations issued not later than twenty-four hours before the function commences.

A list of those attending the function must be kept and made available for inspection by the Garda Síochána.

An occasional licence or special exemption order permitted for this type of event cannot be granted for more than one social function on any day of the festival.

## NIGHT CLUBS

A night club licence, as such, does not exist. Late night entertainment can be operated in a licensed premises only in circumstances where the proprietor is the holder of a collection of appropriate licences, certificates and special exemption orders. When these are obtained, a night club can be operated in a hotel; a public house with a full restaurant certificate; and a premises covered by a wine retailer's on-licence and held together with a full restaurant certificate.

It follows, therefore, that for a proprietor to operate a premises as a night club (where the sale of alcohol and the provision of music and dancing are to feature):

- the premises must be licensed — the licence can be a publican's on-licence, a hotel licence, or a wine retailer's on-licence
- if the premises are not a hotel, they must then be a restaurant and certified by a court as such, under the Intoxicating Liquor Acts
- the occasion must qualify for the grant of a special exemption order and such must be obtained (see special exemption orders, page 182)
- the proprietor must apply for a public dancing licence under the Public Dance Halls Act, 1935 (see page 191).

# Chapter 9

# ENTERTAINMENT LICENCES

## PUBLIC DANCING LICENCES

The law governing the conduct of public dancing and the procedure to be followed in order to obtain a public dancing licence is laid down in the Public Dance Halls Act, 1935. Two types of dancing licence are possible under this legislation: a temporary dance licence and an annual dance licence.

## TEMPORARY DANCE LICENCE

A temporary dance licence may be applied for when the period of time to be covered by it does not exceed one month. Application should normally be made to a District Judge at a sitting of the District Court held in the court area where the dance venue is located. However, if sufficient reason is provided by the applicant, the District Judge has discretion to hear the application at any other court in his/her district.

## Application Procedure

An applicant must give notice in writing of his/her intention to apply for a licence to each of the following:

(a) District Court clerk

(b) Superintendent of the Garda Síochána within whose district the dancing will take place

(c) The fire authority in whose functional area the dancing will take place.

In the case of (a) and (b), at least 48 hours' notice must be given. In the case of (c), the Fire Services Act, 1981 requires one month's notice, or such shorter period as the fire authority may agree to accept in special circumstances.

## ANNUAL DANCE LICENCE

Where a new public dancing licence is required, the application should be made to the Judge of the District Court for the area in which the premises to be licensed are situated. However, if sufficient reason is given, the District Judge may hear the application at a sitting of any other court in his or her district.

In considering an application for a public dancing licence, the District Court Judge, in addition to taking into account any matter that appears to him/her to be relevant, should have regard to the following:

(a) The character of the applicant and his/her financial and other circumstances.

(b) The suitability of the place to be licensed.

(c) The facilities for public dancing existing in the neighbourhood at the time of the application.

(d) The facilities for the parking of vehicles.

(e) The probable age of the clientele.

(f) The ease of supervision by the Garda Síochána of the management and proceedings of the place to be licensed.

(g) The hours during which the applicant proposes that public dancing should be permitted.

Objections to the granting of the licence may be made by any member of the Garda Síochána or indeed by any person who appears to the District Judge to have an interest in the matter.

## Application Procedure

A person wishing to apply for an annual public dance licence (but not a temporary public dance licence) must publish a notice of his/her intention to apply for the licence, in a newspaper circulating in the district in which the dancing is to take place, at least one month before the hearing of the application.

The applicant must give notice in writing to the following:

(a) the superintendent of the Garda Síochána for the district in which the premises to be licensed are situated.

(b) The local authority in whose functional area the premises are situated.

(c) The fire authority in whose functional area the premises are situated.

(d) The clerk of the District Court at which the application is to be made.

At least one month's notice must be given in the case of (a), (b) and (c), and at least 48 hours' notice must be given to the District Court clerk.

When the licence is granted, it comes into force immediately and continues in force (unless it is withdrawn or surrendered) until the next Annual Licensing District Court, whereupon an application for its renewal may be made.

A District Court Judge has the authority to attach such conditions and restrictions as he or she thinks necessary when granting the licence and, for example, could limit the days on which, and the hours during which, the premises may be used for dancing.

## Appeals Procedure

The Circuit Court has jurisdiction to hear appeals in relation to applications for a public dance licence as follows:

(a) By the applicant, where the District Court has refused to grant a licence.

(b) By the applicant against any conditions or restrictions attached to the granting of the licence by the District Court.

(c) By an objector, who appeared and was heard at the court, against an order or part of an order granting a licence.

## General Provisions relating to Public Dance Licences

- A public dance licence cannot be transferred from one person to another.

- A licensee can surrender his/her licence at any time by notifying the District Court clerk in writing and by enclosing the licence.

- It is an offence to use any place for the purpose of public dancing unless a public dance licence has been granted in respect of it.

- Where a public dance licence is in force, the licensee must display conspicuously, at or near the main entrance of the premises, a notice in the following words:

LICENSED UNDER ACT OF THE OIREACHTAS

FOR PUBLIC DANCING

Failure to display this notice is an offence.

- Where a public dance licence is in force, any member of the Garda Síochána in uniform may enter the premises at any reasonable time to make such inspection, examination or inquiry as he or she thinks proper. It is an offence to obstruct a Garda in the exercise of his or her duty.

- The holder of a public dance licence does not require a licence for music and singing in respect of public entertainment that consists mainly of public dancing but includes other entertainment; for example, exhibition dancing, dancing competitions, and vocal or instrumental music.

- In Dublin, where a ballroom is subject to bylaws for premises of public resort, a copy of the bylaws must always be available on the premises while they are in use.

## PUBLIC MUSIC AND SINGING LICENCE

The need for a public music and singing licence arises where Part IV of the Public Health Acts Amendment Act, 1890 has been adopted by the relevant urban authority and where any house, room, garden or other place is used for music, singing or for other public entertainment, irrespective of whether or not it is licensed for the sale of intoxicating liquor. A public music and singing licence is not necessary in areas where Part IV of the 1890 Act has not been adopted by the urban authority nor in rural areas. In cases of doubt, the legal department of a particular local authority should be consulted to ascertain whether Part IV has been adopted, thereby requiring the relevant person to possess a public music and singing licence.

The application for this licence must be made to a District Court Judge for the area in which the premises are situated; the matters to be taken into account by the District Judge are the same as those outlined for applications for annual dance licences (see above). The applicant must give 14 days' notice to the Garda superintendent for the place in which the premises are situated and the same to the District Court clerk.

The District Judge may impose such conditions and restrictions on the public music and singing licence as he or she thinks fit.

## Appeals Procedure

The Circuit Court has jurisdiction to hear appeals in relation to applications for a public music and singing licence as follows:

(a) By the applicant, where the District Court has refused to grant a licence.

(b) By the applicant, against any conditions or restrictions attached to the granting of the licence by the District Court.

(c) By an objector, who appeared and was heard at the court, against an order or part of an order granting a licence.

## General Provisions

- A public music and singing licence may be transferred by a District Judge to such person as he or she thinks fit.

- Application for a renewal of the licence must be made at the Annual Licensing District Court.

## TEMPORARY PUBLIC MUSIC AND SINGING LICENCE

A temporary music and singing licence may be granted by a District Court Judge to permit any house, room, garden or other place to be used for music, singing or other public entertainment for a period not exceeding 14 days. The application may be made at any sitting of the District Court for the court area in which the premises to be licensed are situated. However, if sufficient reason is shown, the District Judge may permit the application to be made at a sitting of any other court in his or her district.

## General Provisions

- It is a condition of every temporary music and singing licence that a notice be displayed in a conspicuous place at the entrance to the premises, and that it should contain the words:

LICENSED IN PURSUANCE OF AN ACT OF THE OIREACHTAS FOR PUBLIC MUSIC AND SINGING

- Where music, singing or other public entertainment are carried on without a licence, such premises will be regarded as a disorderly house and the occupier will be held liable. Running a disorderly house is a ground for the Garda Síochána to object to the renewal of a publican's licence.

- Where a licence has been granted subject to any terms or conditions, contravention of these will be an offence, and the licence is liable to be revoked by court order.

## PERFORMING RIGHTS

The Copyright Act, 1963 grants a number of exclusive rights, known as 'performing rights', to songwriters and composers. Among these rights are:

- the right to perform the work in public
- the right to broadcast the work
- the right to include the work in a cable programme (i.e. piped television).

Before January 1989, the Performing Right Society licensed these rights in Ireland. Since then, however, it has handed over its licensing function to the Irish Music Rights Organisation Limited (IMRO).

IMRO licenses the works of approximately 1,700 Irish composers and publishers and represents some 700,000 copyright owners throughout the world, in association with a network of copyright organisations in other countries. More than 16,000 places of entertainment are covered by IMRO licences in the Republic of Ireland.

As a rule, IMRO does not grant licenses to individual performers, but rather to the proprietors of premises at which there is a 'public performance' of copyright music, or to the promoters of musical entertainments or events. Such proprietors and promoters are legally required to obtain an IMRO licence.

Although it is not defined in the Copyright Act, 1963, the expression 'public performance' has been interpreted by the courts effectively to include any performance that takes place outside the domestic circle. Therefore, the performance of copyright music in hotels, guesthouses, restaurants, public houses, buses, coaches, trains, shops, arcades, hairdressers, factories, clubs and suchlike, are all regarded as public performances. Such an interpretation is not altered even if the audience is confined, as in the case of hotel guests, club members or employees. It does not matter whether a charge is made for admission, whether the performers are paid, or whether the performance is given 'live' or through the medium of radio, television, tape-recorder, record-player, video-player, jukebox or by other means.

The cost of the licence varies, depending on the size and capacity of the premises to be licensed and the circumstances in which the music is being performed. It follows, therefore, that an IMRO licence for a television set in a rural public house will cost much less than for an open air rock concert. It is worth noting that a rebate of one-third is allowable from the first year's rates, where the music user obtains a licence before any music is performed.

Tariffs are agreed, where possible, with representative trade organisations, such as the Irish Hotels Federation and the Restaurants Association of Ireland. However, an evaluation of individual premises or events may be made by an IMRO inspector to calculate the appropriate charge.

Separate rates apply to featured music and background music. Featured music includes cabaret, discos, supper dances, dinner dances and ordinary dances where the music is provided by musicians and singers (whether or not they combine their performances with other activities such as dancing or acting) or by record/tape/compact disc player, primarily intended for entertainment and/or dancing, as distinct from background music. Background music is defined as music provided by record/tape or compact disc player (excluding jukeboxes or video performances, which may be regarded as featured music) or by means of radio or television operated on the premises or by diffusion through a loudspeaker, however conveyed, from another part of the premises or from a source outside the premises.

Where the particular premises are open only for a limited season each year, or the seating capacity is in use only during a limited season, the annual charge is adjusted by a proportionate reduction in respect of the background music rates, subject to a nominal minimum amount.

The charges, which are subject to VAT, are adjusted annually in July and are based on the consumer price index. The royalties thus collected, less only administration costs, are distributed to the song-writers, composers and publishers worldwide.

A current tariff is available by direct application to IMRO, Copyright House, Pembroke Row, Lower Baggot Street, Dublin 2.

Failure to obtain an IMRO licence in circumstances where copy-right music is performed in public could render the user liable to pay damages and costs and be ordered by the court to cease all musical performances.

Apart from music rights, copyright also subsists in sound record-ings, such as films, videos, records, compact discs and tapes (and, of course, in printed matter such as books, although these are not rele-vant in the present context). These copyrights are distinct from and in addition to the music recorded on the film soundtrack or on record, compact disc or tape. Where music is performed in public, using records, compact discs or tapes, a licence from Phonographic Performance Ireland Limited may be required in addition to the IMRO licence. While a film hire contract usually includes a licence to exhibit the film, an IMRO licence is required to cover the music on the soundtrack.

The requirement to hold an entertainment licence (for examples of which see pages 191-96) and/or a television licence is a separate and additional legal requirement to performing rights licences.

# Chapter 10

# EMPLOYMENT LAW — PART I

## THE CONTRACT OF EMPLOYMENT

The legal relationship between an employer and his/her employees is one based on contract. This type of contract is governed by both the general principles of contract law and by a body of labour legislation enacted by the Oireachtas (later reference to which forms a substantial part of this section).

It is important to be able to identify the existence of a contract of employment, often called a 'contract of service', and to distinguish it from a 'contract for services'. This latter expression relates to contracts undertaken between an employer and another self-employed person known in legal terms as an 'independent contractor'. Generally speaking, an independent contractor undertakes to provide a particular service (such as landscaping hotel grounds, or installing double glazing) at an agreed price. The contract continues until such time as the undertaking is completed. It then terminates.

### Control Test

The traditional method employed by the courts to distinguish an employee from an independent contractor is the use of what is known as the 'control test'. Under this test, the employer exercises control over his or her employee to the extent that he or she can tell the employee what to do, and when, how and where he or she must do it. It follows from this that the greater the amount of control exercised by the employer over the employee, the clearer his or her status as an employee. It is worth emphasising that it is not necessary for control to be exercised in person by the employer. It may be as effectively exercised on his or her behalf by a manager or supervisor.

Although the control test is appropriate in the majority of cases, it is not satisfactory for all types of employment. It does not take account of employment where a high degree of skill is required, as, for example, the work of a head chef. In occupations that require special expertise, there are many instances in which an employer (or his or her manager) would be unable to give direct instructions and thus be unable to exercise direct control. Does this mean, therefore, that those engaged in such occupations cannot be regarded as employees? The answer is no.

In recent years the courts have come to recognise that a single test, such as the control test, would not be appropriate for all employees. Instead, consideration must be given to 'the reality of the relationship' and must take into account any number of factors, of which control could be one.

## Consequences of the Employer–Employee Relationship

In view of the foregoing, it would not be unreasonable to pose the question, 'Why is it important to distinguish an employee from an independent contractor?' In the main, statutory employment law applies only to those individuals who have entered into a contract of employment and does not apply to independent contractors. Therefore the recognition of an individual as an employee gives rise to important legal consequences, such as:

- An employer is vicariously liable for the torts of an employee committed in the course of employment.

- An employer must deduct income tax from an employee's wages/salary under schedule E of the income tax code.

- An employee is afforded the protection of a range of legislative provisions, including the Unfair Dismissals Acts, 1977-94, the Minimum Notice and Terms of Employment Acts, 1973-91, and the Redundancy Payments Acts, 1967-91. However, certain categories of employee are excluded from cover by these Acts, details of which are provided under the relevant statutes and are identified as each of the statutes are examined.

- An employer must pay his/her share of PRSI and deduct the employee's contribution from wages/salary.

## Terms of the Contract of Employment

A contract of employment consists of both expressed terms and implied terms.

Expressed terms are those stated and agreed between the employer and the employee and can cover a range of matters, such as rates of pay, hours of work, holidays, sickness benefit, pension scheme, overtime and bonus rates, and notice entitlement. In many cases these can be freely negotiated between the parties.

Implied terms are those which, while not contained in any written or oral agreement, are nevertheless regarded as part of the contract. These may arise from custom and practice, collective agreements between the employer and a trade union, or from statute. In the latter case, many provisions contained in protective labour legislation set down minimum standards which must be met by employers and are automatically imported into the contract of employment.

## Implied Duties of the Employer

1. **To pay wages or salary.** An employer is bound to pay the employee in accordance with the terms of the contract of employment. Where the employer fails to pay within a reasonable period of time, the employee is entitled to regard the contract as terminated and may leave without giving notice. The minimum rates of pay for hotels and other catering enterprises are provided for under employment regulation orders. Employees are entitled to receive a wages and salary slip that shows the gross amount of wages and explains any deductions that have been made. The employer is obliged to make statutory deductions for PAYE and PRSI, or those required by a court order. Certain other deductions for the convenience of the employee may be made at his/her request, e.g. credit union savings, Voluntary Health Insurance contribution, or trade union subscriptions.

2. **To provide work.** Generally speaking, there is no obligation on an employer to provide work for an employee, provided he/she continues to pay the remuneration agreed upon. Where an employee is paid by commission or on a piecework basis, an employer may be required to provide work. Likewise, where the employee is highly skilled, the employer may be obliged to provide work to allow the employee to maintain his or her skill at a satisfactory level.

3. **To ensure safety.** The employer has a duty to take reasonable care of the safety of all employees. This is provided for both by common law (see page 81) and by statute (see page 83). An employer has no automatic common law obligation

to ensure the safety of the employees' personal property.

4. **Right to a reference.** The general rule is that an employer is under no obligation to provide an employee with a reference when the employee is leaving his or her employ. However, it is a matter for the employer and employee to agree to its provision in the contract. Furthermore, employees covered by an employment regulation order of either (a) the Hotels Joint Labour Committee or (b) the Catering Joint Labour Committees are entitled to receive a 'certificate of service'. In the case of (a), the certificate must show the period of employment and the standing of the employment at the date of termination. In the case of (b), the certificate must show the period of employment, length of service and the average weekly hours in each particular grade in which the employee worked.

It should be said that, in circumstances where the employer does provide a reference, a number of legal problems are possible:

(a) If the reference contains anything defamatory regarding the employee and is given directly to a prospective employer, an action may be taken by the employee against the former employer.

(b) Where the employer provides a false reference and knows it to be untrue, he/she may be liable in the tort of deceit.

(c) The employer may also be liable in negligence for a misstatement.

## Implied Duties of the Employee

1. **To attend for work.** The employee has a duty to attend and do the work he or she was contracted to do. He or she must not delegate the duties to anyone else. His or her obligation is a personal one to the employer.

2. **To obey lawful orders.** An employee is not required to do anything that is outside the terms of the employment contract. It follows, however, that he or she must obey all lawful orders in connection with the proper performance of his or her contract. An employer has no right to order his employee to do something that is illegal — for example, selling intoxicating liquor outside the permitted hours — or to require the employee to endanger his or her health or personal safety.

3. **To exercise care and skill.** An employee must exercise reasonable care and skill in carrying out his or her duties under the contract. Under the Safety Health and Welfare at Work Act, 1989, the employee has a statutory duty to take reasonable care for his or her own safety and that of any other person who may be affected by his or her conduct (for further elaboration, see page 85). An employee may be required to indemnify his or her employer for any damage or loss he or she causes the employer.

4. **To give faithful and honest service.** An employee is bound to act in good faith when dealing with the employer's affairs. He or she must act honestly and refrain from divulging trade secrets or giving away confidential information or customer lists.

## Terminating the Employment Contract

An employment contract may be terminated in a number of ways:

1. **By giving notice.** The contract may be terminated by either party giving notice to the other. The length of notice may be provided for in the contract, but it must not be less than that provided for by the Minimum Notice and Terms of Employment Acts, 1973-91 (see page 206). Termination by notice will not protect the employer where the provisions of the Unfair Dismissals Acts, 1977-94 have not been complied with (see page 223).

2. **Expiration of agreed term.** Where an employee is engaged for an agreed period, the employment is terminated when the time has expired. Under the Unfair Dismissals Acts, 1977-94, special conditions apply (see page 226).

3. **Completion of specified purpose.** Where an employee is engaged to carry out a particular task, the contract is at an end when that task is completed. (See, again, the Unfair Dismissals Acts, 1977-94, page 226.)

4. **Frustration.** This occurs where the performance of the contract becomes impossible as a result of an event that is beyond the control of the employer and employee — as, for example, the employee's death.

5. **Breach.** The contract of employment may come to an end by breach. This can happen where the employee leaves without giving the required notice.

# Chapter 11

# EMPLOYMENT LAW — PART II

## EMPLOYMENT LEGISLATION

### Entitlement to Notice

An employee's entitlement to notice on termination of his/her employment is normally determined by the contract of employment. However, such notice must not be less than that laid down in the Minimum Notice and Terms of Employment Acts, 1973-91. Where a specific period of notice is not provided for in the contract of employment, the courts may be required to infer that an appropriate period of notice is implied in the contract, but this, too, will not be less than that provided for by the Act.

## MINIMUM NOTICE AND TERMS OF EMPLOYMENT

Until 1994, the right to minimum periods of notice by both employers and employees when terminating a contract of employment, and the right of an employee to have information concerning the terms of his or her employment set out and given to him or her in writing, were contained in the Minimum Notice and Terms of Employment Acts, 1973-91. These Acts continue to contain the current law with regard to the right to notice and related matters, while the right to have information set out in writing is now to be found in the Terms of Employment (Information) Act, 1994. There are, therefore, now two Acts covering these matters, where there was formerly only one. This division of the contents of the Acts makes it necessary to deal with them separately.

## The Minimum Notice and Terms of Employment Acts, 1973–91

Although the Acts are of general application — that is to say, they apply to most employers and employees — there are some important exceptions:

- employees who work for less than 8 hours per week for the same employer
- the employer's immediate family, provided that they live with him or her and are employed in the same house or farm
- established civil servants
- members of the Permanent Defence Forces
- members of the Garda Síochána
- seamen signing on under the Merchant Shipping Act, 1894 (Part II or Part IV).

### Continuous Service Defined

In order to be entitled to the minimum notice as provided for in the Acts, the employee must have been in 'continuous service' with the same employer for at least thirteen weeks. Service is deemed to have been continuous unless the employee is dismissed or voluntarily leaves the job. Continuity is not usually affected by strikes, lay-offs or lock-outs. The transfer of ownership of a business does not break continuity of service and in these cases an employee's service with the new owner includes service with the former owner. Absence while on statutory maternity leave does not break service.

### Period of Notice

The minimum entitlement of an employee to notice is determined by his/her length of service according to the following table:

| *Length of Service* | *Minimum Notice* |
| --- | --- |
| Thirteen weeks to two years | One week |
| Two to five years | Two weeks |
| Five to ten years | Four weeks |
| Ten to fifteen years | Six weeks |
| Fifteen years or more | Eight weeks |

It follows that the contracting parties — the employer and employee — are free to agree greater periods of notice. Where the contract provides for a shorter period of notice than the statutory minimum, this will have no effect and the contract will be modified to the extent necessary to raise the notice to the minimum provided by the Acts for the period of service in question.

It is important to emphasise that the employer, too, is entitled to a minimum period of notice from an employee who has been in continuous employment by him or her for thirteen weeks or more. However, the employer's entitlement is to a period of at least one week, and there is no provision for this to be increased in line with service. For example, an employee with, say, sixteen years' service has a statutory entitlement on termination of his or her employment to at least eight weeks' notice. On the other hand, should this employee wish voluntarily to leave his or her job, his or her obligation (in the absence of a contract term providing for greater notice) is to give the employer only one week's notice.

The Acts do not require the employer to provide work during the period of notice. Therefore, payment in lieu of notice may be given. Similarly, an employer or employee may waive his/her right to notice.

## Calculating a Period of Service

There is a distinct difference between 'continuity of service' and periods that count towards service. For example, although the following are periods of absence from work, they are permitted to be included towards calculating a period of service and count as though the employee was performing his/her normal duties at work:

- service with the Reserve Defence Forces
- periods of up to twenty-six weeks, if due to
  - lay-offs
  - sickness
  - injury, or if
  - taken by agreement with the employer.

However, any period during which an employee is taking part in a strike in his or her place of work does not count towards a period of service.

## Dispute Procedures

Disputes about such matters as the right to notice or its length, the calculation of a period of service or dismissal due to misconduct may be referred by either the employer or the employee to the Employment Appeals Tribunal. If either party is dissatisfied with a decision arrived at by the Employment Appeals Tribunal, or by the Minister for Enterprise, Trade and Employment, at the request of the Tribunal, he/she may refer an issue to the High Court on a point of law only, i.e. on a question relating to the interpretation of the relevant law, but not on a question of fact.

The Tribunal is empowered to award compensation to an employee for any loss attributable to the employer's failure to give due notice or to observe the employee's rights during notice. However, if no loss has arisen, no compensation is payable.

Since the Acts lay down no time limits for bringing claims, the six-year limit, as provided for by the Statute of Limitations, 1957, operates.

## The Terms of Employment (Information) Act, 1994

The Terms of Employment Information Act, 1994 came into effect on 16 May 1994 and implemented a European Union Directive, No.91/533/EEC of 14 October 1991, requiring employers to provide a written statement to employees setting out particulars of the employee's terms of employment.

The Act applies to any person:

- working under a contract of employment or apprenticeship
- employed through an employment agency, or
- employed in the service of the state, including members of the Garda Síochána and the defence forces, civil servants and the employees of any local authority, health board, harbour authority or vocational educational committee.

The Act does not apply to:

- employment in which an employee is normally expected to work for the employer for less than 8 hours in a week, or

- employment in which the employee has been in the continuous service of the employer for less than one month.

## Provision of Written Statement

Where contracts of employment were entered into on or after 16 May 1994, the written statement of particulars must be provided by the employer within two months of the date of commencement of employment.

In the case of employees whose employment commenced before 16 May 1994, the written statement must be provided by the employer within two months of being requested to do so by the employee.

The written statement must contain the following particulars of the terms of employment:

- the full names of the employer and the employee
- the address of the employer in the state or, where appropriate, the address of the principal place of business or, the registered address of the employer as registered with the Companies Registration Office
- the place of work or, where there is no fixed or main place of work, a statement specifying that the employee is required or permitted to work at various places
- the title of the job or nature of the work for which the employee is employed
- the date of commencement of the employee's contract of employment
- in the case of a temporary contract of employment, the expected duration of employment or, if the contract of employment is for a fixed term, the date on which the contract expires
- the rate or method of calculation of the employee's remuneration,
- whether remuneration is paid weekly, monthly or otherwise
- any terms or conditions relating to hours of work, including overtime
- any terms or conditions relating to paid leave (other than paid sick leave)
- any terms or conditions relating to:
  (i) incapacity for work owing to sickness or injury and paid sick leave, and
  (ii) pensions and pension schemes
- the period of notice which the employee is required to give and entitled to receive; where this cannot be indicated when the written statement is given, the

written statement must state the method for determining the period of notice given

- a reference to any collective agreements which directly affect the terms of employment. Where an employer is not a party to such agreements, the written statement must indicate the bodies or institution which made the agreement.

As an alternative to providing all the details in the written statement, the employer may use the statement to refer the employee to certain other documents containing the particulars. For example, the employer may refer the employee to the provisions of any relevant legislation, Employment Regulation Order of the Labour Court, an employment agreement registered in the Labour Court, or a collective agreement, provided that the information is reasonably accessible to the employee.

The statement must be signed by or on behalf of the employer, and a copy of the statement must be retained by the employer during the period of the employee's employment and for at least one year after the employment has ceased. If the employee leaves the employment within the 2-month period for giving the notice, the statement must, nevertheless, be given to the employee.

Where an employee is required to work outside the state for a period of not less than one month, the employer is required to add the following particulars to the written statement:

- the period of employment outside the state
- the currency in which the employee is to be remunerated in respect of that period
- any benefits in cash or kind for the employee in respect of the employment outside the state
- any terms and conditions governing the employee's repatriation.

The complete particulars must be provided to the employee before his or her departure from the state. Here again, the employer's obligations are fulfilled where the written details refer the employee to legislation, administrative provisions or collective agreements.

## Notification of Changes in the Written Particulars

An employer must notify an employee of the date and nature of any change to the particulars contained in the written statement not later than one month after the change comes into effect. The requirement to notify the employee of any change in the particulars does not apply if the change is to legislation, administrative provisions or collective agreements to which the employee has already been referred by the employer.

## Procedure for Making a Complaint

The Act provides the employee with a right of complaint to a Rights Commissioner where an employer fails to provide a written statement of the terms of his or her employment. There is a right of appeal by either party to the Employment Appeals Tribunal from a recommendation of a Rights Commissioner.

A complaint to a Rights Commissioner may be initiated by an employee by giving notice of it in writing on the appropriate form. The Rights Commissioner, on receiving the complaint, is required to send a copy of the notice of complaint to the employer. An opportunity is then afforded both parties to be heard by the Rights Commissioner and to present any relevant evidence. The hearing is held in private and, after which, the Rights Commissioner will issue a written recommendation. A recommendation of a Rights Commissioner will do one or more of the following:

- declare that the complaint was or was not well founded
- confirm all or any of the particulars contained or referred to in any statement furnished by the employer
- alter or add to the written statement for the purpose of correcting any inaccuracy or omission in the statement
- require the employer to give the employee a written statement containing such particulars as may be specified by the Rights Commissioner
- order the employer to pay the employee such amount (if any) as is just and equitable, but not exceeding four weeks' remuneration.

An employee may bring a complaint at any time during his or her employment and for up to six months from the date of the termination of employment.

Either party may appeal the recommendation of a Rights Commissioner to the Employment Appeals Tribunal within six weeks of the date on which the Rights Commissioner issued his or her recommendation to the parties.

A further appeal may be made to the High Court from a determination by the Employment Appeals Tribunal, but only on a point of law. The Minister for Enterprise, Trade and Employment, at the request of the Tribunal, may refer a question of law to the High Court for a determination.

Failure to appear before the Employment Appeals Tribunal where a subpoena is served, and/or failure to produce documentation, is a criminal offence and the offender is liable, on summary conviction, to a fine of up to £1,000.

An employer must carry out a Determination of the Employment Appeals Tribunal within six weeks, unless it is under appeal to the High Court. The employee, the employee's trade union, or the Minister on behalf of the employee, may apply to the District Court for an order seeking enforcement of the Employment Appeals Tribunal Determination and an order compelling the employer to pay interest on the amount of any compensation awarded.

## WORKING TIME, REST AND HOLIDAYS

The enactment of the Organisation of Working Time Act, 1997 brought about the repeal of the Holidays (Employees) Act, 1973 in its entirety and of Section 4 of the Worker Protection (Regular Part-time Employees) Act, 1991. (This section made provision for the holidays of part-time workers.) The Act sets out the rights of employees in regard to:

- maximum working time
- periods of rest
- holidays.

These new rights will be applied using the following mechanisms, as relevant, in any particular case:

- by the law as set out in the Act itself
- in regulations created under the authority of the Act
- through legally binding collective agreements.

(Note: these collective agreements may allow for variations in such matters as the times at which a rest period is taken or the averaging period over which weekly working time is calculated.)

The implementation of this Act fulfils Ireland's obligations under Council Directive 93/104/EC concerning the organisation of working time and related matters.

## Non-application of the Act

As a general rule the Act applies to all employees. However, there are some important exceptions. The Garda Síochána and Defence Forces are exempt entirely from this statute. The following are excluded from the rest and working-time provisions but (most importantly) are not excluded from the holidays provisions:

- the activities of a doctor in training
- persons engaged in sea fishing or other work at sea
- transport employees
- a person whose working time is permitted to be determined by himself/herself
- a person who is employed by a relative and is a member of that relative's household and whose place of employment is a private house or farm where both employer and employee reside.

(Note: 'Relative' in this context means spouse, father, mother, grandfather/ mother, stepfather/mother, son, daughter, grandson/daughter, stepson/daughter, brother, sister, half-brother/sister.)

## Maximum Weekly Working Time

An employer must not permit an employee to work, in each period of 7 days, more than an average of 48 hours, that is to say, an average of 48 hours calculated over a reference period. The reference period may be over 4, 6 or 12 months depending on the circumstances.

For employees generally, the reference period will be 4 months. The 6-month reference period will apply to employees engaged in activities involving the need for continuity of service or production, including hospital and prison services; dock and airport workers; press, radio, television; emergency services; utilities (gas, water, electricity); research and development; agriculture; security and surveillance activities. The 6-month reference period will also apply where there is a foreseeable surge in activity, for example, in the postal services or in tourism. The 12-month reference period will apply to all employees who enter into a collective agreement with their employer which is approved by the Labour Court.

A reference period must not include:

- Any period of annual leave (except so much of it as exceeds the minimum leave required to be given by the Organisation of Working Time Act, 1997).
- Any absences from work by the employee authorised by the Maternity Protection Act, 1994 or the Adoptive Leave Act, 1995.
- Any sick leave taken by the employee concerned.

## Transitional Arrangements — Working Hours

The 48-hour week will become fully effective in the third year following the commencement of the Act. In the first year, 1998, employees may work a maximum of 60 hours per week and in the second year, 1999, employees may work up to 55 hours per week. In order to work these hours, employees must sign a written agreement with their employers.

In circumstances where the employee is represented by a trade union, the agreement must be signed through the union. Where the employee is not represented by a trade union, the agreement to work up to 60 hours (or 55 hours, as the case may be) must be signed directly with the employer. Any such agreement to work in excess of 48 hours requires the approval of the Labour Court.

## Minimum Rest Periods

The main provisions concerning periods of rest are as follows:

- All workers are entitled to a rest period of not less than 11 consecutive hours in each period of 24 hours (known as a daily rest period).
- All workers are entitled to a rest break of 15 minutes for each consecutive working period of 4 hours and 30 minutes; and a rest break of 30 minutes for each consecutive working period of six hours (the latter period may include the already mentioned 15-minute break, and the Minister for Enterprise, Trade and Employment may, by separate regulations, provide for this break to be more

than 30 minutes (but not more than 1 hour) for a specified group or groups of employee).

- All workers are entitled to a minimum uninterrupted rest period of 24 hours plus 11 hours for each 7-day period (known as a weekly rest period).

- An employer may, in lieu of granting the rest period described in the previous point, grant to the employee, in the next following period of 7 days, two rest periods. Each rest period must be of at least 24 consecutive hours and, generally speaking, if the rest periods are consecutive, the time at which the first of these periods commences must be such that that period is immediately preceded by a daily rest period (11 hours). If, however, the rest periods are not consecutive, the time at which each of them commences must be such that each of them is immediately preceded by a daily rest period. Unless otherwise provided for in the contract of employment, a rest period, as described, must include a Sunday.

These rest periods may be subject to variation where there is a collective agreement in place, approved by the Labour Court, and, similarly, where a regulation aimed at a particular sector or sectors has been made. It follows that where variations are in place, at least equivalent compensatory rest periods must be provided by the employer.

## Sunday Work

An employee who is required to work on a Sunday, and this fact has not been taken into account in the determination of his or her pay, must be compensated by his or her employer as follows:

- by the payment of an allowance of such an amount that is reasonable in the circumstances, or

- by otherwise increasing the employee's rate of pay by such an amount that is reasonable in the circumstances, or

- by granting the employee such paid time off as is reasonable in the circumstances, or

- by a combination of two or more of the means referred to.

## Nightly Working Hours

The Act defines 'night time' as the hours between midnight and 7 a.m. and 'night work' as work carried out during these hours. A night worker means an employee

- who normally works at least 3 hours of his or her daily working time during night time, and

- the number of hours worked by whom during night time, in each year, equals or exceeds 50 per cent of the total number of hours worked by him or her during that year.

An employer must not permit a night worker whose work involves special hazards or a heavy physical or mental strain to work more than 8 hours in any 24-hour period. In any other case, the night worker must not work more than an average of 8 hours in each period of 24 hours, calculated over a reference period of two months, or a longer period specified in a collective agreement which must be approved by the Labour Court.

## Providing Information about Working Time

If neither the contract of employment nor any employment regulation order, registered employment agreement or collective agreement in force specifies the normal or regular starting and finishing times of work of an employee, the employer is required to give the employee 24 hours' notice, prior to the start of the working week, of these times. The employer is also required, at the same time, to inform the employee of the days on which he/she will be required to work additional hours.

## 'Zero-hour' Contracts

'Zero-hour' contracts are those where employers require employees to make themselves available for work even though, on the day in question, they may not be asked to work. Under the 1997 Act, an employee who suffers a loss by not working the hours for which he or she was requested to be available, is entitled to be paid a minimum of 25 per cent for either the contract hours for which he or she was to be available or 15 hours, whichever is the lesser. For example, an employee is required to be available for 20 hours and is not required to work that week. The employee is, nevertheless, entitled to a minimum payment for 5 hours' work.

## Holidays — Annual Leave

An entitlement to paid holidays is directly related to time worked. All employees, whether full-time, part-time, temporary or casual, earn holiday entitlements from the time their work is commenced. An employee is entitled under the Act to paid annual leave equal to:

- four working weeks in a leave year (a leave year runs from 1 April to 31 March) in which he or she works at least 1,365 hours (unless it is a leave year in which he or she changes employment) or

- one-third of a working week (a 'working week' is a reference to the number of days that the employee concerned usually works in a week) for each month in the leave year in which he or she works at least 117 hours, or

- 8 per cent of the hours he or she works in a leave year (but subject to a maximum of four working weeks).

(Note: Because these holiday entitlements are not yet fully implemented, see page 218 for transitional arrangements from 1997 to 2000.)

If more than one of the preceding options is applicable in a particular case and the period of annual leave of the employee, determined in accordance with each of those options, is not identical, the annual leave to which the employee will be entitled will be whichever of those periods is the greater.

Where an employee is ill on any day or days during annual leave and he or she furnishes a medical certificate to his or her employer in respect of the illness, the day or days covered by the certificate will not count as annual leave.

The annual leave of an employee who works eight or more months in a leave year must include an unbroken period of two weeks. This is subject to any provisions contained in an employment regulation order, registered employment agreement, collective agreement or any agreement entered into between the employee and his or her employer.

The times at which annual leave is granted to an employee will be determined by his or her employer having regard to work requirements and subject —

- to the employer taking into account

    (i) the need for the employee to reconcile work and family responsibilities

(ii) the opportunities for rest and recreation available to the employee

- to the employer, having consulted the employee or the trade union (if any) of which he or she is a member, not later than one month before the day on which the annual leave (or a portion of it) is due to commence, and

- to the leave being granted within the leave year to which it relates or, with the consent of the employee, within the six months following the end of the year.

The pay in respect of an employee's annual leave shall:

- be paid to the employee in advance of his or her taking the leave

- be at the normal weekly rate or, as the case may be, at a rate which is proportionate to the normal weekly rate, and

- in a case in which board and/or lodging constitute part of the employee's remuneration, include compensation, calculated at the prescribed rate, for any board and/or lodging that will not be received by the employee while on annual leave.

Nothing in the Act prevents an employer and employee from entering into arrangements that are more favourable to the employee with regard to the times of, and the pay in respect of, his or her annual leave.

## Transitional Holiday Arrangements

The Organisation of Working Time Act, 1997 provides for transitional arrangements over the period 1997 to 1999 because the new holiday entitlement to 20 days is not fully implemented until the year 2000. The build-up of the new entitlements is outlined in the following schedule:

| Year | 5-Day Week | Other | Part-Time |
|------|-----------|-------|-----------|
| 1997/98 | 16 days | 3.2 weeks | 6.4% of |
| 1998/99 | 18 days | 3.6 weeks | 7.2% hours |
| 1999/2000 | 20 days | 4.0 weeks | 8.0% worked |

It may be useful for those concerned to calculate holiday entitlements by multiplying the number of days worked per week by 3.2 for 1997/98, 3.6 for 1998/99 and 4.0 for 1999/2000. How this works in practice is demonstrated as follows:

| Year | 2-Day Week | 3-Day Week | 4-Day Week | 5-Day Week |
|------|-----------|-----------|-----------|-----------|
| 1997/98 | 2x3.2=6.4 days | 3x3.2=9.6 days | 4x3.2=12.8 days | 5x3.2=16 days |
| 1998/99 | 2x3.6=7.2 days | 3x3.6=10.8 days | 4x3.6=14.4 days | 5x3.6=18 days |
| 1999/2000 | 2x4.0=8.0 days | 3x4.0=12.0 days | 4x4.0=16.0 days | 5x4.0=20 days |

## Public Holidays

In respect of a public holiday, an employee will be entitled to whichever one of the following his or her employer determines:

- a paid day off on that day
- a paid day off within a month of that day
- an additional day of annual leave
- an additional day's pay.

It should be noted that an employee may, not later than 21 days before a public holiday, request an employer to make a decision on which of the options the employer wishes to exercise and to notify the employee of the decision at least 14 days before the holiday.

The options listed above do not apply, in respect of a particular public holiday, to an employee (not being an employee who is employed whole-time) unless he or she has worked for the employer concerned for at least 40 hours during the period of five weeks ending on the day before that public holiday.

Each of the following days are public holidays for the purposes of the 1997 Act:

| | |
|---|---|
| Christmas Day | The first Monday in May |
| St. Stephen's Day | The first Monday in June |
| 1 January | The first Monday in August |
| St. Patrick's Day | The last Monday in October |
| Easter Monday | |

Any other day or days as may from time to time be prescribed.

The Minister for Enterprise, Trade and Employment may by regulations substitute, for any day referred to above, another day.

An employer may, for the purpose of fulfilling any relevant obligation imposed by this part of the Act, treat as a public holiday, in lieu of a public holiday as identified above, either

- the Church holiday falling in the same year immediately before the public holiday, or

- the Church holiday falling in the same year immediately after the public holiday or, if the public holiday is St. Stephen's Day, the 6th January next following.

The employer must give the employees concerned notice of his or her intention to do so not less than 14 days before the Church Holiday (where that holiday is before the public holiday) or before the public holiday (where that holiday is before the Church Holiday or, as the case may be, 6 January).

Each of the following are Church Holidays for the purposes of the Act:

- 6 January, except when falling on a Sunday
- Ascension Thursday
- Feast of Corpus Christi
- 15 August, except when falling on a Sunday
- 1 November, except when falling on a Sunday
- 8 December, except when falling on a Sunday
- any other day or days as may be prescribed.

The Minister may, by regulations, vary the above by deleting any day or by substituting, for any day referred to, another day.

## Compensation for Loss of Annual Leave

Where an employee ceases to be employed and the whole or portion of annual leave remains to be granted, the employee must be paid, as compensation for the loss of that annual leave, an amount equal to the pay, calculated at the normal weekly rate (or at a proportionate rate) that he or she should or would have received had he or she been granted annual leave.

## Compensation for Loss of Public Holiday

Similarly, where an employee ceases to be employed during the week ending on the day before a public holiday and the employee has worked for his or her employer during the four weeks preceding that week, the employee must be given an additional day's pay.

## Double Employment

An employer must not employ a person to do any work in a 'relevant period' during which the employee has done work for another employer that would result in the total hours of work from the combined employment exceeding the maximum working hours during a daily 'relevant' period (24 hours), weekly 'relevant' period (7 days) or yearly 'relevant' period (12 months).

## Keeping Records

An employer must keep such records as will show whether the provisions of the Act are being complied with, including details of annual and public holidays. The records must be kept safely on the premises where the employees concerned work and must be retained for a period of three years from the date of their making. These records must be available for inspection by inspectors of the Department of Enterprise, Trade and Employment.

## Inspectors

Inspectors, who are appointed by the Minister for Enterprise, Trade and Employment, have wide-ranging powers under the Act, including the right to:

- enter at all reasonable times any place of employment
- make such examination or inquiry as may be necessary to ascertain whether the provisions of the Act are being complied with
- require the production of any records that may be relevant
- require any person to furnish such information as the inspector may reasonably request.

However, an inspector must not, other than with the consent of the occupier, enter a private dwelling (other than a part of a dwelling used as a place of work) unless he or she has obtained a warrant from the District Court authorising such entry.

Where he or she considers it necessary, an inspector may be accompanied by a member of the Garda Síochána when exercising any powers conferred on an inspector by this Act.

Any person who

- obstructs or impedes an inspector in the exercise of his or her powers
- refuses to produce any record which an inspector lawfully requires to be produced
- produces or knowingly allows to be produced any record which is false or misleading
- gives to an inspector any information which, knowingly, is false or misleading
- fails or refuses to comply with any lawful requirement of an inspector

shall be guilty of an offence.

## Complaints and Proceedings

Proceedings under this Act are initiated by way of a complaint by an employee or, with his or her consent, the employee's trade union, to a Rights Commissioner within six months of the alleged breach of the legislation. The proceedings are conducted in private.

A decision of the Rights Commissioner will do one or more of the following:

- declare that the complaint was or, as the case may be, was not well founded
- require the employer to comply with the relevant provisions
- require the employer to pay the employee compensation up to an amount not exceeding two years' remuneration.

Either party may appeal the decision of the Rights Commissioner to the Labour Court, within six weeks of the date of that decision being communicated to the party taking the appeal. If an employer fails to carry out a determination by the Labour Court within six weeks from the date on which the determination is communicated to the parties, the Circuit Court will, on an application made to it by

(a) the employee concerned,

(b) with the consent of the employee, any trade union of which the employee is a member, or

(c) the Minister, if he or she considers it appropriate to make the application, having regard to all the circumstances,

without hearing the employer or any evidence (other than in relation to the matters aforesaid) make an order directing the employer to carry out the determination in accordance with its terms.

An employer must not penalise an employee for having in good faith opposed by lawful means an act which is unlawful under this legislation. If the penalisation constitutes a dismissal of the employee within the meaning of the Unfair Dismissals Acts, 1977 to 1994, the employee must decide under which statute he or she will seek redress. Relief will not be granted to an employee in respect of penalisation both under the Organisation of Working Time Act, 1997 and the Unfair Dismissals Acts, 1977 to 1994.

## Penalties

A person guilty of an offence under this Act is liable on summary conviction to a fine not exceeding £1,500.

If the contravention in respect of which a person is convicted of an offence under this Act is continued after conviction, that person shall be guilty of a further offence on every day on which the contravention continues, and for each offence the person will be liable on summary conviction to a fine not exceeding £500.

Notwithstanding Section 10 (4) of the Petty Sessions (Ireland) Act, 1851, proceedings for an offence under this Act may be instituted within twelve months from the date of the offence.

## UNFAIR DISMISSAL

The concept of unfair dismissal is a relatively recent one in Irish law, achieving recognition for the first time in the Unfair Dismissals Act, 1977 and further enhancement in the Unfair Dismissals (Amendment) Act, 1993. Other minor adjustments were introduced by virtue of the Maternity Protection Act, 1994. These Acts may be cited together as the Unfair Dismissals Acts, 1977-94. It is important at the outset to distinguish an 'unfair dismissal' as defined and provided for in these Acts from the common law action for 'wrongful dismissal'. The latter is a remedy still available and made use of, but it must be pursued through the ordinary courts. As will be seen later, the Unfair Dismissals Acts provide mechanisms for redress additional to the courts. An aggrieved employee therefore must decide (and should seek professional legal advice on this) whether to pursue his/her claim under the common law or under the Unfair Dismissals Acts. Opting for one necessarily excludes the other.

The purpose of the Acts is to afford protection to employees from being unfairly dismissed from their employment. The Acts lay down the criteria by which dismissals are to be judged to be unfair and provide a system of adjudication and redress for employees whose dismissals have been found to be unfair.

In general, the Acts apply to all employees who are normally expected to work eight hours or more per week and who have had at least one year's continuous service with the same employer. The Acts also apply to anyone employed through employment agencies. The third party (the hirer/user) is deemed to be the employer for purposes of redress under the Acts.

## Excluded Categories

The Acts do not apply to the following:

- Employees who have reached normal retiring age or who are not covered by the Redundancy Payments Acts because of age.
- Individuals working for a close relative in a private house or farm, provided that both also live in the same house or farm.
- Members of the Defence Forces and the Garda Síochána.
- FÁS trainees and apprentices (see below for specific provisions).
- Most civil servants and officers of health boards (other than temporary officers), vocational education committees and committees of agriculture.
- Employees with less than one year's continuous service with the same employer (continuous service is defined under the Minimum Notice and Terms of Employment Act, 1973).

## Special Provisions Relating to Apprenticeship, Training and Probation

1. The Acts apply to persons engaged in a statutory apprenticeship, except during

   (a) the first six months of the apprenticeship and

   (b) the period of one month following completion of the apprenticeship.

   *NOTE: Statutory apprenticeship in this context is an apprenticeship in an industrial activity designated by FÁS.*

2. The Acts do not apply to the dismissal of an employee during a period at the beginning of employment when he/she is on probation or undergoing training, provided that

   (a) the contract is in writing

   (b) the duration of probation or training is one year or less and is specified in the contract.

3. The Acts do not apply to persons undergoing training for certain professions, in particular those, such as nursing, that are connected with the health services.

## Bringing an Action for Unfair Dismissal

The following requirements must be satisfied by an employee seeking redress under the Acts:

- To have at least one year's continuous service with the employer (this requirement is not necessary where the dismissal is due to pregnancy or for exercising rights under the Maternity Protection Act, 1994 or trade union activity, but in the latter case the onus rests with the employee to prove that the dismissal was unfair). In determining if an employee has the necessary service, a Rights Commissioner or the Employment Appeals Tribunal may consider whether the employment of a person on a series of two or more contracts of employment (between which there has been no more than twenty-six weeks of a break) was for the purpose of avoidance of liability by the employer under the Acts. Where this is found to be the case, the length of the various contracts may be added to assess the length of service of an employee for eligibility under the Acts.

- To be normally expected to have worked at least 8 hours per week.

- To lodge the claim for unfair dismissal in writing to either a Rights Commissioner or to the Employment Appeals Tribunal within six months of the date of dismissal. The time limit for hearing a claim may be extended to twelve months in cases where exceptional circumstances prevented the lodgment of the claim within the normal limit of six months. The notice of claim must contain certain particulars. (A form which sets out the particulars may be obtained from the Department of Enterprise, Trade and Employment, from local offices of FÁS or from employment exchanges.)

Although the Acts require that the employer be notified within the same six-month limit, there is no requirement that this notification should come specifically from the employee.

The date of expiry of the six-month time limit often gives rise to confusion and contention. To arrive at this date, it is necessary to be certain about the date of dismissal. The generally accepted position is that the date of dismissal is deemed to be one of the following:

- The date on which notice (if served) runs out.
- If notice has not been given but should have been, dismissal occurs on the earliest date that would comply with the minimum entitlement set down in the Minimum Notice and Terms of Employment Acts, 1973-91 or that provided by the contract of employment, whichever is the longer.
- Where an employee accepts payment in lieu of notice, the date on which the notice, if given, would have expired.

The time limit is based on calendar months and runs from the actual date of dismissal. Therefore, the time limit of an employee who was dismissed on 1 February will expire on the same date six months hence, i.e. 1 August.

## Establishing the Fact of Dismissal

Before the fairness or otherwise of a dismissal can be adjudicated upon, the fact that a dismissal has occurred must be ascertained. An employee is regarded as having been dismissed if any of the following occur:

- The termination by the employer of the employee's contract of employment (with or without notice).
- The termination by the employee of his/her contract of employment (with or without notice) because of the misconduct of the employer. This is known in law as constructive dismissal.
- The expiration of a fixed-term employment contract which is not being renewed.
- The completion of a specified purpose employment contract.

In relation to the last two matters, dismissals arising only from the expiry of a fixed term or the completion of a specified purpose will not be covered by the Acts provided that

- the contract is in writing
- it is signed by both the employer and employee
- it contains a statement that the Unfair Dismissals Acts, 1977-94 shall not apply to the dismissal.

Where a fixed term has expired and the particular employee is re-employed within three months in similar employment by the same employer, a Rights Commissioner (Employment Appeals Tribunal, or Circuit Court) may examine any second or subsequent fixed-term contract of employment and take a view as to whether or not the fixed nature of the contract was wholly or partly connected with the avoidance of liability under unfair dismissals legislation. If so, the employee will be able to benefit from the protection of the Acts and make a claim for unfair dismissal at the expiry of the contract.

## Establishing the Burden of Proof

In cases where the fact of dismissal is in dispute, the burden is on the employee to establish that the dismissal actually took place. When this initial hurdle is overcome (or where the dismissal is not disputed), the Acts impose upon the employer the burden of proving that the dismissal was fair. There exists, therefore, the presumption that the dismissal is unfair and it is for the employer to prove the contrary.

## Unfair Dismissals Identified

The Acts identify a range of situations in which a dismissal will be held to be unfair:

- The employee's trade union membership or activities either outside working hours or at those times during working hours when the employer permits.
- The employee's membership of the travelling community.
- The employee's religious or political opinions.
- The employee's race, colour or sexual orientation.
- Civil or criminal proceedings either taken or proposed against the employer and to which the employee is a party or a witness.
- The age of the employee.
- Unfair selection of the employee for redundancy.

**(NOTE: The Unfair Dismissals Acts, 1977-94 provide that a dismissal wholly or mainly because of redundancy is not deemed to be an unfair dismissal. However, if an employee is unfairly selected for redundancy, the dismissal is deemed to be unfair.)**

- The employee's pregnancy, giving birth or breastfeeding or any matters connected therewith.

- Where the employee has been locked out by the employer and is not offered re-engagement or reinstatement when work is resumed.

- Where an employee has been dismissed for taking part in a strike or industrial action and other participants were either not dismissed or were subsequently offered reinstatement or re-engagement.

- An employee's exercise of her rights under the Maternity Protection Act, 1994.

## Fair Dismissal Identified

The dismissal of an employee from his/her employment may be justified if it can be shown that it resulted from one or more of the following cases or that there are other substantial grounds:

- The employee's competence or qualification for the work undertaken.
- The employee's misconduct.
- Redundancy (where the correct policy and procedures are adhered to).
- Where continuation of the employment would break the law.
- The expiry of a fixed-term or specified purpose employment contract, provided the rules relating to these (mentioned above) are adhered to.

## Making a Claim for Unfair Dismissal

The stages through which a claim of unfair dismissal may be processed are to:

(a) a Rights Commissioner

(b) the Employment Appeals Tribunal.

Where the claim is brought first before a Rights Commissioner, either party may appeal the result of the hearing to the Employment Appeals Tribunal. Where an employer has neither implemented nor appealed a recommendation of a Rights Commissioner, the employee may bring the claim before the Employment Appeals Tribunal. The Tribunal will issue a determination confirming the Rights Commissioner's recommendation without rehearing the claim. Where either the employer or the employee objects to the claim being made before a Rights Commissioner and notifies the Rights Commissioner in writing of the objection, the claim may be made to the Employment Appeals Tribunal. A decision of the Tribunal may be appealed to the Circuit Court and, although not specifically provided for in the Acts, the High Court has determined that a further appeal may be made to it from the Circuit Court.

An appeal by either party from a recommendation of a Rights Commissioner to the Employment Appeals Tribunal must be notified in writing to the Tribunal within six weeks.

The Employment Appeals Tribunal may hear a claim coming before it directly or arising out of an appeal from a determination by a Rights Commissioner. Either party, at its own expense, may appeal within six weeks to the Circuit Court and, if necessary, from there to the High Court.

If an employer does not carry out within six weeks the terms specified in a determination of the Employment Appeals Tribunal, which has not been appealed, or an order made by the Circuit Court on appeal, the employee or the Minister for Enterprise, Trade and Employment on behalf of the employee may apply to the Circuit Court for an order directing the employer to implement the determination. In these circumstances, the Circuit Court has the power to make an order against an employer which would include interest on the amount of any financial compensation awarded.

In cases where an order for reinstatement or re-engagement is concerned, the Circuit Court may direct the employer to pay the employee financial compensation in respect of the period during which the employer failed to implement the order. The Circuit Court may also vary a determination of reinstatement or re-engagement to one of financial compensation.

The written notice of a claim to a Rights Commissioner should be sent to the Rights Commissioner Service, Labour Relations Commission, Tom Johnson House, Haddington Road, Dublin 4. An appeal to the Employment Appeals Tribunal should be sent to the Employment Appeals Tribunal, Davitt House, 65A Adelaide Road, Dublin 2.

## Forms of Redress for Unfair Dismissal

Where an employee has been deemed to be unfairly dismissed, the Acts provide for one of the following forms of redress to be awarded:

- reinstatement of the employee in his or her former job and thereby entitling the employee to benefit from any improvement in terms and conditions of employment which may have occurred between the date of dismissal and the date of reinstatement, or

- re-engagement of the employee in his or her former job or in a suitable alternative job on conditions which the adjudicating bodies (Rights Commissioner, Employment Appeals Tribunal or Court, as the case may be) consider reasonable, or

- financial compensation within a maximum of two years' pay, the exact amount of which can depend on a variety of factors, e.g. where the responsibility for the dismissal lay; the measures taken to reduce financial loss; the extent to which negotiated dismissal procedures were followed. Under the Acts, compensation may also be awarded for unfair dismissal in cases where no financial loss was incurred by the employee. In such circumstances, the maximum amount of compensation is limited to four weeks' pay.

Where the ownership of the business that dismissed an employee is transferred to new ownership, the award of compensation to the employee is not affected. The Acts require the new owner of the business to take on liability for any claim that may be pending for unfair dismissal against the former employer.

In calculating financial loss for the purpose of compensation, payments to an employee under the Social Welfare and Income Tax Codes will be disregarded.

## Reasons for Dismissal Given in Writing

An employee who has been dismissed from his/her employment is entitled to demand in writing the reasons for the dismissal. The employer must provide this information within 14 days of such demand. However, in any hearing of a claim for unfair dismissal, account may be taken of any other substantial grounds which would have justified the dismissal.

## Notification of Dismissal Procedures

An employer must provide each employee with a written notice of dismissal procedures, which the employer will implement in the event of the employee's dismissal. Such information must be given to the employee within 28 days of starting work and any alteration must be notified in writing also within 28 days of such alteration.

## Actions at Common Law

An employee retains the right to claim damages under common law for wrongful dismissal up to the time that either a Rights Commissioner makes a recommendation in the case or a hearing by the Employment Appeals Tribunal has commenced. Similarly, an employee retains the right of redress under the Unfair Dismissals Acts up to the time that his/her claim for damages for wrongful dismissal in the civil courts has commenced.

## Illegal Contracts

In the case of a contract of employment tainted with illegality, e.g. where an employer or employee colluded to make some or all of the wage payments 'informally' to evade tax or, where an employee was working and drawing unemployment benefit at the same time, a dismissed employee will, nevertheless, be entitled under the Unfair Dismissals Acts to redress for unfair dismissal. However, the Rights Commissioner, Employment Appeals Tribunal or the Circuit Court (as the case may be) is required to notify the Revenue Commissioners or the Minister for Social, Community and Family Affairs, as appropriate, of the illegal activities.

## EMPLOYMENT OF CHILDREN AND YOUNG PERSONS

The Protection of Young Persons (Employment) Act, 1996 repealed in total the 1977 Act of the same title. The Act gives effect to international rules on the protection of young employees, drawn up by the International Labour Organisation and the European Union. The Act sets out to protect the health of young workers and to ensure that work undertaken during school years does not adversely affect a child's or young person's education. The Act applies generally to workers under the age of 18 years and covers such important issues as the minimum age for entry into employment, limits on working hours, the provision of rest intervals and the prohibition on late night work. Under the Act, a 'child' is defined as a person who is under 16 or the school-leaving age (whichever is higher). And a 'young person' is defined as a person who has reached the age of 16 or the school-leaving age (whichever is higher) but is less than 18 years old.

## Employment Conditions for Children

There is a general prohibition on the employment of those under the age of 16 in regular full-time work. Children between the ages of 14 and 16 may, however, be employed on 'light work', subject to certain requirements. 'Light work' is defined in the Act as work which is not industrial work and which, on account of the inherent nature of the tasks which it involves and the particular conditions under which they are performed, is not likely to be harmful to the safety, health or development of children, their schooling, vocational guidance or training. It should be noted that the Act reserves to the Minister for Enterprise, Trade and Employment the right to declare any form of work to be industrial work for the purposes of the Act.

An employer may employ a child who is over the age of 14 years to do light work during any period outside the school term provided that

- the hours of work do not exceed 7 hours in any day or 35 hours in any week
- the work is not harmful to the safety, health and development of the child, and
- during the summer holidays the child does not do any work for an uninterrupted period of at least 21 days.

A child over the age of 14 who is a full-time student at an institute of secondary education may be employed on a work experience or educational programme approved by the Minister for Education, provided that the hours of work do not exceed 8 hours in any day or 40 hours in any week.

A child over the age of 15 may be employed to do light work during school term time, provided that the hours of work do not exceed 8 hours in any week.

The Minister for Enterprise, Trade and Employment may, by licence (or, by regulations where the child is over the age of 13), authorise in individual cases the employment of a child in cultural, artistic, sports or advertising activities which are not likely to be harmful to the safety, health or development of the child and which are not likely to interfere with the child's schooling. The minister may attach to a licence or provide in regulations such conditions as he or she thinks fit.

An employer must not employ any person under the age of 16 to do any work between the hours of 8 p.m. on any one day and 8 a.m. on the following day. Furthermore, an employer must ensure that such a person receives a minimum rest period of 14 consecutive hours in each period of 24 hours. For example, where the employer requires the child to start work at the earliest time permitted by the statute, i.e. 8 a.m., he or she must ensure that the child did not work after 6 p.m. on the previous day. (However, the 14 consecutive hours of rest may be interrupted by the employer in the case of a child employed on activities that do not extend beyond 2 hours a day, provided that in each period of 24 hours the child receives a minimum rest period of 14 hours.) In any period of 7 days, a child is entitled to a minimum rest period of 2 days, which must, as far as practicable, be consecutive. (The minister may, but only by issuing specific regulations, reduce the minimum period of rest to 36 consecutive hours in respect of any class of employees or any class of work where, in the opinion of the minister, this is justified for technical or organisational reasons.)

Finally, employers must provide a thirty-minute rest period after every 4 hours of work by children under the age of 16 years of age, although there is no entitlement to payment for such a break.

## Employment Conditions for Young Persons

A young person must not be employed for more than 8 hours in any day or 40 hours in any week, or between the hours of 10 p.m. on any day and 6 a.m. on the following day. However, during school holidays and on weekend nights where the young person has no school the next day, he or she may work up to 11 p.m., but must not be required to work again until after 7 a.m. the next day. In this case the Minister for Enterprise, Trade and Employment must be satisfied, following consultation with appropriate representatives of employers and employees, that there are exceptional circumstances warranting departure from the normal requirements.

An employer must ensure that a young person receives a minimum rest period of 12 consecutive hours in each period of 24 hours. (However, the minimum consecutive hours of rest may be interrupted by an employer in the case of a young person employed on activities that do not extend beyond 2 hours each day, provided that in each period of 24 hours the young person receives a minimum rest period of 12 hours.) In any period of 7 days, a young person is entitled to a minimum rest period of 2 days which must, as far as is practicable, be consecutive. Employers must provide a thirty-minute break after every 4$^{1}/_{2}$ hours of work by young persons. There is no entitlement to payment for such breaks.

## Prohibition on Combined Employments

An employer is under an obligation not to permit an employee (covered by this Act) to work for him or her on any day where the work for that employer, when combined with the work done for any other employer, exceeds the statutory limits referred to above.

Failure to comply with this requirement is a criminal offence not only for the employer, but also for the employee (if over age 16) and for a parent or guardian who aids a breach of this requirement.

It will be a defence for an employer to prove either that he or she did not know, or could not by reasonable enquiry have known, that the employee had done work for any other employer on the day in respect of which the prosecution is brought, or that he or she did not know, or could not have known, that the aggregate of the periods for which the employee did work exceeded the period for which he or she could lawfully be employed to do work for one employer on that day.

## Formalities

- Before employing anyone under the age of 18, an employer must see that person's birth certificate or other satisfactory evidence of age.

- Before employing a child, the employer must obtain written permission from the parent or guardian.

- The employer is required to keep a record of the following particulars for each employee under the age of eighteen years:

  - full name

  - date of birth

  - starting and finishing times of work each day

  - rates of pay per day, week, etc.

  - total amount paid.

- An employer must retain all records for at least a period of 3 years at the place of employment.

- Every employer must display the prescribed abstract of this Act at the principal entrances to the premises where any of his or her employees work, and, in such other places as an inspector may require, in such a position that it may be easily read by employees.

Any person guilty of an offence under this Act will be liable on summary conviction to a fine not exceeding £1,500.

Where a person, after conviction for an offence under this Act, continues to contravene the provision(s) concerned, he or she will be guilty of an offence for every day on which the contravention continues, and for each offence will be liable on summary conviction to a fine not exceeding £250.

Notwithstanding section 10 (4) of the Petty Sessions (Ireland) Act, 1851, summary proceedings for an offence under this Act may be instituted within 12 months from the date of the offence.

It will be a defence to any proceedings taken against an employer for a breach of any of the provisions of this Act in relation to an employee who is a young person, if the employer can show that a breach of the Act was necessitated by the occurrence or reasonable anticipation of fire, flood, storm, violence, a breakdown of plant or machinery, or any other emergency, provided that:

- the work is of a temporary nature and has to be performed immediately

- adult workers are not available

- the young person is allowed equivalent compensatory rest time within 3 weeks of the date of the occurrence of the breach, and
- the young person is paid at the rate of time plus a quarter for any time worked as a result of the emergency.

Money due from an employer to an employee under the provisions of the Act may be sued for in court by the employee concerned. It is also open to a parent or guardian of the employee or his or her trade union to institute proceedings to recover money due to the employee. Where a prosecution is brought under this Act and it appears that money is due to an employee, the court may order the employer to pay over this money in addition to any fine it imposes on the employer.

## MATERNITY PROTECTION

The Maternity Protection of Employees Acts, 1981-91 have been repealed and replaced by the Maternity Protection Act, 1994. This change in the law was necessary to comply with the provisions of Council Directive 92/85/EEC on the introduction of measures to encourage improvement in the safety and health at work of pregnant workers and workers who have recently given birth or are breast feeding.

All female employees under a contract of employment are entitled to the protection afforded by the Maternity Protection Act, 1994. This includes apprentices, employees on probation and employment agency workers.

While all female employees under a contract of employment are entitled to maternity leave, some may not be entitled to the full amount. Where a woman is employed on a fixed-term contract and her contract ends while she is still on maternity leave, the maternity leave will end on the same day as the contract ends. (For example, an employee who is contracted for one year's service and who goes on maternity leave eight weeks before her contract ends, will have her maternity leave end after eight weeks.)

## Scope of the Benefits of the Act

The Act provides for a range of legal rights for female employees. These include the right to:

- take maternity leave
- take additional maternity leave
- return to work
- take time off for ante-natal and post-natal care
- leave for fathers in the event of the death of the mother if the death occurs within a set period after the birth of the child
- health and safety leave
- protection of certain employment rights while on leave under this Act
- protection against dismissal from the beginning of pregnancy to the end of maternity leave (if the dismissal results from pregnancy or any connected matter)
- provide a means for resolving disputes.

## Right to Pay under the Act

While an individual employee's contract of employment may make provision for paid maternity leave, an employer is otherwise not obliged to pay an employee during maternity leave, additional maternity leave, father's leave of any kind or after the first 21 days of health and safety leave (health and safety leave will be more fully explained later — suffice it to say at this point that an employee who is granted health and safety leave under this Act must be paid her usual wage/salary by her employer for the first 21 days of her leave). However, pregnant employees and employees who have recently given birth are entitled to time off work without loss of pay for ante-natal and post-natal medical visits. It should be noted that there is no maximum or minimum amount of time specified for these visits. The employee is entitled to as much time off as is necessary to attend each appointment/visit. This includes the time to travel to and from the appointment, as well as the time taken for the appointment itself.

Furthermore, a woman who takes maternity leave may be entitled to maternity benefit from the Department of Social, Community and Family Affairs, subject to her PRSI contributions. To qualify for maternity benefit, the employee must have:

- at least 39 weeks' PRSI paid in the 12 months prior to the first day of maternity leave, or

- 39 weeks' PRSI paid since the employee started working and also 39 weeks' PRSI paid or credited in the relevant income tax year.

(Note: 'the relevant tax year' means the last complete year (1 January to 31 December) prior to the year during which the maternity leave is taken. Thus, if the employee goes on maternity leave during 1998, 'the relevant leave year' is 1997.)

Maternity benefit is normally paid for a period of 14 weeks. This period may be extended in certain cases where there has been a late birth. The maximum amount of maternity benefit payable is 70 per cent of an employee's average weekly earnings in the relevant tax year. (There is, however, a minimum and maximum payment and, because these are subject to change, it is necessary to obtain up-to-date information from the Department of Social, Community and Family Affairs.) It is worth noting that maternity benefit is tax free and, in addition, the employee may be able to obtain a tax refund or tax credit.

## Maternity Leave Entitlement

A pregnant female employee is entitled to a minimum of 14 weeks' maternity leave. Of this, at least 4 weeks must be taken before the end of the week in which her baby is due to be born, and 4 weeks after that week. The remaining 6 weeks may be taken either before or after the birth and in whatever combinations best suit her, as long as they run consecutively.

## Requirements to be Met

In order to exercise her right to maternity leave, the employee is required to do the following:

1. Notify the employer in writing at least 4 weeks before she intends to take maternity leave (the notification may be given by the employee herself or by someone else on her behalf) the date on which the leave is due to commence.

2. At the same time as he or she is notified, the employer must be given, or have

produced for his or her inspection, a medical certificate confirming the employee's pregnancy and indicating the expected week of confinement.

## Revocation of Maternity Notification

If a woman has notified her employer that she intends to take maternity leave and then changes her mind, she may revoke the notification by sending a further written notice to the employer stating that she no longer wishes to take maternity leave from the date specified.

## Birth Earlier than Expected

If confinement is 4 weeks or more earlier than expected, and before the employee has taken maternity leave, her employer must be notified in writing within 14 days of the birth. The employee in this case is then entitled to 14 weeks' maternity leave, beginning on the date of the birth.

## Birth Later than Expected (Extended Leave)

If the late confinement results in the employee having less than 4 weeks' maternity leave remaining after the week in which the baby is born, she may extend her leave accordingly. The maximum extension is 4 weeks.

The employer must be notified in writing by the employee (or her representative) as soon as possible after such an extension appears likely. When an extension is certain to be required, the employee herself must:

- confirm to the employer in writing that she is extending her maternity leave, and
- indicate how long the extension will be.

This must be done as soon as possible after the confinement.

## Effect of Miscarriage

There is no entitlement to maternity leave under this Act where a miscarriage occurs up to and including the 24th week of pregnancy. Any confinement occurring after the 24th week, even if it does not result in a live birth, is covered by the Act.

## Additional Maternity Leave

An employee may choose to take up to 4 consecutive weeks' additional maternity leave immediately after normal maternity leave and can do so even where that has been extended (as above) for a late birth (there is no entitlement to social welfare maternity benefit during this period). To be entitled to take this leave, the employee must notify her employer of her intention to do so not later than 4 weeks before the end of the maternity leave period.

## Right to Time Off

An employee is entitled to such time off (both ante-natal and post-natal) as to enable her to keep appointments for medical examinations and tests, and without loss of pay.

An employee must give her employer written notice of taking time off at least two weeks beforehand (on each occasion) and, except for the first appointment, must produce her appointment document, if requested by the employer. In urgent cases, where it is not possible to comply with these requirements, the employee must explain, not later than one week after the appointment, why notification was not possible and provide evidence of having kept the appointment.

## Preservation of Rights during Leave

Employees availing of entitlements under this Act other than 'additional' leave or 'further' leave are held to be in the employ of the employer. Generally speaking, therefore, maternity leave is regarded as reckonable service. Employment rights — e.g. annual leave, increments, seniority — are preserved and continue to build up. Protective leave cannot be counted against any other leave entitlement, such as annual leave or sick leave. (Under the Maternity Protection Act, 1994, protective leave is defined as maternity leave, additional maternity leave, time off for ante-natal and post-natal medical visits, father's leave, and health and safety leave.)

An employee on 'additional' maternity leave, 'additional' father's leave or 'further' father's leave is not considered to be in work, and such an employee does not benefit from employment rights during this leave. Continuity of employment is not broken, but such leave is not counted as reckonable service.

Employees on maternity leave (or father's leave) are entitled to be credited for any public holiday that occurs during their leave. This also applies in circumstances where the employer continues to provide full pay to the employee who is on such leave. The employee is still entitled to the benefit of public holidays occurring during maternity leave (or father's leave). This means that the employer must give the employee either:

- an extra day's pay, or
- a paid day off within one month, or
- an extra day's annual holiday,

as the employer may decide, for every public holiday that occurs during their period of leave. Employees absent on health and safety leave do not have an entitlement to time off in lieu of public holidays that occur during such leave.

## Right to Return to Work

The Act imposes no obligation on the employee to return to work after protective leave. However, the Act preserves her right to do so if she wishes.

Where the employee wishes to exercise her right to return to work, she must comply with the notification procedure set down in the Act. A written notification of intention to return to work must be given at least four weeks before the due date of return. This notification must state the employee's return date and may be written by another person on the employee's behalf.

The employee is entitled to return not only to her employer, but to a new employer where there has been a change of ownership of the business. Furthermore, she is entitled to return to the same job, although if for good reason this is impracticable, she must be provided with suitable alternative employment. On her return to work, a probationer, trainee or apprentice must complete whatever period had not expired before taking maternity leave.

Strict compliance with the return-to-work notification procedure is essential. Failure to issue the required notification will deprive the employee of her statutory right to return to work. In certain exceptional circumstances a rights commissioner or employment appeals tribunal may extend the time limit for giving notice of return.

## Father's Leave Entitlement

If a woman (the mother) who has been delivered of a living child herself dies at any time during the fourteen weeks following the week of her confinement, the father of the child (providing he is employed under a contract of employment) is entitled to a period of leave from his employment.

If the mother's death occurs within ten weeks of the birth, the father will be entitled to leave up to the end of the ten weeks. This means that if the mother dies, say, four weeks after the week of confinement, the father is entitled to six weeks' leave (father's leave). If the mother dies at childbirth, the father is entitled to ten weeks' leave.

If the mother's death occurs after the tenth week but before the end of the fourteenth week following confinement, the father is also entitled to leave. In this case, the period of leave ends at the end of the fourteenth week. This means that if the mother dies eleven weeks after the week of confinement, the father is entitled to three weeks' leave (referred to as additional father's leave).

If the mother dies before the tenth week following confinement and the father commenced leave within this period, the father is entitled to take a further four weeks' leave, if he wishes to do so. (This is similar to a mother's 'additional maternity leave' — as previously described — and may be conveniently referred to as 'further' leave.)

The father must produce, within seven days, a copy of the death certificate of the mother and the birth certificate of the child, if requested to do so by his employer. Any leave to which the father is entitled must commence within seven days of the death of the mother.

Notice in writing of the father's intention to take leave must be given to the employer no later than the day the leave commences. If the father intends to take 'further' leave, he must notify his employer of this either at the time of taking leave or, if this is not possible, no later than four weeks before the end of father's leave proper.

## Health and Safety Leave

Health and safety leave may be provided to:

- pregnant employees
- employees who have recently given birth
- employees who are breast feeding.

Regulations under the Safety, Health and Welfare at Work Act, 1989 (S.I. 446 of 1994) require that an employer must assess the workplace for risks to pregnant workers, workers who have recently given birth or who are breast feeding. If a risk is established, the employer must put in place such measures as are necessary to remove the risk. If it is not possible for the employer to do this, the employee must be granted suitable alternative work. But if

- it is not technically or objectively feasible for the employer to move the employee, or
- such a move cannot reasonably be required on duly substantiated grounds, or
- the other work to which the employer proposes to move the employee is not suitable for her,

the employee must be granted leave from her employment.

Where an employee is granted health and safety leave, she is entitled to receive a certificate to this effect from her employer, if she so requests. The certificate must state the reason she has been granted health and safety leave, the date the leave commences and how long it is expected to last. This certificate may be required for presentation to the Department of Social, Community and Family Affairs to allow a claim for health and safety benefit to be made.

An employee who is granted health and safety leave must be paid her usual wage by her employer for the first twenty-one days of her leave. Where health and safety leave extends beyond this period, the employee may be entitled to benefit, subject to her PRSI contributions.

## Ending Health and Safety Leave

Health and Safety leave for pregnant employees ends:

- if the risk to health and safety no longer exists or is no longer an issue
- if suitable alternative work becomes available
- where maternity leave commences
- for women on fixed-term contracts, on the day the contract ends
- for a breast-feeding mother, if she ceases to breast-feed her child; if she has not ceased breast-feeding her child by the twenty-sixth week following the birth of her child, the health and safety leave ends after that week.

If an employee on health and safety leave ceases to be pregnant or ceases breast-feeding, she must give written notice to her employer immediately. On receipt of such notice, the employer must enable the employee to return to work as soon as possible. But, at the same time, the employer must be satisfied that it is safe for the employee to return to work. The employee must return to work within seven days from receiving a notice to return from her employer.

If the health risk is removed while the employee is on health and safety leave and she is notified of this, she must return to work within seven days of receiving the notification. Similarly, the employer is obliged to notify an employee on health and safety leave when suitable alternative work becomes available, whereupon the employee has seven days to return to work.

## Protection against Dismissal

An employee who is on protective leave cannot be dismissed, made redundant or suspended while on such leave. Notice of any kind of dismissal or redundancy cannot be given to an employee who is on protective leave. Similarly, an employee cannot be dismissed on grounds of pregnancy, for having recently given birth or for breast-feeding, and cannot be dismissed for exercising rights under the Maternity Protection Act, 1994.

## General Protection

A provision is void in any agreement or contract of employment which allows for less favourable entitlements than those provided by the Act. However, nothing in the Act prohibits any agreement from containing provisions more favourable to the employee than those set out in the Act.

## Dispute Settlement Procedure

An employee or employer can refer a dispute that relates to entitlements under this Act to a Rights Commissioner. There are, however, two important exceptions to this rule:

- disputes related to dismissal must be referred under the Unfair Dismissals Acts, 1977-94
- disputes related to health risks must be referred to the Health and Safety Authority.

A dispute must be referred to a Rights Commissioner in writing within six months of the issue arising. The details sent to a Rights Commissioner include the following:

- the name and address of the complainant
- the name and address of the respondent (other party)
- the details and facts of the issue in dispute
- the reason for the dispute.

When the Rights Commissioner receives notice of dispute, details will be sent by the Rights Commissioner to the respondent. The respondent must reply to the Rights Commissioner within 14 days if the dispute is contested. A private hearing is arranged for the resolution of the dispute. The Rights Commissioner will then reach a decision on the dispute.

Either party is entitled to appeal the decision of the Rights Commissioner to the Employment Appeals Tribunal, within four weeks of the Rights Commissioner's decision. The Tribunal will consider the case and issue its determination. Once again, either party may appeal from the determination of the tribunal to the High Court on a point of law.

A Rights Commissioner or the Employment Appeals Tribunal may award an employee leave for a specified period and/or compensation. If compensation is awarded, it must not exceed twenty weeks' remuneration.

## ADOPTIVE LEAVE

The Adoptive Leave Act, 1995, came into operation on 20 March 1995, and entitles female employees, and in certain circumstances male employees, to employment leave for the purpose of child adoption. It also extends to them the protection against unfair dismissal conferred by the Unfair Dismissals Acts, 1977-93.

The Act applies many of the provisions of maternity leave as it already exists for natural mothers to adoptive mothers and, in very limited circumstances, to adoptive fathers, who are employed under a contract of employment.

An employed adopting mother (or sole adopting father) is entitled to adoptive leave from her employment for a period of not less than ten consecutive weeks, during which time she will be entitled to an allowance from the Department of Social, Community and Family Affairs. If she so requests, an adopting mother is entitled to further leave, referred to in the Act as 'additional leave', for a maximum period of four weeks.

All employment rights of the adopting mother, except those relating to remuneration, are preserved during the period of leave, and any notice of termination of employment given during the period of leave is void.

The adopting mother has the right to return to her job on terms and conditions not less favourable than those pertaining before she took adoptive leave. Where this is not possible, she must be offered suitable alternative employment under terms and conditions not substantially less favourable to her.

A dismissal on grounds of taking, or contemplating taking, adoptive leave will be adjudged automatically unfair even where the employee does not have the requisite one years' service with her employer.

## Notification Requirements

The employee must give her employer written notice of her intention to take adoptive leave as soon as is reasonably practicable, but not later than four weeks before the expected placement of the child. Where an adopting mother intends to seek additional adoptive leave, she must inform her employer, in writing, at least four weeks beforehand. Similarly, an employee must inform her employer, in writing, at least four weeks beforehand, of the date on which she intends to return to work after adoptive leave or additional adoptive leave. However, a Rights Commissioner, or the Employment Appeals Tribunal, can extend that time period where there are 'reasonable grounds'. Failure to give the requisite notice will be a matter to be taken into account 'in determining the adoptive parent's rights under the Unfair Dismissals Acts, the Adoptive Leave Act or any other enactment'.

## Evidence of Placement of Child

In the case of Irish adoptions, an eligible employee who has commenced adoptive leave must furnish her employer with a certificate of placement. The certificate must be furnished as soon as is reasonably practicable, but no later than four weeks after the day of placement of the child. The certificate may be obtained by the employee from the appropriate Health Board or the adoption society which arranged the placement. An Bord Uchtála will issue the certificate of placement in other Irish placement cases.

In the case of foreign adoptions, an eligible employee must give her employer a copy of the declaration of eligibility and suitability (issued under the Adoption Act, 1991) before the commencement of the adoptive leave or additional adoptive leave (whichever is the earlier). Particulars of the placement must be furnished as soon as is reasonably practicable thereafter.

## Qualifying Male Adopters

The Adoptive Leave Act, 1995 allows an adopting father to take leave where the adopting mother has died either before or during her period of leave. The Act also makes provision for a man who is adopting alone (known as a sole male adopter) to be treated in the same way as an adopting mother.

## Foreign Adoptions

In the case of foreign adoptions, the Act allows some or all of the additional leave to which an employee is entitled to be taken before the date of the placement for the purposes of familiarisation with the child. If the placement does not take place, some of the additional leave having already been taken, the employee must return to work at the latest on the date that the notified period of that additional leave expires, and must notify the employer of the intended date of return as soon as is reasonably practicable.

## Right of Redress

Any dispute under the Act, other than one relating to unfair dismissal, redundancy or minimum notice rights, may be referred to a Rights Commissioner, who will hear the parties and deliver a decision. This may be appealed to the Employment Appeals Tribunal. The Employment Appeals Tribunal will then issue its determination. From there an appeal may be made to the High Court on a point of law only.

A decision or determination will give directions to the parties for the resolution of the dispute and may include an award of compensation to the employee, not exceeding 20 weeks' remuneration. The decision or determination can be enforced by the Circuit Court.

A reference to a Rights Commissioner must be made in writing within six months of the date of placement or, where no placement occurs, within six months of the date on which the employer first receives written notification of the employee's intention to take adoptive leave or, where an adoptive mother has died, within six months of the date of death.

Where the Rights Commissioner is satisfied that 'exceptional circumstances' prevented the giving of the notice within six months, the notice period may be extended to twelve months.

## REDUNDANCY

A considerable body of legislation deals with redundancy. The principal Act is the Redundancy Payments Act, 1967, but this was amended by Acts of the same title in 1971, 1973, 1979 and by the Protection of Employees (Employers Insolvency) Act, 1984. Futher amendments occurred in 1990 and 1991. These Acts may be collectively referred to as the Redundancy Payments Acts, 1967-91.

### Redundancy Defined
An employee is regarded as dismissed by reasons of redundancy

- where the employer has ceased to do the business that the employee was employed for, or
- where the employer has ceased to do the business in the particular place, or
- where the requirements of the business have changed, or
- where the business requires fewer employees, or
- where the work now requires someone with different qualifications.

### Establishing Eligibility
In order to establish eligibility for redundancy payment under the Acts, employees must meet the following requirements:

- be aged between 16 years and 66 years at the time of the redundancy
- have 104 weeks' continuous service
- be normally expected to work at least 8 hours per week for the same employer
- be in employment which is insurable under the Social Welfare Acts.

### Benefit Entitlement
The benefit to which an employee is entitled on being made redundant is a lump sum payment and is calculated on the basis of:

- length of service
- amount of earnings
- age.

The lump sum is computed as follows:

- one week's normal pay

  *plus*

- half-a-week's pay for each year of continuous employment between the ages of 16 and 41 years

  *plus*

- one full week's pay for each year of continuous employment worked from age 41 to the date of dismissal (subject to the maximum age of 66).

The lump sum calculations are regulated from time to time by the Minister for Finance. At present, the maximum amount allowable for calculating the lump sum payment is £15,600 per year or £300 per week.

Individual employees or their trade union representatives are free, through the bargaining process, to seek payments in excess of those provided for under the relevant statutes.

An employee may lose the right to redundancy payment if, in the two weeks before the day of dismissal, the employer offers him/her a new contract on the same terms or on suitable alternative terms.

## Effect of Non-Payment of Benefit by Employer

Irrespective of the capacity of the employer to pay redundancy benefit, the employee will be paid his entitlements. Where the employee has taken all reasonable steps (other than legal proceedings) to obtain his/her lump sum from the employer, he/she will be paid out of the redundancy fund. The Minister for Enterprise, Trade and Employment then assumes the rights and remedies to pursue the employer, or his/her estate if he/she is deceased.

## Rebate for Employers (Form RP3)

The employer is normally entitled to recover 60 per cent of statutory redundancy payments from the redundancy fund, which was set up under the Redundancy Payments Act, 1967. The employer's 60 per cent refund may be reduced to 40 per cent if the employer fails to give the employee at least two weeks' notice in writing of his or her intention to dismiss him for reasons of redundancy. A copy of the notice must also be sent to the Minister for Enterprise, Trade and Employment. Applications for rebate must be made within 6 months of the date on which redundancy payment is made to the employee.

## Time Off to Look for Work

An employee who is being made redundant is entitled to reasonable time off during working hours (on full pay) for the purpose of securing new employment or training. An employee may be entitled to compensation where the employer unreasonably refuses time off.

## Statutory Procedures

In addition to at least two weeks' notice in writing (Form RP1) which the employer must give the employee and the Minister for Enterprise, Trade and Employment, the employer must also give the employee a Redundancy Certificate (Form RP2). Otherwise, his or her statutory duty is not necessarily discharged.

A longer period of notice may be required under the Minimum Notice and Terms of Employment Acts, 1973-91 and by the contract of employment.

As soon as the redundancy dismissal takes place, the employer must pay the lump sum due.

It is important to note that different notification requirements to those above must be fulfilled when a collective redundancy within the meaning of the Protection of Employment Act, 1977 is proposed.

## Dispute Settlement Procedures

Disputes arising under the Redundancy Payment Acts may be referred to the Employment Appeals Tribunal and from there may be appealed to the High Court on a point of law only.

## COLLECTIVE REDUNDANCIES

Special provisions apply in cases where an employer dismisses by reason of redundancy not one worker but a number. These provisions are contained in the Protection of Employment Act, 1977.

The Act applies to persons in an establishment employing more than 20 people (including those not entitled to redundancy benefits) but with the following exceptions:

- Employees under a contract for a fixed term or specified purpose, except where the collective redundancies take place before the completion of the term or purpose.
- Employees of the state, other than industrial grades.
- Local authority officers.
- Seamen signing on under the Merchant Shipping Act, 1894.
- Employees in an establishment where employment ceases because of bankruptcy or winding-up procedures, or for any other reason as a result of a court decision.
- Such classes of employees as may be identified by the Minister for Enterprise and Employment at his or her discretion.

## Collective Redundancy Defined

In order to be regarded as a 'collective redundancy', a minimum number of employees must be subjected to dismissal for one or more reasons not related to the individual workers concerned. The number varies with the size of the workforce. The Act defines a 'collective redundancy' as the dismissal for redundancy reasons over any period of 30 consecutive days of at least:

- five persons in an establishment normally employing more than 20 and less than 50 employees
- ten persons in an establishment normally employing at least 50 but less than 100 employees
- ten per cent of the number of employees in an establishment normally employing at least 100 but less than 300 employees
- thirty persons in an establishment normally employing 300 or more employees.

*NOTES:*
*1. Where an employer operates his/her business in more than one location, each location is treated separately.*
*2. The number of persons 'normally' employed in an establishment is taken to be the average of the number employed in each of the twelve months preceding the date on which the first dismissal takes effect.*

## Obligations Imposed on the Employer

The employer must consult with the representatives (usually, a trade union) of the employees at least 30 days before the first dismissal takes effect. In particular, these consultations must include discussion of the possibility of avoiding the proposed redundancies or at least of reducing their number or consequences. An explanation of the basis for selecting particular employees for redundancy must also be given. A second requirement of the Act is that the Minister for Enterprise, Trade and Employment must be notified of the proposed redundancies in writing, again not less than 30 days before the first dismissal takes effect. The formal notification to the Minister, a copy of which must also be sent to the employees' representatives, must include the following information:

- The name and address of the employer and an indication of whether he or she is a sole trader, a partnership or a company.

- The address of the establishment where the collective redundancies are proposed.

- The number of persons normally employed at that establishment.

- The number and descriptions or categories of the employees it is proposed to make redundant.

- The period during which the collective redundancies are proposed to be effective, i.e. the starting dates on which the first and final dismissals are expected to take effect.

- The reasons for the proposed collective redundancies.

- The names and addresses of the trade unions and/or staff associations representing employees affected by the proposed redundancies and with which it has been the practice of the employer to conduct collective bargaining negotiations.

- The date on which consultations with each trade union and/or staff association commenced and the progress achieved in these consultations to the date of the notification.

*N.B. The proposed collective redundancies must not begin to take effect before the expiry of a period of thirty days, beginning on the date of the notification to the Minister.*

## Further Provisions

The Act does not affect the individual rights of employees, to which they may be entitled either under statutes or under their contract of employment.

Authorised officers, appointed by the Minister for Enterprise, Trade and Employment, have powers of inspection and investigation for the purpose of ensuring compliance with the requirements of the Act. To show that the Act is being complied with, employers are required to retain all relevant and necessary records for at least three years.

## Offences under the Act

Offences are committed where an employer fails:

- to consult the employees' representatives
- to delay redundancies for 30 days following notice to the Minister
- to permit authorised inspection and investigation
- to keep the required records.

## Cannot Contract Out of Act

Any provision in a contract of employment or other agreement which purports to exclude or limit the operation of any provision of the Protection of Employment Act, 1977 will be null and void.

## Proceedings and Penalties

Proceedings may be taken by the Minister for Enterprise, Trade and Employment. On conviction on indictment by the courts, the maximum fine for failing to delay collective redundancies is £3,000; for each of the other offences, the maximum fine is £500.

## PAYMENT OF WAGES

The Payment of Wages Act, 1991 came into operation on 1 January 1991 and repealed the Truck Acts, 1743-1896 and the Payment of Wages Act, 1979. The Truck Acts required that manual workers should be paid in 'ready money' or in 'current coin of the realm', and limited the circumstances in which deductions from wages could be made. Their purpose was to eliminate abuses in the payment of wages to manual workers, such as payment in kind instead of 'ready money'. However, in recent times, the provisions of the Truck Acts became an obstacle to modern methods of paying wages.

Under the provisions of the Payment of Wages Act, 1991, all employees are entitled to a range of rights in connection with the payment of wages. These are:

- a right to the payment of wages in a form set down in the Act
- an entitlement to a written statement of wages and any authorised deductions
- protection from unlawful deductions from wages.

These rights extend to any person working under a contract of employment or apprenticeship, employed through an employment agency or subcontractor, or in the service of the state (including members of the Garda Síochána and the Defence Forces, civil servants, employees of any local authority, health board, harbour authority or VEC). These rights may be examined individually.

1. **Form or method of paying wages**

   The Act identifies a wide range of legally acceptable methods of paying wages of which the following are examples: cheque, cash, bank draft, postal order, money order, payable order warrant and credit transfer. The Act also permits the Minister for Enterprise, Trade and Employment, in consultation with the Minister for Finance, to add by regulation any other mode of payment not already provided for in the Act.

   For the purposes of the Act, the following are regarded as wages: basic pay (including overtime); any fee, bonus or commission; holiday pay, sick pay, maternity pay; shift payments; pay in lieu of notice. The following, however, are not regarded as wages: any payment in respect of expenses incurred by the employee in carrying out his or her employment; any payment by way of a pension, allowance or gratuity in connection with the death, retirement or resignation of the employee or as compensation for loss of office; any payment referable to the employee's redundancy; any payment to the employee otherwise than in his/her capacity as an employee; any payment in kind or benefit in kind.

2. **Statement of wages**

   Employers must provide a written statement of wages for every employee and, except in the case of a payment by credit transfer, the statement must accompany the payment. Where wages are paid by credit transfer, the statement of wages must be given to the employee as soon as possible after the credit transfer has taken place. The Act requires the statement to specify clearly the gross amount of the wages payable to the employee and the nature and amount of any deduction. Furthermore, there is a statutory obligation on the employer to take such reasonable steps as are necessary to ensure that the wages statement and the information contained in it are treated with confidentiality by the employer, his/her agents and by any other employees. Where a wages statement contains an error or omission, it will not, for those reasons, be invalid if it is shown that the error or omission was made by way of a clerical mistake or was otherwise made accidentally and in good faith.

3. **Deductions from wages**

The most extensive section in the Act is that dealing with deductions from wages. The following deductions may be made by an employer:

- any deduction authorised by law (e.g. PAYE and PRSI)
- any deduction authorised by a term of the employee's contract (e.g. an Occupational Pensions Scheme contribution)
- any deduction agreed in writing in advance by the employee (e.g. VHI premium)

Where deductions from wages (a) arise from any act or omission of the employee (e.g. breakages, money shortages, bad workmanship) or (b) relate to the supply by the employer to the employee of any goods or services which are necessary to the employment (e.g. the provision of a uniform), the following conditions must be satisfied:

- The deduction must be provided for in a term (whether express or implied and if express, whether oral or in writing) of the contract of employment.
- The deduction is of an amount that is fair and reasonable, having regard to all the circumstances, including the amount of the wages of the employee.
- The employee must be given at some time prior to the act or omission or the supply of the goods or services, written details of the terms in the contract of employment governing the deduction from wages. Where a written contract exists, a copy of the term of the contract which provides for the deduction must be given to the employee. In any other case, the employee must be given written notice of the existence and effect of the term.
- The employee must be furnished with particulars in writing of the act or omission, and the amount of the deduction, at least one week before the deduction is made.
- Where a deduction is made in respect of compensation for loss or damage

sustained by the employer as a result of an act or omission of the employee, the deduction must be of an amount not exceeding the loss or damage sustained by the employer.

- Any deduction from wages must be made no later than six months after the act or omission became known to the employer. Where a series of deductions are to be made in respect of a particular act or omission, the first deduction in the series must be made within the six-month period. This condition also applies to any deduction from wages for the supply to an employee of goods or services which are necessary to the employment — the deduction must not exceed the cost to the employer of providing the goods or services.

*Note: While reference is made exclusively in the foregoing to 'deductions from wages', it is, nevertheless, important to note that the same conditions (as outlined above) apply in circumstances where an employee makes 'direct payment' to an employer in respect of any act or omission of the employee or for the supply by the employer to the employee of any goods or services necessary to the employment. It is also important that, where an employer accepts such a payment, he/she is satisfied that the payment is lawful. Upon acceptance of the payment, the employer must immediately issue a receipt for it to the employee.*

Non-payment of wages or any deficiency in the amount of wages properly payable is regarded as an unlawful deduction from wages unless the deficiency or non-payment is attributable to an error in computation.

## Complaints Procedure

An employee who alleges that an employer made an unlawful deduction from his/her wages may make a complaint to a Rights Commissioner. The complaint must be made within six months of the date of the deduction. This period may be extended for up to a further six months. After hearing the parties, the Commissioner will give a decision in writing and advise both parties of the outcome. Where the complaint is upheld, the Rights Commissioner will order the employer to pay compensation to the employee. The maximum compensation which the Rights Commissioner can award is:

(a) the net wage, after all lawful deductions that would have been paid to the employee in respect of the week immediately preceding the unlawful deduction (or, if the complaint by the employee related to a payment made by him/her, the net wages that were paid to the employee in respect of the week immediately preceding the date of the payment), or

(b) if the amount of the deduction or payment is greater than the wage referred to at (a), twice the amount of the deduction.

Proceedings under this Act before a Rights Commissioner are conducted in public unless the Rights Commissioner, at the request of one of the parties, decides otherwise.

An appeal from a decision of a Rights Commissioner may be made by an employer or employee to the Employment Appeals Tribunal within six weeks of the date of the decision.

A further appeal from a determination of the Tribunal may be made to the High Court on a point of law and the decision of the High Court is final and conclusive.

Finally, any provision in an agreement (whether it is a contract of employment or not) that purports to preclude or limit the application of any provision in the Payment of Wages Act, 1991 will be void. However, it is important to note that certain deductions (and payments) are outside the complaints procedure.

These are:

- **Statutory Deductions** — These are deductions from wages imposed on an employer by any statutory provision or order of a court (examples of which would be PAYE, PRSI, or an Attachment of Earnings Order). This category of deduction is outside the scope of the complaints procedure, providing it is made in accordance with the relevant statutory authority.

- **Deductions Paid Over to a Third Party** — These are deductions from wages which the employer pays over to a third party on the employee's behalf (e.g. VHI subscriptions, trade union subscriptions, contributions to a savings plan or scheme). This type of deduction is excluded from the complaints procedure so long as the employer pays the correct amount to the third party by the appropriate date.

- **Deductions (or payments) to Recoup Overpayments** — These deductions are to reimburse the employer for any overpayment of wages or expenses but are excluded from the complaints procedure only if the amount of the deduction (or payment) does not exceed the amount of the overpayment.

- **Deductions (or payments) arising from Industrial Action**
- **Deductions relating to Statutory Disciplinary Proceedings**
- **Deductions (or payments) resulting from Court Orders**

Authorised officers appointed by the Minister for Enterprise, Trade and Employment have the power to enter premises, inspect documents and take copies or abstracts from them, and to question any person. Impeding or obstructing an authorised officer in the performance of his or her duty is an offence which, on summary conviction, carries a fine not exceeding £1,000.

## EQUAL PAY

The right to equal pay is firmly enshrined in the Anti-Discrimination (Pay) Act, 1974, which provides that 'It shall be a term of the contract under which a woman is employed in any place that she shall be entitled to the same rate of remuneration as a man who is employed in that place by the same employer if both are employed on like work.' The aim of this Act, therefore, is to ensure equality of treatment between men and women in relation to remuneration. This is achieved first by establishing the right of a woman to equal pay for 'like work' and, secondly, by providing the means by which such a right can be enforced.

It is clear from the content of the Act that, where there is no physical contract of employment or there is a contract, but no express reference in it to the right to equal pay for 'like work', such a term is implied automatically into the contract to establish the right.

While undoubtedly the principal object of the Act was to provide equality of treatment for women in regard to pay, it also applies to men where there is discrimination based on sex.

## Defining 'Like Work'

Under the Act, a man and woman are regarded as being employed in 'like work' in the following circumstances:

(a) Where both perform the same work under the same or similar conditions, or where each is in every respect interchangeable with the other in relation to work, or

(b) Where the work performed by one is of a similar nature to that performed by the other, and any differences between the work performed or the conditions under which it is performed by each occur only infrequently or are of small importance in relation to the work as a whole, or

(c) Where the work performed by one is equal in value to that performed by the other, in terms of the demands it makes in relation to such matters as skill, physical or mental effort, responsibility and working conditions.

It seems clear from these provisions that while (a) and (b) are reasonably straightforward, compliance with (c) is very complex indeed. The Act does not detail how work of equal value is to be determined.

## Establishing the Right to Equal Pay

In order to secure the right to equal pay with a man who allegedly is doing a comparable job, a woman must establish the following:

- that both are employed under a contract of service or apprenticeship or a contract personally to execute any work or labour

- that both are employed by the same employer or any associated employer (in comparisons involving associated employers, the employees must have common terms and conditions of employment)

- that both work in a place located in the same city, town or locality

- that both are employed on like work.

It is important to stress that the Act does not prevent the payment of different rates of remuneration, provided that such differentiation is not based on the sex of the employee. For example, rates of pay based on qualifications, length of service and experience are permissible. Remuneration is defined in the Act as any consideration, whether in cash or in kind, which an employee receives either directly or indirectly from the employer. This means that bonuses, holiday pay, sick pay and suchlike must all be paid on the basis of equality between the sexes.

## Pursuing a Claim for Equal Pay

When a dispute arises about the right to equal pay, a woman may refer the matter to an equality officer of the Labour Relations Commission for investigation or, alternatively, her trade union may act on her behalf. Similarly, the dispute may be referred to the equality officer by the employer or the employer organisation to which he or she belongs. The Employment Equality Agency, established under the Employment Equality Act, 1977, is empowered to refer a case to an equality officer for investigation where it appears that an employer has failed to comply with the Act and where it is not reasonable to expect the employee to refer the case. An investigation is conducted in private, although for the purposes of carrying it out, the equality officer has the power to enter the premises, examine records and seek information.

## Making an Appeal

It is open to both the employee and the employer to appeal against what they consider to be an unsatisfactory outcome from the recommendation of the equality officer. Such an appeal must be made to the Labour Court not later than 42 days from the date of the equality officer's recommendation. Appeals are heard in private unless either party requests otherwise. An appeal against a Labour Court decision may be made to the High Court on a point of law by either party.

If a determination of the Labour Court has not been implemented by the employer, the employee may complain again to the Labour Court, whereupon, after due consideration, the Labour Court may direct, by order, the employer to implement the determination. An employer who fails to carry out such an order within two months is guilty of an offence.

## Dismissal Arising from an Equal Pay Claim

It is an offence for an employer to dismiss an employee solely or mainly because a claim for equal pay was made. Where such dismissal arises, proceedings may be taken either in a court of law or through the Labour Court. If proceedings are taken in a court of law, the option of going to the Labour Court is no longer open.

In a court of law, the onus is on the employer to prove that the claim for equal pay was not the reason for the dismissal. In addition to imposing a substantial fine, the court may direct the employer to pay compensation and may order the reinstatement or re-engagement of the employee.

The complaint must be lodged with the Labour Court within six months of the date of dismissal, but it is possible to have this limit extended where reasonable grounds exist.

It is an offence to fail to pay compensation for dismissal arising from an equal pay claim.

## EMPLOYMENT EQUALITY

The Employment Equality Act, 1977 makes it unlawful for an employer to discriminate on the grounds of sex or marital status, whether such discrimination is direct or indirect. While the main thrust of the Act is directed at eliminating discrimination by employers, it is also concerned with activities related to the employment (e.g. in the provision of training, the services of employment agencies) and the advertising of jobs. Admissions to trade unions and professional organisations and associations are also covered.

While most emphasis is usually placed upon eliminating discrimination against female employees, it should be stressed that the Act applies equally to men and women. Certain categories of person, however, are excluded. These are:

- members of the prison service, the Garda Síochána and the Defence Forces
- persons employed in a private residence
- persons employed by a close relative
- persons whose sex is a genuine occupational qualification, e.g. a model or an actor.

The Act provides that where a woman's contract does not include an equality clause (a term of the contract that entitles a woman whose work is materially the same as a man's to be treated as favourably as a man, where both are employed by the same employer), it will be deemed to include one. However, this rule will not apply where the employer can show that any difference in the woman's contract is genuinely due to reasons other than her sex or marital status.

The Act declares as discriminatory the dismissal (or any other act of victimisation by way of retaliation) of an employee who took any action in pursuit of rights under this Act, or the Anti-Discrimination (Pay) Act, 1974.

## Enforcement Procedures

The Employment Equality Act gives an aggrieved individual direct access to the Labour Court or, alternatively, a trade union may act on the employee's behalf. While the case normally must be referred to the Labour Court within six months of the act of discrimination, this time limit may be extended where reasonable cause is shown. The Labour Court will endeavour to resolve the dispute through one of its industrial relations officers. If efforts at conciliation fail, the Labour Court will refer the case to an equaliy officer for determination.

Either the employer or the employee may appeal to the Labour Court against an equality officer's recommendation. The appeal must be lodged in the Labour Court not later than 42 days from the date of the equality officer's recommendation.

A further appeal is permitted from the Labour Court, on a point of law or in respect of the assessment of damages, to the Circuit Court or High Court.

## Remedies

In reaching a determination on the matter in dispute, the Labour Court may:

- state that unlawful discrimination did or did not take place
- recommend a specific course of action to be taken
- award compensation to the complainant.

In arriving at the amount of compensation payable, the Labour Court will make an award based on what it considers reasonable, having regard to all the circumstances of the case, but subject to a maximum of 104 weeks' pay. Where an employer fails to implement a determination of the Labour Court, the employee may complain again to the Court. If the Court is satisfied that the determination has not been carried out, it may direct its implementation by order.

## Penalties

An employer who fails to carry out an order of the Labour Court is guilty of an offence and is liable on conviction in a court of law to a fine for each day the offence is allowed to continue.

In addition to a fine for failing to comply with an order of the Labour Court, a court of law, at its discretion, may award damages for loss of remuneration to the person who suffered the unlawful discrimination.

## Employment Equality Agency

The Employment Equality Agency was set up under the Employment Equality Act, 1977. Broadly speaking, its main functions can be summarised as follows:

- To work towards the elimination of discrimination in regard to employment.
- To promote equality of opportunity between men and women generally.
- To keep under review the operation of the Employment Equality Act, 1977, the Anti-Discrimination (Pay) Act, 1974, and such other protective legislation as the agency or the Minister for Enterprise, Trade and Employment considers appropriate.

To assist in fulfilling its functions, the Agency may conduct or sponsor research and may draft and publish information aimed at eliminating discrimination between men and women in employment.

The Agency consists of a chairman and ten ordinary members appointed by the Minister for Enterprise, Trade and Employment. Two of the ordinary members are workers' members, two are employers' members; of the remaining six, three are representatives of women's organisations.

The Agency has the power to carry out formal investigations into any matter in relation to employment. Where such investigations reveal conduct that violates either the Employment Equality Act or the Anti-Discrimination (Pay) Act, it will have authority to issue what is known as a 'non-discrimination notice' (see below).

The Agency is empowered to obtain a High Court injunction where necessary to combat persistent discrimination and to enforce a non-discrimination notice. It may do this at any time within five years from the date on which a non-discrimination notice becomes operative.

## Non-Discrimination Notices

The purpose of a non-discrimination notice is to bring to an end a discriminatory practice before a penalty may be incurred. Even before serving a non-discrimination notice, the Employment Equality Agency must notify the person concerned in writing of its intention to do so and must specify the reasons for it. It must allow 28 days for the recipient to respond and then take into account any representations made.

Where the Agency is satisfied that there has been a contravention of the Employment Equality Act, 1977, and/or the Anti-Discrimination (Pay) Act, 1974, it may proceed to serve the non-discrimination notice. The recipient may appeal to the Labour Court within 42 days against any requirement of the notice. The Labour Court may uphold the appeal and quash the notice, may vary the requirements of the notice, or may confirm the notice without amendment of any kind.

A non-discrimination notice becomes binding when an appeal against it has failed or when the time for lodging an appeal expires without an appeal being made.

## Penalties

A person who fails to comply with a notice requiring the production of information or to attend as a witness and give evidence at a formal investigation commits an offence punishable on summary conviction to a fine of up to £100, or £1,000 if convicted on indictment.

The penalty for the concealment or destruction of relevant documents or for deliberately making a false statement is a fine of up to £100 on summary conviction.

## SEXUAL HARASSMENT

As long ago as 1985, the Labour Court interpreted the Employment Equality Act, 1977 in such a way as to ensure that many successful cases were taken by victims of sexual harassment. The Labour Court stated 'freedom from sexual harassment is a condition of work which an employee of either sex is entitled to expect. The Court will

accordingly treat any denial of that freedom as discrimination within th
terms of the Employment Equality Act, 1977.'

It is very widely agreed that the term 'sexual harassment' is difficult t
define. Speaking at a seminar in Dublin in May 1993, the then Ministe
for Equality and Law Reform stated, 'there is no universally accepted defi
nition of sexual harassment and there are different views about where th
boundaries lie. What one person regards as sexual harassment may not
therefore, be considered harassment by another. Similarly an individua
may tolerate or even welcome comments or actions from one person, bu
resent to the point of complaining about the same comments or action
from somebody else. Further complicating the situation is the fact tha
men and women have a very different perspective on the issue of sexua
harassment. This gender division makes it even more difficult to arrive at a
generally acceptable definition of the term "sexual harassment". This brie
quotation  succinctly identifies the enormity of the difficulty of arriving a
an acceptable and satisfactory definition.

In both the Resolution of the Council of Ministers (29 May 1990) an
the European Commission Code of Practice, sexual harassment is define
as 'unwanted conduct of a sexual nature or other conduct based on se
affecting the dignity of men and women at work'. The Employmen
Equality Agency defines it as 'behaviour which includes unreciprocate
and unwelcome comments; looks; jokes; suggestions or physical contac
which might threaten a person's job security or create a stressful or intimi
dating working environment'.

In the absence of a specific Act of the Oireachtas aimed at sexual harass
ment, the main avenue for victims remains a complaint within the provi
sions of the Employment Equality Act, 1977. However, in Septembe
1994, the government introduced a code of practice entitled 'Measures t
Protect the Dignity of Women and Men at Work'. Its provisions are no
legally binding, although at the time of its publication the then Ministe
for Equality and Law Reform expressed the hope that it would receiv
statutory recognition in forthcoming employment equality legislation. S
far, this has not happened.

The aims of the code are stated to be:

- to provide guidance towards creating a work environment free of sexual harassment

- to provide a framework for dealing effectively with complaints of sexual harassment when they arise.

The code identifies examples of some forms of sexual harassment and categorises them as follows:

(i) non-verbal/visual sexual harassment
- sexually suggestive or pornographic pictures and calendars
- leering, offensive gestures and whistling.

(ii) verbal sexual harassment
- unwelcome sexual advances
- unwelcome pressure for social contact
- sexually suggestive jokes, remarks or innuendo.

(iii) physical sexual harassment
- unwelcome physical contact, such as groping, pinching, patting or unnecessary touching.
- unwelcome fondling and/or kissing
- sexual assault or rape.

Sexual harassment may create an intimidating, hostile or humiliating environment for an employee and may occur outside the workplace, e.g. in a hotel, a person's home, a car, or on the street. The degree of control available to the employer in the particular circumstances is a relevant factor. It is also important for an employer to be aware that the perpetrator of sexual harassment need not necessarily be senior to the victim but may be at the same level, a junior colleague or even a non-employee — a client, a customer or supplier. While the sexual harassment of women by men is the focus of most attention, sexual harassment of men by women or same sex harassment may also occur.

Sexual harassment in employment may contravene the Employment Equality Act, 1977, if it is unwelcome and offensive to the victim and the perpetrator knew or ought reasonably to have known that the conduct complained of was unwelcome and offensive to the victim. An employer may, in certain circumstances, be liable for such conduct. Employers have a duty to seek to ensure that the working environment is free of sexual harassment. Therefore, in sex discrimination cases alleging sexual harassment, the case is brought against the employer and not the perpetrator-employee.

The code of practice exhorts employers to develop strategies aimed at prevention. Employers should be aware, too, that the Labour Court may take into account, when assessing an employer's liability for discrimination, the fact that an employer has implemented a code of practice to counteract sexual harassment in the workplace. Furthermore, it is important for employers to keep in mind that determining whether sexual harassment is unlawful in particular circumstances is a matter, not for employers, but for the courts.

## SAFETY, HEALTH AND WELFARE AT WORK

The requirements of the Safety, Health and Welfare at Work Act, 1989 (referred to at page 83) have been extended by the Safety, Health and Welfare at Work (General Application) Regulations, 1993. These regulations, which came into operation on 22 February 1993, implement Council Directive 89/391/EEC of 12 June 1989 on the introduction of measures to encourage improvements in the health and safety of workers at the workplace. The regulations also implement five related directives which set down minimum requirements for health and safety in specific aspects of working activities:

1. Council Directive 89/654/EEC of 30 November 1989, on minimum health and safety requirements for the workplace.

2. Council Directive 89/655/EEC of 30 November 1989, on minimum health and safety requirements for the use of work equipment by workers at work.

3. Council Directive 89/656/EEC of 30 November 1989, on minimum health and safety requirements for the use by workers of personal protective equipment.

4. Council Directive 90/269/EEC of 12 May 1990, on minimum health and safety requirements for the manual handling of loads where there is a risk, particularly of back injury, to workers.

5. Council Directive 90/270/EEC of 29 May 1990, on minimum health and safety requirements for work with display screen equipment.

*Note: Also implemented by these regulations is Council Directive 91/383/EEC of 25 June 1991, on measures to improve safety and health at work of workers with a fixed duration or temporary employment relationship.*

The Safety, Health and Welfare at Work (General Application) Regulations, 1993 also revise and update existing legal requirements concerning the safe use of electricity in the workplace, the provision of first-aid facilities and the procedures governing the notification of accidents and dangerous occurrences to the National Authority for Occupational Safety and Health.

The regulations impose general and specific obligations on employers with regard to the evaluation and reduction of the exposure of employees to occupational risk and hazards, the development of risk prevention policies, consultation, training and information of workers and health surveillance.

While it is not possible here to examine in detail the provisions of these regulations, there are some aspects worthy of mention. Under the regulations, it is the duty of every employer to ensure that any measures taken by him or her which are related to safety, health and welfare at work do not involve financial cost to an employee. Furthermore, where personal protective equipment is required to be provided by the regulations, this must be supplied by the employer free of charge where the equipment is exclusively for use at the place of work. However, where the equipment is not used exclusively at the place of work, an employer may request the employee concerned to contribute towards the cost of such equipment, the contribution being in proportion to the cost to the employer resulting from its use outside the place of work.

Every employer has an obligation to designate one or more employees to carry out activities specified by him or her which are related to the protection from and the prevention of occupational risk at the place of work and to ensure that any such employee is not placed at any disadvantage in relation to his or her employment.

Finally, and most importantly, these regulations apply, of course, to an employer, but they also apply to a self-employed person as if that self-employed person was an employer and his or her own employee.

## PART-TIME WORKERS

Part-time workers, a hitherto largely unprotected section of the Irish workforce, received a major enhancement to the legislative protection afforded them in employment with the enactment of the Worker Protection (Regular Part-time Employees) Act, 1991. The purpose of this Act is to extend to part-time workers who satisfy certain criteria the scope of a range of protective legislation.

The individual statutes whose provisions now extend to part-time employees were activated on different dates:

- the Unfair Dismissals Act, 1977
- the Minimum Notice and Terms of Employment Acts, 1973 and 1984
- the Worker Participation (State Enterprises) Acts, 1977 and 1988

were all extended fully to regular part-time employees on 6 April 1991;

- the Redundancy Payments Acts, 1967-90
- the Protection of Employees (Employers' Insolvency) Acts, 1984 and 1990

have effect and fully apply to regular part-time employees from 17 June 1991.

Broadly speaking, therefore, it can be seen that the intention of the Act is to extend to regular part-time employees legal rights to minimum notice, redress for unfair dismissal, worker participation (where appropriate), and redundancy and employer insolvency protection.

### Regular Part-Time Employee Defined

A regular part-time employee is defined for the purposes of the Worker Protection (Regular Part-time Employees) Act, 1991, as one who has been

- in the continuous service of his/her employer for at least thirteen weeks
- is normally expected to work at least eight hours a week
- does not already come within the provisions of the various Acts mentioned above which this Act amends.

It should be appreciated that continuous service is defined in accordance with the provisions of the Minimum Notice and Terms of Employment Acts (for which refer to page 206).

### Effect of Act on Rights to Notice and Terms

Provided the part-time employee has completed thirteen weeks' continuous service and is expected to work at least eight hours a week, he/she is entitled to the periods of notice and a statement of terms and conditions of employment provided for in the Minimum Notice and Terms of Employment Acts, 1973-91 and the Terms of Employment (Information) Act, 1994 (refer to pages 205 and 208 respectively).

Employers cannot avoid their obligations under the Worker Protection (Regular Part-time Employees) Act, 1991 by dismissing an employee with less than thirteen weeks' service and then re-employing him/her after a brief interval (or within twenty-six weeks) or employing him/her for just less than eight hours a week. In circumstances where re-employment takes place within twenty-six weeks or an employee works less than eight hours a week with the purpose of avoiding the provisions of the Act, the Employment Appeals Tribunal is enabled to decide that the employee is protected by the Act.

### Effect of Act on Unfair Dismissals Protection

A regular part-time employee who has completed thirteen weeks' service is protected against unfair dismissal on the grounds of pregnancy, trade union membership or activity, or the exercise of rights by the employee under the Maternity Protection Act, 1994. Where dismissal is for any other reason, the employee must have completed one year's continuous service to be able to make a claim for unfair dismissal.

### Effect of Act on Redundancy Entitlement

A regular part-time employee is entitled to redundancy payments on the same basis as that applied to full-time workers. This means that part-time employees will have an entitlement to a redundancy lump sum based on service, provided that they have a minimum of one hundred and four (104) weeks' continuous service.

## Effect of Act on Other Rights

Regular part-time employees are permitted to vote in elections for employee representatives on the boards of designated state enterprises under the Worker Participation (State Enterprises) Acts, 1977 and 1988, provided they have completed one year's continuous service and are over 18 years of age. They are also entitled under the Protection of Employees (Employers Insolvency) Act, 1984, to claim arrears of pay from the insolvency fund administered by the Department of Enterprise, Trade and Employment, if their employer becomes insolvent.

## Dispute Settlement under the Act

Any dispute arising in respect of the calculation of the thirteen weeks' continuous service requirement, or any dispute relating to the number of hours a week actually worked or normally expected to be worked, must be referred to the Employment Appeals Tribunal.

The decision of the Tribunal is final, subject to a right of appeal to the High Court on a question of law.

## JOINT LABOUR COMMITTEES

For those engaged in employment in the Irish hotel and catering industry, minimum rates of pay and statutory conditions of employment are dictated by employment regulation orders, which are drafted by Joint Labour Committees and put into force by the Labour Court. A Joint Labour Committee, or JLC as it is often called, is a statutory body set up by the Labour Court, provided it receives an application to do so from the Minister for Enterprise, Trade and Employment, a trade union or any group claiming to be representative of the workers or employers concerned.

The Industrial Relations Act, 1990 provides that a Joint Labour Committee shall be made up of an equal number of worker and employer members, who will be appointed by the Labour Court following consultations with the employer and trade union organisations and of such number as the Court thinks fit. The JLC will have one independent member, appointed by the Minister for Enterprise, Trade and Employment, who will be the chairman and who will hold office during the pleasure of the Minister. Where a representative member of a JLC ceases, in the opinion of the Labour Court, to be representative of employers or workers, as the case may be, the Court shall terminate his/her membership.

There are four JLCs representing the Irish hotel and catering industry, two for hotels and two for catering. One of each kind covers areas known until 1 January 1994 as the County Borough of Dublin and the Borough of Dun Laoghaire. The remaining two, again one of each kind, cover the rest of the country.

## Procedure for Making an Employment Regulation Order

The Act sets out the procedure to be followed for the making of an Employment Regulation Order (ERO):

- The Joint Labour Committee drafts and publishes proposals for the ERO.
- Representations with respect to the proposals may be made within twenty-one days following publication.
- The JLC, having considered any representations made to it, may submit to the Labour Court such proposals as it thinks proper.
- The Labour Court may give effect to the proposals and make an Employment Regulation Order, or where the Court is not satisfied, it may submit to the committee amended proposals which it is willing to accept.
- Where the Labour Court refers amended proposals back to the committee, the committee may resubmit these to the Court in an amended or an unamended form.
- The Labour Court may then accept the proposals in full and make an Employment Regulation Order, or reject the proposals and refuse to make an Order.

It is interesting and important to note that the Act provides for the exclusion by the Labour Court of an undertaking, to which an Employment Regulation Order applies, from the scope of the Order for as long as a registered employment agreement, with terms as good as, or better than, those provided for in the Employment Regulation Order, applies to that employment. Where an exclusion order is made, it will automatically cease to have effect if the pay and conditions become less favourable than those provided for in the Employment Regulation Order. The Labour Court will give consideration to granting the exclusion of an undertaking on the request of both the employer and the workers concerned.

## Employment Regulation Orders for Hotels and Catering

Employment regulation orders define the workers covered and detail the minimum rates of pay, normal working hours, holidays and other conditions of employment.

Since there are two separate Joint Labour Committees for catering and two for hotels, it follows that there are separate Employment Regulation Orders relating to each JLC (four in all).

Before November 1993, there were no JLCs for either catering or hotels in the areas formerly known as the County Borough of Dublin and the Borough of Dun Laoghaire. In November 1993, a catering JLC was formed to cover those areas and, more recently, in April 1997, one was also formed for hotels. These areas were excluded from the two long-established JLCs (one each for catering and hotels) which are unaffected by the new JLCs and continue to operate in and apply to the rest of Ireland.

Once put into operation, an employment regulation may not be amended or revoked unless it has been in force for at least six months. Normally they are updated annually, usually in July or August.

An employer of workers covered by these orders must keep all relevant records and retain these for at least three years. The employer must also post up in a prominent place in the hotel or catering establishment a prescribed notice setting out particulars of pay and conditions, in accordance with the current, relevant employment regulation order.

## LABOUR RELATIONS COMMISSION

The Labour Relations Commission was established under the Industrial Relations Act, 1990 and came into being on 21 January 1991. The Commission is given a broad range of functions which are intended to promote improved industrial relations and to assist in the resolution of industrial disputes.

The main functions of the Labour Relations Commission are:

- to provide a conciliation service
- to provide an industrial relations advisory service
- to prepare codes of practice relevant to industrial relations after consultation with unions and employer organisations
- to offer guidance on codes of practice and help to resolve disputes concerning their implementation
- to appoint equality officers of the Commission and provide staff and facilities for the Equality Officer Service
- to select and nominate persons for appointment as Rights Commissioners and provide staff and facilities for the Rights Commissioner service
- to conduct or commission research into matters relevant to industrial relations
- to review and monitor developments in the field of industrial relations
- to assist Joint Labour Committees and Joint Industrial Councils in the exercise of their functions.

In a number of matters, the Commission has taken over responsibility for providing a service which was formerly provided by the Labour Court (e.g. the Conciliation Service, the Equality Officer Service, the Rights Commissioner Service and the servicing of Joint Labour Committees and Joint Industrial Councils).

One of the main functions of the Labour Relations Commission is to prepare codes of practice relating to industrial relations matters. Such codes are not directly enforceable because there is no criminal sanction for a breach of a code of practice nor can any civil proceedings be taken against a person alleged to have breached a code of practice. However, there are ways in which codes of practice can be enforced indirectly. Where proceedings come before a court of law, the Labour Court, the Labour Relations Commission, the Employment Appeals Tribunal, a Rights Commissioner or an Equality Officer, a code of practice will be admissible in evidence and will be taken into account in deciding the matter in hand.

Where a breach of a code of practice is alleged, the complaint may be referred to the Labour Relations Commission, and if the complaint is not resolved, it can be referred to the Labour Court. The Court has the power to interpret a code of practice and make a recommendation on whether or not it has been breached.

## Constitution of the Labour Relations Commission

The Labour Relations Commission consists of a chairman, appointed by the Minister for Enterprise, Trade and Employment, and six ordinary members. The ordinary membership of the Commission is composed as follows:

- two workers' members, nominated for appointment by the Minister by such organisations as the Minister determines to be representative of trade unions of workers

- two employers' members, nominated for appointment by the Minister by such organisations as the Minister determines to be representative of employers

- two members nominated by the Minister for Enterprise, Trade and Employment.

The terms, conditions and duration of appointment of the members of the Commission are determined by the Minister for Enterprise, Trade and Employment, who, with the consent of the Minister for Finance, may appoint such staff as he/she thinks necessary to assist the Commission in the performance of its functions.

## THE LABOUR COURT

The Labour Court was established under Section 10 of the Industrial Relations Act, 1946. Its constitution and operations were later amended by the Industrial Relations Acts of 1969 and 1976 and its functions further extended by the provisions of the Anti-Discrimination (Pay) Act, 1974 and the Employment Equality Act, 1977. Yet further changes occurred under the Industrial Relations Act, 1990.

The Court consists of a chairman, three deputy chairmen and eight ordinary members. Four of the ordinary members are nominated by trade unions and four are nominated by employers' organisations. All the members of the Court are appointed by the Minister for Enterprise, Trade and Employment. There is no requirement for members of the Court to hold formal legal qualifications.

While the Court may function with the chairman and all the ordinary members sitting together, it is almost always the case that it sits in a division comprising the chairman (or a deputy chairman) with one employer representative and one trade union representative. This composition permits four divisions, which in turn expedites the business of the Court.

The main functions of the Court include the following:

- the investigation of trade disputes and the issuance of recommendations for their settlement

- deciding on appeals in disputes in which the recommendations of a Rights Commissioner have been rejected.

Unlike the formality of the ordinary courts of law, Labour Court hearings are conducted with as little formality as possible. Although the Labour Court is entitled to summon witnesses and to take evidence under oath, these powers have never been exercised. Investigations of the court must be in private, unless one of the parties concerned requests a public hearing. When a public hearing takes place, the Court is empowered to hear any part of the case in private.

When the Court has reached its decision on any case, it is pronounced by the chairman or such other member authorised by the chairman.

In general, all disputes must first go through the conciliation service of the Labour Relations Commission before they can be referred to the Labour Court. The Industrial Relations Act, 1990 provides that the Labour Court may not investigate a dispute unless it receives a report from the Commission stating that it is satisfied that no further efforts on its part will help to resolve the dispute. All the parties to the dispute must also request a Labour Court investigation. However, there are a number of very important exceptions to these provisions:

- Where the chairperson of the Commission (or any member or officer of the Commission authorised by the chairperson) notifies the Court that, in the circumstances specified in the notice, the Commission waives its function of conciliation in the dispute and all the parties to the dispute so request, the Labour Court may investigate.

- The Court may hear an appeal from a recommendation of a Rights Commissioner or an Equality Officer without the matter being referred to the Commission.

- Where the Court, following consultation with the Commission, is of the opinion that there are exceptional circumstances which warrant doing so, the Court may investigate the dispute without the parties requesting it to do so and without the dispute first going to the Commission.

- The Labour Court may investigate a trade dispute (where the employer does not agree to a Court investigation) in circumstances where the union indicates in advance that it will accept the recommendation of the Court. In such circumstances, the dispute can be investigated without first going to the Commission. (It is also the case that where both parties agree in advance to accept a Labour Court recommendation, the dispute can be investigated directly by the Labour Court.)

- Where the Minister for Enterprise, Trade and Employment believes that a particular dispute affects the public interest, he/she may refer the dispute to the Commission or to the Court. Where the dispute is referred directly to the Court by the Minister, the Court may investigate without first going to the Commission.

## RIGHTS COMMISSIONERS

Since the passing into law of the Industrial Relations Act, 1990, Rights Commissioners operate as a service of the Labour Relations Commission. While Rights Commissioners continue to be appointed by the Minister for Enterprise, Trade and Employment, the Act requires that, where the Minister proposes to appoint a Rights Commissioner, he or she must request the Labour Relations Commission to submit to him or her a panel of persons (the Act does not specify a minimum or maximum number of persons on the panel) from which an appointment is to be made. The Minister cannot appoint as a Rights Commissioner any person not included on the panel.

The term of office of a Rights Commissioner is normally a period not exceeding three years, but a Rights Commissioner may be reappointed by the Minister for a further term or terms. A Rights Commissioner is independent in the performance of his or her duties and functions and travels throughout the country hearing cases as and when required. The hearings are normally conducted in private. The Rights Commissioner is empowered to investigate all trade disputes other than those connected with:

- rates of pay (as distinct from unlawful deductions from pay under the Payment of Wages Act, 1991)
- hours or times of work
- annual holidays.

When the Rights Commissioner has investigated a particular dispute, he/she will issue a recommendation to the parties concerned, giving his/her opinion on the merits of the dispute and putting forward suggested solutions. A recommendation of this kind is not binding on the parties.

Any recommendation issued by a Rights Commissioner can be appealed by either party to the Labour Court or to the Employment Appeals Tribunal as provided for by law, in the specific case.

A party to a dispute who wishes to object to an investigation of the dispute by a Rights Commissioner must notify the Commissioner within three weeks after the notice of the reference of the dispute to the Commissioner has been sent by post to that party.

A party wishing to appeal a Rights Commissioner's recommendation to the Labour Court, must notify the Court in writing, within six weeks of the Rights Commissioner's recommendation. In the case of an objection to a Rights Commissioner's investigation, the three-week period will begin to run from the date on which a notice is sent to the party wishing to object, informing that party of the reference of the dispute to the Commissioner. In the case of an appeal, the six-week period will begin to run from the date on the Rights Commissioner's recommendation. These time limits relate only to cases dealt with by the Rights Commissioner under the Industrial Relations Act, 1990 and do not affect the time limits set out for objecting to a Rights Commissioner's investigation or an appeal from a Rights Commissioner's recommendation to the Employment Appeals Tribunal under the Unfair Dismissals Acts, 1977-93.

A Rights Commissioner, in addition to notifying the Labour Court, is required to apprise the Minister for Enterprise, Trade and

Employment and the Labour Relations Commission of every recommendation made by him/her.

## EMPLOYMENT APPEALS TRIBUNAL

The Tribunal consists of a chairman, who must be a practising barrister or solicitor of at least seven years' experience, and 14 vice-chairmen, who also hold formal legal qualifications. An equal number of members are nominated by the various employers' organisations and by the Irish Congress of Trade Unions. The Tribunal sits in divisions consisting of the chairman (or vice-chairman) and one member each from the employer and trade union sides of industry. While two of the vice-chairmen are based in Cork and the others in Dublin, the Tribunal travels to other towns throughout the country as and when required. The hearings are open to the public unless requested otherwise by one of the parties.

The jurisdiction of the Employment Appeals Tribunal extends to disputes under the following statutes:

- the Redundancy Payments Acts, 1967-91
- the Minimum Notice and Terms of Employment Acts, 1973-91
- the Terms of Employment (Information) Act, 1994
- the Unfair Dismissals Acts, 1977-94
- the Maternity Protection Act, 1994
- the Protection of Employees (Employers' Insolvency) Acts, 1981-91.

Claims or appeals to the Employment Appeals Tribunal are made on forms for the purpose, which are available from the Department of Enterprise, Trade and Employment. In bringing a case, the employee must observe the time limits, where specificd, under each of the Acts relevant to the case.

# SELECT BIBLIOGRAPHY

It is hoped that readers of this book will have found much to interest them among the variety of topics covered. Perhaps curiosity and a thirst for deeper and more specialised legal information will encourage some to tackle further reading. The following books are all highly regarded in their field and are enthusiastically recommended.

Brennan, Olive, *Laying Down the Law — A Practical Guide*, published by Oak Tree Press, 1993.

Byrne, Raymond and Paul McCutcheon, *Irish Legal System,* 3rd edition, published by Butterworth (Ireland) Ltd., 1996.

Cassidy, Constance (editor), *Licensing Handbook*, published by Roundhall Sweet and Maxwell, 1996.

Clark, Robert, *Contract*, 3rd edition, published by Sweet and Maxwell, 1992.

Doolan, Brian, *Principles of Irish Law*, 4th edition, published by Gill and Macmillan, 1996.

Doolan, Brian, *A Casebook on Irish Business Law*, published by Gill and Macmillan, 1989.

Doolan, Brian, *A Casebook on Irish Contract Law*, published by Gill and Macmillan, 1989.

Faulkner, Mary, Gerry Kelly and Padraig Turley, *Your Guide to Irish Law*, published by Gill and Macmillan, 1993.

Fennell, Caroline and Irene Lynch, *Labour Law in Ireland*, published by Gill and Macmillan, 1993.

Gunnigle, Patrick, Thomas Garavan, Gerard FitzGerald, *Employee Relations and Employment Law in Ireland*, published by the Open Business School, Plassey Management and Technology Centre, Limerick, 1992.

Harvey, Noel and Adrian Twomey, *Sexual Harassment in the Workplace*, published by Oak Tree Press, 1995.

Keane, Ronan, *Company Law in the Republic of Ireland*, 2nd edition, published by Butterworth (Ireland) Ltd, 1991.

McDonald, Marc, *Hotel, Restaurant and Public House Law*, published by Butterworth (Ireland) Ltd., 1992.

McMahon, Bryan and William Binchy, *Casebook on the Irish Law of Torts*, published by Butterworth (Ireland) Ltd, 1983 (reprinted 1988).

McMahon, Bryan and William Binchy, *Irish Law of Torts*, 2nd edition, published by Butterworth (Ireland) Ltd, 1990.

Meenan, Frances, *Working Within the Law*, published by Oak Tree Press, 1994.

Murdoch, Henry, *A Dictionary of Irish Law*, 2nd edition, published by Topaz Publications, 1993.

O'Malley, Thomas, *Sources of Law — An Introduction to Legal Research and Writing*, published by Round Hall Press, 1993.

Woods, James, *Liquor Licensing Laws of Ireland*, 2nd edition, published by James Woods, 1992, 12 Elsinore, Castletroy, Limerick.

# INDEX

## A

accident, inevitable
  defence in tort, 92
Accidental Fires Act, 1943, 101
act of God
  defence in tort, 92
actual or express authority, 20
adjectival law, 1
Adoption Act, 1991, 247
Adoptive Leave Act, 1995, 214, 246-9
  evidence of placement of child, 247
  foreign adoptions, 248
  notification requirements, 247
  qualifying male adopters, 247-8
  right of redress, 248
agency by estoppel, 63
agreement
  discharge of contract, 65
alcohol, *see* intoxicating liquor licensing
Aliens Order, 1946, 102
annual dance licence, 192
Annual Licensing District Court, 155-7
Anti-Discrimination (Pay) Act, 1974, 259-62, 264-5, 276
  defining 'like work', 259-60
  dismissal arising from claim, 261-2
  establishing right to equal pay, 260
  making appeal, 261
  pursuing claim for equal pay, 260-1
apprenticeship, 225
area exemptions, 185-6
Articles of Association, 27, 63
assault, 90
Attorney General, 14

## B

barristers, 14-15
battery, 90

betting
  on licensed premises, 162
Bord Fáilte Éireann, 35-6, 95
Bord Uchtála, An, 247
breach of contract, 66
  remedies for, 66-7
  tort distinguished from, 93
brothel, premises used as, 161
buildings
  potentially dangerous, 120-1
business, types of, 17-30
  companies, 23-30
  general partnership, 19-22
  limited partnership, 22-3
  sole trader, 17-18
business agreements, 59
business insurance, 49-51
business names
  index of, 33
  offences and penalties, 33-4
  passing off, 34-5
  registration of, 31-4

C
cancellation of registration, 40-1, 47-8
case law, *see* common law
catering
  Joint Labour Committee, 274
Central Criminal Court, 4, 13
charges, display of, 43
children, employment of, 231-6
Church Holidays, 220
Circuit Court, 4
  description, 11-12
  on-licence applications, 166-7
civil law, 2
Civil Liability Act, 1961, 75
collective redundancies, 251-5
  cannot contract out of Act, 254
  defined, 253
  further provisions, 254
  obligations imposed on employer, 253

offences under Act, 254
  proceedings and penalties, 254
commercial agreements, 59
common law, 4-5
companies
  business name registration, 31-4
  capacity to contract, 63
  members of, 25
  options, 24
  private limited, 24-30
Companies Act, 1963, 24
Companies Act, 1990, 25
Companies Acts, 1963-90, 23, 26, 29, 85
Companies (Amendment) Act, 1983, 24
Companies (Amendment) Act, 1990, 26
Companies Registration Office, 23, 29, 209
Company Law Review Group, 30
Conciliation Service, 275
consent
  defence in tort, 92
consideration, 59-61
Constitution, 1937, 2-3
consumer contract
  Small Claims procedure, 9
Consumer Information Act, 1978, 107-10
  defences available, 109
  false or misleading indication of prices or charges, 108-9
  false statements, 108
  penalties, 110
  prosecutions, 109
consumer information and protection, 107-19
  Consumer Information Act, 1978, 107-10
  Package Holidays and Travel Trade Act, 1995, 110-19
  Sale of Goods and Supply of Services Act, 1980, 110
continuous service, 206
contract, law of, 53-72
  concept of contract, 53-4
  contract form, 54-67
  unfair terms, 67-72
contract of employment, 199-203
  consequences of employer-employee relationship, 200
  control test, 199-200

implied duties of employee, 202–3
implied duties of employer, 201–2
terminating, 203
terms of, 201
contracts
 capacity to contract, 61–3
 essential elements of, 54–61
  agreement, 55–8
  consideration, 59–61
  intention to be legally bound, 58–9
 invalid, 63–4
 remedies for breach, 66–7
 termination or discharge of, 64–6
control test, 199–200
Copyright Act, 1963, 196–8
counter offer
 lapse of offer, 57
Court of Criminal Appeal, 13
Courts Act, 1996, 11
Courts and Courts Officers Act, 1995, 12–13, 14
Courts (No. 2) Act, 1986, 155, 156
Courts (Supplemental Provisions) Act, 1961, 101
credit, sale of liquor on, 162
credit card
 not 'sale on credit', 162
crime
 tort distinguished from, 93
criminal law, 1
Customs and Excise, Collector of, 156, 157
Customs and Excise authority
 and on-licences, 167, 169, 176


D
damage and loss insurance, 50
death
 lapse of offer, 57
defamation, 88–9
Defence Forces
 excluded from Unfair Dismissals Acts, 224
 exempt from Working Time Act, 213
defences
 in tort, 91

Director of Consumer Affairs, 71-2, 109
Director of Public Prosecutions, 1, 14
directors, restriction on, 25
District Court, 4
    Annual Licensing, 178-81
    description, 8-11
    liquor licences, 155-6
domestic agreements, 58-9
double employment, 221
drinking-up time, 158-9, 160
Dublin Metropolitan District Court, 156
duty of care, 74-5
    place of assembly, 125-6
    to visitors, 77-8

E
Education, Minister for, 232
employees, *see also* contract of employment
    duties of, 85
    food hygiene, 143
    food workers, 133
    on licensed premises, 154
employer's liability, 81-8
    common law position, 81-2
    consultations between employers and employees, 86
    duties of designers, manufacturers, importers, suppliers, 85
    general duties of employees, 85
    general duties of employers, 84
    inspectors, 87
    NAOSH, 86-7
    offences, 88
    powers of inspectors, 87-8
    provision of competent staff, 82
    provision of proper equipment, 82-3
    provision of safe place of work, 82
    provision of safe system of work, 83
    safety statement, 85-6
    statutory position, 83-4
employer's liability insurance, 50
Employment Appeals Tribunal, 208, 211-12, 275
    address, 229
    adoptive leave, 247-8

functions, 280
maternity protection, 245-6
part-time workers, 271, 272
redundancy, 251
and Rights Commissioners, 279
unfair dismissals, 225, 227-31
Employment Equality Act, 1977, 262-5, 276
Employment Equality Agency, 264
  enforcement procedures, 263
  non-discrimination notices, 264-5
  penalties, 263-4, 265
  remedies, 263
  sexual harassment, 265-8
Employment Equality Agency, 264-5
employment law, 199-280
  adoptive law, 246-9
  contract of employment, 199-203
  employment equality, 262-5
  employment of children and young persons, 231-6
  equal pay, 259-62
  JLCs, 272-4
  Labour Court, 276-8
  LRC, 274-6
  maternity protection, 236-46
  minimum notice and terms of employment, 205-12
  payment of wages, 254-9
  redundancy, 249-54
  Rights Commissioners, 278-80
  safety, health and welfare at work, 268-9
  sexual harassment, 265-8
  working time, rest and holidays, 212-23
Employment Regulation Order (ERO), 272-3
Enterprise, Trade and Employment, Department of, 280
  part-time workers, 272
Enterprise, Trade and Employment, Minister for, 23, 71, 87, 109
  employment of young persons, 232-4
  holidays, 220
  and JLCs, 272-3
  and Labour Court, 276-8
  and LRC, 276
  payment of wages, 258-9
  redundancies, 250-1, 254

and Rights Commissioners, 278-80
terms of employment, 208
unfair dismissals, 229
working hours, 212, 214-15, 221-2
entertainment licences, 191-8
dancing licences, 191-4
music and singing licences, 194-6
performing rights, 196-8
Environment, Department of the
codes of practice, 126
equal pay, *see* Anti-Discrimination (Pay) Act, 1974
Equality and Law Reform, Minister for, 266
Equality Officer Service, 275
Equality Officers
and Labour Court, 278
European Commission, 6-7
Code of Practice, 266
European Communities (Hygiene of Foodstuffs) Regulations, 1998, 135, 140-4
food rooms, 141-2
food waste, 142-3
general provisions, 141
guides to good hygiene practice, 143-4
Hazard Analysis and Critical Control Points, 140
hygiene training and supervision, 143
movable and other premises, 142
offences and penalties, 144
personal hygiene, 143
vehicles and containers, 142
water, ice and steam, 143
European Communities (Official Control of Foodstuffs) Regulations, 1998, 135-9
co-operation and assistance, 139
enforcement, 138-9
offences and penalties, 139
powers of authorised officers, 137
sampling, 137-8
European Communities (Single-Member Private Limited Companies)
Regulations, 1994, 29-30
European Communities (Unfair Terms in Consumer Contracts)
Regulations, 1995, 67-72
European Community, 5
European Council, 7
European Court of Justice, 7

European Parliament, 7
European Union, 231
  Budgetary Treaties, 6
  law of, 5–7
    decision, 6
    directive, 6
    regulation, 6
  treaties, 5–6
excise duty
  hotels, 170
  publican's licence, 169
  special restaurant licence, 175
  wine retailer's on-licence, 178

F
false imprisonment, 90
Farm and Country Standards Ltd, 37
FÁS, 224, 225
festival clubs, 188
fidelity insurance, 50
Finance, Minister for, 250, 276
Finance Act, 1992, 150
Fire Authorities (Emergency Operations) Regulations, 1987, 119
Fire Safety in Places of Assembly (Ease of Escape) Regulations, 1985, 119, 125–6
fire safety legislation, 119–27
  appeal against fire safety notice, 123
  Department of the Environment codes of practice, 126
  fire safety notices, 121–2
  potentially dangerous building, 120–1
  power of inspection, 123–5
Fire Services Act, 1981, 119, 126–7, 172, 191
Fire Services Act, 1981 (Prescribed Premises) Regulations, 1987, 119
Food Hygiene (Amendment) Regulations, 1989, 130
Food Hygiene Regulations, 1950–89, 18, 45, 48, 127–35, 172
  employment of infected persons, 134
  further regulations, 135
  general provisions relating to food stall licences, 131–2
  licensing procedure for food stalls, 131
  other food businesses, 133
  penalties, 135
  power of health board CEO, 134–5
  regulations governing food premises, 127–9

regulations governing food stalls, 129-31
regulations governing food vehicles, 132-3
regulations governing food workers, 133
food premises, registration of, 45-9
frustration
    discharge of contract, 65

G
gambling
    on licensed premises, 162
Gaming and Lotteries Acts, 1956-79, 127
Garda Siochána, 1
    bribery of, 162
    dance licences, 191-4
    event licensing, 185-6
    excluded from Unfair Dismissals Acts, 224
    exempt from Working Time Act, 213
    festival clubs, 188
    harbouring on premises, 161
    inspection of hotel register, 102
    inspections, 222
    intoxicating liquor licences, 155, 156
    obstructing entry of, 162
    restaurant certificate, 180
general exemption order, 181-2
    application procedure, 181
    permitted hours, 181-2

H
Hazard Analysis and Critical Control Points, 140
health
    employment of infected persons, 134
Health and Children, Minister for, 45-7, 139
    food hygiene, 143-4
    smoking restrictions, 146-7
health boards
    food hygiene, 45-7
    power of CEO, 134-5
health insurance, 50
High Court, 11
    description, 12-13
holidays, 217-21

Holidays (Employees) Act, 1973, 212
hotel licences, 169-70
  excise duty for, 170
Hotel Proprietors Act, 1963, 95-102, 111
  coming into force, 95
  definitions, 95-6
  duties imposed by, 96
  duty regarding safety of guests and premises, 97
  duty to receive all-comers, 96-7
  duty to receive the property of guests, 97-8
  general provisions, 101-2
  liability for guest's property, 98-9
  limiting liability, 99-100
  right of lien, 100
  right of sale, 100-1
  rights of the proprietor, 100
hotels
  definition of, 95-6
  exemptions on hours of trading, 159
  Joint Labour Committee, 274
  register of guests, 102


I
illegal contracts, 231
improvement notice, 87-8
Industrial Relations Act, 1946, 276
Industrial Relations Act, 1969, 276
Industrial Relations Act, 1976, 276
Industrial Relations Act, 1990, 272-4, 277-8
inevitable accident
  defence in tort, 92
infants
  capacity to contract, 61-2
injunction
  remedy for breach of contract, 67
inspection
  fire safety legislation, 123-5
insurance for business, 49-51
intention
  in tort, 91
International Labour Organisation, 231
Intoxicating Liquor Act, 1927, 179

Intoxicating Liquor Act, 1960, 170
Intoxicating Liquor Act, 1988, 36, 37, 152-3
Intoxicating Liquor Acts, 1833-1995, 149
intoxicating liquor licensing, 149-89, *see also* liquor licence
  categories of licence, 149-50
  children on licensed premises, 152-3
  employment of persons under 18, 154
  exemption for special events, 185-6
  festival clubs, 188
  general considerations and offences, 160-4
  general exemption order, 181-2
  hotel licences, 169-70
  hours of trading, 158-60
  limited restaurant certificate, 180-2
  night clubs, 188-9
  objections to granting of declaration, 155
  objections to renewal of, 156
  obtaining a declaration relating to proposed premises, 154
  occasional licence, 186-7
  procedure for objecting to renewal of, 157
  procedure for obtaining declaration, 155
  procedure for renewal of licence, 155-6
  prohibition on sale to persons under 18, 152
  restaurant certificate, 178-80
  special exemption order, 182-5
  special restaurant licence, 171-5
  spirits retailer's on-licence, 165-9
  tax clearance certificates, 150-1
  wine retailer's on-licence, 175-8
intoxication
  capacity to contract, 63
Iris Oifigiúil, 4, 71
Irish Congress of Trade Unions, 280
Irish Hotels Federation, 197
Irish Music Rights Organisation Limited (IMRO), 196-8

J
Joint Industrial Councils, 275
Joint Labour Committees, 272-4
judges, appointment of, 15
Justice, Minister for, 102

# L

Labour Court, 222
  employment equality, 263-4
  equal pay claim, 261-2
  functions, 276-8
  JLCs, 272
  and Rights Commissioners, 279
  sexual harassment, 265-8
  working hours, 214, 215, 216
Labour Relations Commission, 274-6, 277
  constitution of, 276
  and Rights Commissioners, 279-80
lapse of time
  termination of offer, 57
law
  classification of, 1-2
  courts of, 8-14
  personnel of, 14-15
  sources of, 2-7
Law Reform Commission, 12
leasing
  of licensed premises, 163
legislation, 3-4
liability, *see also* occupier's liability
  of hotel proprietors, 98-100
  registration of business name, 34
  travel trade, 111-12
libel, 88-9
Licensing Acts, 1833-1995, 127
Licensing (Ireland) Act, 1902, 149, 170
lien, right of
  hotel proprietor, 100
limited liability, 24-5
Limited Partnership Act, 1907, 22
limited restaurant certificate, 180-1
  application procedure, 180
  court jurisdiction, 180
  granting of, 181
liquor licence
  betting and gaming on licensed premises, 162
  bribing a Garda, 162
  clearing of premises, 164

custody of, 160
endorsements, 163
extension or alteration of premises, 164
forfeiture of, 163
harbouring a Garda, 161
holding of, 161
intoxicated persons on premises, 161
leasing of premises, 163
obligation to serve, 162
obstructing entry of Garda, 162
premises used as brothel, 161
prostitutes on premises, 161
sale of, 160
sale of liquor on credit, 162
Local Government (Planning and Development) Acts, 1963-93, 172

M
Maastricht Treaty, 5
married women
  capacity to contract, 62-3
Maternity Protection Act, 1994, 214, 224, 225, 236-46, 271, 280
  additional maternity leave, 240
  birth earlier than expected, 239
  birth later than expected, 239
  dispute settlement procedure, 245-6
  effect of miscarriage, 239
  ending health and safety leave, 244
  father's leave entitlement, 242-3
  general protection, 244-5
  health and safety leave, 243
  maternity leave entitlement, 238
  preservation of rights during leave, 240-1
  protection against dismissal, 244
  requirements to be met, 238
  revocation of maternity notification, 239
  right to pay under, 237-8
  right to return to work, 241-2
  right to time off, 240
  scope of benefits of, 237
Maternity Protection of Employees Acts, 1981-91, 236
meal, definition of, 159-60
Memorandum of Association, 27, 63

mentally ill
  capacity to contract, 63
Minimum Notice and Terms of Employment Act, 1973, 224
Minimum Notice and Terms of Employment Acts, 1973-84, 271
Minimum Notice and Terms of Employment Acts, 1973-91, 200, 203, 205-12,
    226, 251, 280
  calculating period of service, 207-8
  continuous service defined, 206
  dispute procedures, 208
  period of notice, 206-7
money insurance, 50
music and singing licences, 194-6

N
National Authority for Occupational Safety and Health, 86-7
National Standards Authority of Ireland, 144
necessity
  defence in tort, 92
negligence, 74-5
  breach of duty of care, 74-5
  contributory, 75
  duty of care, 74
  ensuing damage or injury, 75
  scope of, 75
night clubs, 188-9
night work, 215-16
notice, period of, 206-7
nuisance, 89-90
  private nuisance, 89-90
  public nuisance, 90

O
obligation to serve, 162
occasional licence, 186-7
  procedure for obtaining, 187
  rules applying to, 187
occupier's liability, 76-81
  duty of visitors, 77-8
  duty to recreational users and trespassers, 78-80
  general provisions, 81
  modification of duty to entrants, 80-1
  'recreational user' defined, 78

'trespasser' defined, 78
'visitor' defined, 77
Occupier's Liability Act, 1995, 76-81
offer, termination of, 56-7
Oireachtas
  legislation, 3-4
on-licence, *see* spirits retailer's on-licence; wine retailer's on-licence
Organisation of Working Time Act, 1997, 212-23
  compensation for loss of annual leave, 220
  compensation for loss of public holiday, 221
  complaints and proceedings, 222-3
  double employment, 221
  holidays - annual leave, 217-18
  inspectors, 221-2
  keeping records, 221
  maximum weekly working time, 213-14
  minimum rest periods, 214-15
  nightly working hours, 215-16
  non-application of, 213
  penalties, 223
  providing information, 216
  public holidays, 219-20
  Sunday work, 215
  transitional arrangements, 214
  transitional holiday arrangements, 218
  'zero-hour' contracts, 216
ostensible or apparent authority, 20

P
Package Holidays and Travel Trade Act, 1955
  contract price revision, 116-17
Package Holidays and Travel Trade Act, 1995, 110-19
  alteration or cancellation by organiser, 117-18
  complaints, 118
  definition of 'organiser', 112-13
  definition of 'package holiday', 112
  essential terms of contract, 115-16
  failure of package, 118
  holiday brochure content, 113-14
  limitation of liability, 111-12
  offences and penalties, 119
  pre-contractual requirements, 114-15

pre-holiday information, 115
prosecutions, 119
protection against insolvency, 118
transfer of booking, 116
part-time workers, *see* Worker Protection (Regular Part-time
    Employees) Act, 1991
partnership, general, 19-22
  advantages, 21-2
  authority, 20
  disadvantages, 22
  dissolution, 21
  forming, 19
  liability, 19
  power of partners, 20-1
partnership, limited, 22-3
  defined, 22
  Registration requirement, 23
  rules, 22-3
Partnership Act, 1890, 19
passing off, 34-5
paternal leave, 242-3
Payment of Wages Act, 1991, 254-9, 279
  complaints procedure, 257-9
  deductions from wages, 256-7
  form or method of paying, 255
  statement of wages, 255-6
penalties
  company law, 30
pension-type insurances, 50
performance
  discharge of contract, 65
performing rights, 196-8
Performing Rights Society, 196
permanent health insurance, 50
personal accident insurance, 50
Petty Sessions (Ireland) Act, 1851, 139, 223, 235
Phonographic Performance Ireland Limited, 198
place of assembly
  duty of care, 125-6
premises, registration of, 35-45
prices, *see* Retail Prices Display Order, 1976 and 1984
private limited companies, 24-30

advantages, 28
appointment of examiner, 26
disadvantages, 28-9
formation of, 26-8
restriction on directors, 25
single-member, 29-30
probation, 225
prohibition notice, 88
prostitutes
  on premises, 161
Protection of Employees (Employers' Insolvency) Act, 1984, 249, 272
Protection of Employees (Employers' Insolvency) Acts, 1981-91, 280
Protection of Employment Act, 1977, 251
Protection of Young Persons (Employment) Act, 1996, 231-6
  employment conditions for children, 232-3
  employment conditions for young persons, 233-4
  formalities, 235-6
  prohibition on combined employments, 234
Public Dance Halls Act, 1935, 127, 183, 189, 191-4
  appeals procedure, 193
  application procedure, 192-3
  general provisions, 193-4
Public Enterprise, Minister for, 112
Public Health Acts Amendment Act, 1890, 127, 194
public holidays, 219-21
public liability insurance, 50
public music and singing licence, 194-5
pubs, *see* intoxicating liquor licensing

Q
Quality Approved Bed and Breakfast Ltd, 37

R
recision
  remedy for breach of contract, 67
recreational user, 78-80
rectification
  remedy for breach of contract, 67
redundancy
  and unfair dismissal, 228
Redundancy Payments Acts, 224
Redundancy Payments Acts, 1967-91, 200, 249-54, 280

benefit entitlement, 249-50
collective redundancies, 251-5
dispute settlement procedures, 251
effect of non-payment of benefit by employer, 250
establishing eligibility, 249-50
rebate for employers, 150-1
redundancy defined, 249
statutory procedures, 251
time off to look for work, 251
register
of hotel guests, 102
Registrar of Companies, 23, 27, 29-30
particulars required by, 32
safety statement, 85
registration, certificate of, 32
Registration of Business Names Act, 1963, 18, 19, 27, 31-4
Registration of Clubs Acts, 1904-86, 127
registration of food premises, 45-9
alteration and cancellation of register entries, 46-7
cancellation and suspension of, 47-8
occasional food premises, 49
procedure, 45-6
procedure after provisional registration, 46
registration of premises, 35-45
application procedure, 38-9
cancellation of, 40-1
display of certain information, 43-4
display of charges, 43
external signs, 44
grading, 42
inspection, 42-3
inspection of register, 43
publication of list of registered premises, 44
range of registers, 37-8
restriction on description, 41-2
rules relating to, 40
service of notice, 44-5
remedies
in tort, 92-3
restaurant certificate
application procedure, 178-9
benefits of obtaining, 179

granting of, 179-80

permitted hours, 179

restaurants

certificate, 178-80

exemptions on hours of trading, 159

limited certificate, 180-1

special licence, 171-5

Restaurants Association of Ireland, 197

restraint of trade, 64

Retail Prices (Beverages in Licensed Premises) Display Order, 1976, 105-7

display of notices, 106

penalties, 107

references to prices charged, 106

refund of deposit on bottles, 106-7

requirements of, 105-6

Retail Prices (Food in Catering Establishments) Display Order, 1984, 103-5

defence to proceedings, 104

foods defined, 103

manner in which notices displayed, 104

penalties, 105

prices and charges to be displayed, 103-4

Revenue Commissioners, 150-1, 173

restaurant licences, 173-4, 175

revocation

lapse of offer, 57

Rights Commissioner Service, 275

address, 229

Rights Commissioners, 211-12, 222

adoptive leave, 247-8

functions, 278-80

and Labour Court, 278, 279

maternity protection, 245-6

unfair dismissals, 225, 226, 228-31


S

Safety, Health and Welfare at Work Act, 1989, 83-8, 243, 268-9

Safety, Health and Welfare at Work (General Applications)
    Regulations, 1993, 268-9

safety statement, 85-6

sale, right of

hotel proprietor, 100-1

Sale of Goods Act, 1893, 101

Sale of Goods and Supply of Services Act, 1980, 110, 111
service, period of, 207–8
sexual harassment, 265–8
signs, external, 44
Single European Act, 1986, 6
single-member company, 29–30
slander, 88–9
Small Claims Procedure, 9–11
smoking, prohibition and restriction on, 144–7
Social, Community and Family Affairs, Department of, 237–8, 243, 246
social agreements, 58–9
sole trader, 17–18
 advantages, 18
 disadvantages, 18
solicitors, 14–15
sources of law
 common law, 4–5
 Constitution, 2–3
 EU law, 5–7
 legislation, 3–4
Special Criminal Court, 4, 13
special events, exemption for, 185–6
special exemption order, 182–5
 application procedure, 183
 conditions relating to, 184–5
 meaning of 'special occasion', 183
'special occasion', meaning of, 183
special restaurant licence, 171–5
 excise duty, 175
 further provisions, 175
 hours of trading, 174
 offences, 175
 powers of Tourism Quality Services, 174
 procedure for obtaining, 171–3
 renewal of, 173–4
Special Restaurant Licence (Standards) Regulations, 1988, 172
Specialist Accommodation Approvals, 37
specific performance
 remedy for breach of contract, 67
spirits retailer's on-licence, 165–9
 excise duty for publican's licence, 169
 grounds for objections, 168

notifying county registrar, 169
objections to granting, 168
procedure for obtaining, 166
procedure for obtaining court certificate, 166-7
procedure for obtaining on-licence, 167
right of appeal, 168
in rural area, 165-6
in town or city, 166
Standard Time Act, 1968, 158
Statute of Limitations, 1957, 208
and contracts, 67
in torts, 92
statutory authority
defence in tort, 92
Statutory Declaration, 28
statutory instruments, 3
substantial meal, definition of, 159-60
substantive law, 1
summer time, 158
Sunday work, 215
Supreme Court, 4, 12, 13
description, 14

T
tax clearance certificates, 150-1
temporary dance licence, 191
temporary public music and singing licence, 195-6
tenancy
Small Claims procedure, 9
termination of contract, 64-6
Terms of Employment (Information) Act, 1994, 205, 208-12, 271, 280
notification of changes in written particulars, 210-11
procedure for making complaint, 211-12
provision of written statement, 209-10
Tobacco (Health Promotion and Protection) Act, 1988, 144
Tobacco (Health Promotion and Protection) Regulations, 1995, 144-7
defence to a prosecution, 147
enforcement, 146-7
penalties, 147
prohibition on smoking, 145-6
restriction on smoking, 146

tort
  Small Claims procedure, 9
torts, law of, 73–93
  defamation, 88–9
  defences in tort, 92
  distinguished from breach of contract, 93
  employer's liability, 81–8
  intention in tort, 91
  negligence, 74–5
  nuisance, 89–90
  occupier's liability, 76–81
  remedies in tort, 92–3
  specific torts, 73–4
  tort distinguished from crime, 93
  trespass, 90–1
Tourism, Sport and Recreation, Minister for, 35
Tourism Quality Services (Ireland) Ltd, 36–45, 95
  powers of, 174
  restaurant licences, 171–5
Tourist Traffic Acts, 18, 95–6
  registration of premises, 35–45
trade union activity, 225
training, 225
travel, *see* Package Holidays and Travel Trade Act, 1995
travel insurance, 50
Treaty of European Union (TEU), 5, 6
trespass, 90–1
  to goods, 91
  to land, 91
  to the person, 90
trespassers, 78–80, 91


U
unfair contracts, 67–72
  application and exclusions, 68–9
  defined, 68
  enforcement, 71–2
  examples of unfair terms, 69–71
  general provisions, 71
Unfair Dismissals Acts, 1977–93, 200, 203, 246, 279, 280
Unfair Dismissals Acts, 1977–94, 223–31
  actions at common law, 231

bringing action for, 225-6
establishing burden of proof, 227
establishing fact of dismissal, 226-7
excluded categories, 224
forms of redress, 230
illegal contracts, 231
making a claim, 228-9
notification of dismissal procedures, 230-1
reasons for dismissal given in writing, 230
special provisions, 225
unfair dismissals identified, 227-8

V
visitor, 77-8
voidable contracts of infants, 62
voluntary health insurance, 50

W
wine retailer's on-licence, 175-8
  application procedure, 176
  excise duty, 178
  hours of trading, 177-8
  objections to granting, 176-7
  transfer of, 177
Worker Participation (State Enterprises) Acts, 1977, 272
Worker Protection (Regular Part-time Employees) Act, 1991, 212
  dispute settlement under, 272
  effect on other rights, 272
  effect on redundancy entitlement, 271
  effect on rights to notice and terms, 271
  effect on unfair dismissals protection, 271
  regular part-time employee defined, 270
working hours, *see* Organisation of Working Time Act, 1997

Y
young persons, employment of, 231-6

Z
'zero-hour' contracts, 216

# CERT: STATE TOURISM TRAINING AGENCY

CERT is the state agency responsible for the recruitment, education and training of staff at all levels in the hotel, catering and tourism industry with priority for the needs of tourism. Its objective is to ensure high operational standards in the industry and to develop a skilled, professional workforce.

Tourism is now one of Ireland's largest industries, with tourism earnings contributing up to 6.2% of GNP and over 188,000 people directly employed in the industry. Employment in the industry increased by an estimated 20% between 1992 and 1996.

CERT provides its services through a network of regional offices, third-level colleges, hotel schools and temporary training centres. It has two operational divisions, School Training and Research and Industry Training, which provide the following services:

- identification of employment and training needs, through research studies and on-going consultation with industry
- recruitment, training and formal education of those preparing for careers in the industry
- continuing training for existing industry personnel
- support services to industry businesses
- development of national curriculums and certification for tourism, through the National Tourism Certification Board.

A range of training publications and resources are developed by CERT Curricula Section and are available for training purposes to lecturers, instructors, students and industry personnel.